BEST BETS

Recipe for cover photograph is on page 113.

Nathan Adelson Hospice Foundation

The Nathan Adelson Hospice Foundation was established in 1978 to raise funds to help meet the needs of the Nathan Adelson Hospice. The Foundation currently contributes nearly a million dollars each year to insure that the Hospice can maintain the fundamental policy that every terminally ill patient is accepted into the Hospice program without regard to race, religion, sex, age, disease, or *ability to pay.*

By purchasing this cookbook, you are contributing to the private funding base that allows the Nathan Adelson Hospice to continue serving the growing number of terminally ill patients and their families. Proceeds from the sale of *BEST BETS* go directly to the Nathan Adelson Hospice Foundation and will assist the Hospice in achieving its mission: *"To be a friend to the terminally ill and their families who are concerned with quality of life and compassionate support. We're here to care."*

Published by: Nathan Adelson Hospice

Copyright© Nathan Adelson Hospice
4141 South Swenson Street
Las Vegas, Nevada 89119
(702) 733-0320

Library of Congress Number: 93-072353
ISBN: 0-87197-383-9

Edited, Designed and Manufactured in the United States of America by:
Favorite Recipes® Press
P.O. Box 305142
Nashville, Tennessee 37230
1-800-358-0560

First Printing: 1993   7,500 copies

Acknowledgments

The Nathan Adelson Hospice thanks each person who submitted a recipe. Because of them, *BEST BETS* was made possible. Please note that *BEST BETS* is a collection of favorite recipes which are not necessarily original recipes.

We are deeply appreciative for the advice, counsel and time commitment given by our Trustee and *Las Vegas Sun* Food Editor, Muriel Stevens. She not only helped select the recipes in this cookbook, but also prepared the dishes pictured on the cover.

Credit is also given to the following for their support of the Nathan Adelson Hospice. Their work was truly invaluable to the completion of *BEST BETS*. Thank you to: Ron Bell and Rob Cornely at Bell Agency for cover layout, Danny Rose at Graphics West for color separations, Greg and Sharon at Sampsell/Preston Studios for cover photography, and Lee Eames for the sketch of the Hospice building.

We gratefully acknowledge the hard work and dedication of each cookbook committee member. Their hard work and enthusiasm made *BEST BETS* a reality.

Cookbook Committee Members

Terrie Bergman
Bonnie Crosby
Susie Epstein — Gary Gardia
Ike H. Hancock
Jerry J. Kaufman
Dee King — Carol Rumbolz
Mary Jo Sugden
Toni Walo, Chair

Nathan Adelson Hospice

Las Vegas is a city that lives—Hospice affirms life. How truly fitting that one of the nation's foremost hospice programs, the Nathan Adelson Hospice, calls Las Vegas its home.

Founded on November 22, 1978, we began serving terminally ill patients and their families at home in 1980. In 1983, a 20-bed freestanding inpatient unit was added to our program of care. The program focuses on the whole patient and their family—their medical, emotional and spiritual needs, working to elevate the quality of life for patients through comfort seeking measures and support. Hospice helps family and friends prepare for the loss and cope with issues surrounding death and dying. It involves the family in the care of the patient, enriching their experience and memories.

The Nathan Adelson Hospice is recognized as one of the world's leading programs. There are more than 2,000 hospice programs in the United States. Our staff regularly provides information and guidance to communities planning or already supporting hospices throughout the country.

Hospice is a concept of personalized care for those with a life-shortening illness whose goal is comfort and dignity when a cure is no longer possible. Care is based upon a philosophy of unconditional love and acceptance. The hospice interdisciplinary team—physicians, nurses, social workers, counselors, clergy, volunteers and staff—work with the patient and family to achieve a pain-free, gentle close to life's journey.

We embellish this concept of care by providing an environment of living designed to meet the sensitive needs of the terminally ill, their family and friends. Hospice is first and foremost a wonderful, specialized home care program. We offer a cost effective alternative program of care where the needs of the patient and family are our primary concern. When acute-symptom management or respite care are required, the natural home-like surroundings of the hospice facility provide a peaceful, dignified setting for those approaching the final stages of life.

While the majority of our patients are more than 65 years of age, we serve a growing population of infants, children and younger adults who are in need of a compassionate, comfortable way to live their final days.

The Founders created a living memorial to Nathan Adelson, one of Las Vegas' leading citizens and a great humanitarian who passed away from terminal cancer in 1978. It stands as a most fitting memorial to a very special man.

Contributors

Due to limited space we were unable to use every recipe which was submitted, but again we want to thank everyone who contributed recipes and made this cookbook possible.

Marty Allen
Mary Allred
Carole Annexstein
Chef Lucio Arancibia
Bob Barengo
Chef Alan Barnum
Chef Todd Berg
Terrie Bergman
Laura Biggers
Karon Kate Blackwell
Chef Ken Bozzo
Mary Bredlau
Chef Arnauld Briand
Mary L. Browder
Chef Robert A.
    Camerota
Paul V. Carelli III
Lene Carpenter
The Castricone Family
Michael Cherubino
Christina Christensen
Chef John Ciborski
Bonnie Crosby
Donna Jo Day
Chef Robert DeLillo
Elsie Dorsett
Susan Drongowski
Alan & Beverly
    Duncan
Chef Barbara Endrezze
Jan Fleshman
Gary Gardia
Jill Gardiner
Sally Garvelink
Mike Gornet
Chef John Guyer

Ginger Hanson
Ilene Hanson
Susan Harrison
Margaret G. Henley
Chef Stanton Ho
Dottye Hulsberg
Chef Tom Janarone
Jeanne R. Jones
Jerry J. Kaufman
Marion Keltner
Dee King
Chef Eric Kornbluh
Betty Lee Lamping
Leland Lewis
Heinz O. Lottermoser
Sister Tim Malone
Chef Miguel Maganak
Chef Tom Martinez
Chef Scott McCarter
Sue McNutt
Tina Megason
Wendy Messer
Susan Molasky
Tija E. Muntean
Evelyn Newman
Elvis (Jerry) Olds
Wilma Palmer
Carol Paxinos
Chef Mark Piludo
Beryl B. Pinney
Chef Sammy Pollack
Dee Powers
Chef Wolfgang Puck
Shirley B. Putz
Sarah C. Rausch
Debra Rhodes

Michelle Ridout
Jean Rodgriguz
Peggy Romanoski
Joan Rumble
Carol Rumbolz
Chef George Sanchez
Chef Chris Sbrascia
Chef Mai Shao
Dorothy E. Sims
Chef Kerry Slagle
Dee Snyder
Donald D Snyder
Larry L. Spitler
Muriel Stevens
Vito J. & Adele Stolfa
Jeannine Stroth
Beth Sudderth
Mary Jo Sugden
Pam Sugden
Terese Sugden
Chef Michael Ty
Mickey Ubbink
Chef David
    Ventimiglia
Anna Marie Virgilio
Magel Walo
Toni Walo
Barbara Wardlaw
Chef Bruno Wehren
Chef Rene Werner
Ming See Woo
Chef Walter Worotylko
Stacey L. Yahraus
Chef Christopher
    Young
Patti Zielinski

Contents

Foreword

If you are like me, you buy cookbooks in search of that special recipe. Special to you because it can be made in 10 minutes so you can spend more time relaxing and with family. Or maybe you buy cookbooks for the special recipes that will make a dinner party memorable. Whether it's easy preparation, healthy food, unique cuisine—cookbooks provide it. They provide an opportunity for gathering—for sharing a meal with family or friends.

Those who submitted a recipe for *BEST BETS* did so because it held a special memory for them. It may have been handed down through generations; it may have been their child's favorite dessert; it may have been the "big success" at a dinner party. Whatever the memory, it involved people—family and friends, and it portrayed moments of sharing and caring for one another.

The Founders of the Nathan Adelson Hospice felt a special need in their heart—to provide such moments for terminally ill patients. When time is short, the use of that time or the quality of that time, becomes very important. The Founders developed a special kind of caring for these individuals, one that offered the opportunity for creating an environment where family and friends can be together and enjoy their time remaining. Comfort, serenity, and a peaceful family environment are the hallmarks of such heartfelt endeavors. Through medical and psychological support, terminally ill patients and families are comforted so they may have lasting memories of sharing tender loving care.

It is our hope *BEST BETS* helps you create your own lasting memories. As you explore the recipes in this book, please remember from time to time that it is intended to be shared with those you care about. Spend that extra moment to pick the right menu that will help everyone remember the great times together.

Betsy Peirson Gornet
Chief Executive Officer

Restaurants

PEPPERED TURKEY POBLANO YOLANDO

1 shallot, minced
1 chipotle chili, minced
1 clove of garlic, minced
6 sprigs of cilantro, chopped
1 cup honey
1 tablespoon lemon juice
1 tablespoon red wine vinegar
1/8 ounce cumin
1/8 ounce cracked pepper
1 1/2 pounds turkey
1 shallot, chopped
3 green onions, chopped

2 poblano peppers, coarsely
    chopped
1 green yolando pepper, coarsely
    chopped
1 red yolando pepper, coarsely
    chopped
12 pearl onions
1/8 ounce each thyme and
    coriander buds
Salt and pepper to taste
Cornstarch or arrowroot

Combine 1 shallot, chipotle chili, garlic, cilantro, honey, lemon juice, wine vinegar, cumin and pepper in bowl; mix well. Adjust lemon juice to taste. Cut turkey into strips; rinse and pat dry. Add to marinade. Marinate in refrigerator for 1 hour or longer. Drain, reserving marinade. Sauté 1 shallot and green onions lightly in large skillet. Add turkey, peppers and pearl onions. Sauté until turkey is cooked through. Season with thyme, coriander, salt and pepper. Mix reserved marinade with enough cornstarch or arrowroot to thicken in saucepan. Cook until thickened, stirring constantly. Serve with turkey and peppers. Yield: 2 to 3 servings.

Bacchanal
Caesars Palace Hotel
Chef Alan Barnum

BACCHANAL
A Roman Feast

WARM SHRIMP AND SPINACH SALAD WITH BALSAMIC VINAIGRETTE

8 ounces fresh spinach
4 Roma tomatoes, sliced
16 to 20 shrimp, peeled, deveined
1/4 teaspoon chopped garlic
1 teaspoon chopped red onion
1/2 teaspoon Dijon mustard
1 1/2 ounces balsamic vinegar

3 ounces high quality extra-virgin olive oil
1/2 teaspoon chopped fresh basil
1/4 teaspoon salt
1/4 teaspoon freshly cracked pepper
Freshly grated Parmesan cheese

Arrange spinach and sliced tomatoes on 4 salad plates. Sauté shrimp in heated nonstick sauté pan for 1 minute on each side or until cooked through. Remove to warm plate in warm oven. Sauté garlic in same sauté pan until light brown. Add onion. Sauté until tender. Add mustard and vinegar. Cook for 20 seconds. Stir in olive oil. Bring to a boil; season with basil, salt and pepper. Arrange shrimp over salad; spoon vinaigrette over top. Sprinkle with Parmesan cheese. Yield: 4 servings.

Bistro
The Mirage
Chef Scott McCarter

BROILED SALMON WITH SPINACH FETTUCINI

1 6-ounce salmon filet	¹/₂ teaspoon Mrs. Dash seasoning
2 tablespoons chopped onion	Salt and pepper to taste
1 teaspoon chopped garlic	1 cup chopped fresh spinach
¹/₄ cup sliced mushrooms	4 ounces spinach fettucini, cooked
3 tablespoons margarine	3 ounces grated Parmesan cheese
2 ounces Chablis	2 lemon slices
Worcestershire sauce to taste	2 lime slices

Broil or grill salmon until it flakes easily; keep warm. Sauté onion, garlic and mushrooms in margarine in sauté pan until mushrooms are almost tender. Add next 5 ingredients. Sauté for 1 minute. Add spinach. Sauté until tender. Add fettucini. Cook until heated through. Toss with 2 ounces Parmesan cheese. Place fettucini on serving plate; sprinkle with remaining Parmesan cheese. Place salmon next to fettucini on serving plate; garnish with lemon and lime slices. Yield: 1 serving.

Cantina Charlie's
Chef Barbara Endrezze

Cantina Charlie's
Sahara &
Decatur

MEXICAN VEGETARIAN LASAGNA

1 onion, chopped
1 clove of garlic, minced
5 or 6 mushrooms, sliced
1 green bell pepper, chopped
2 cups cooked beans
1½ cups stewed tomatoes
½ cup dry red wine
1 tablespoon chili powder
1 teaspoon ground cumin seed
½ cup part-skim ricotta cheese
¼ cup low-fat yogurt
8 whole wheat tortillas
¼ cup shredded part-skim
   mozzarella cheese
6 black olives, sliced

Sauté onion, garlic, mushrooms and green pepper in nonstick saucepan. Add beans, tomatoes, wine, chili powder and cumin seed; mix well. Simmer for 30 minutes. Combine ricotta cheese and yogurt in bowl. Alternate layers of tortillas, bean sauce, mozzarella cheese and yogurt mixture in 1½-quart baking dish until all ingredients are used, ending with bean sauce and yogurt mixture. Top with olives. Bake at 350 degrees for 15 to 20 minutes or until bubbly. Yield: 6 servings.

Cariba Charlie's
Chef Todd Berg

Tropicana & Rainbow

CHICKEN MARSALA

4 8-ounce chicken breast filets
2 cups flour
Salt and pepper to taste
6 ounces oil
1 tablespoon minced garlic

5 ounces Marsala
2 cups brown sauce
6 ounces mushrooms, sliced
6 ounces chicken broth
1 tablespoon butter

Rinse chicken and pat dry; coat with mixture of flour, salt and pepper. Sauté in hot oil in skillet on both sides until light brown. Add garlic, 4 ounces wine, brown sauce, mushrooms and chicken broth. Simmer for 10 to 15 minutes or until chicken is tender, stirring occasionally; remove from heat. Stir in remaining 1 ounce wine and butter. Yield: 4 servings.

Charlie's Lakeside
Chef Robert DeLillo

W. Sahara & Durango

FRUIT-FILLED COCOA TACOS

1/4 cup flour
1/4 cup sugar
1 tablespoon baking cocoa
2 tablespoons 2% milk
2 tablespoons oil
1 egg white
1 teaspoon vanilla extract
Salt to taste

8 ounces fruit-flavored low-fat
  yogurt
4 kiwifruit, peeled, sliced
6 large strawberries, sliced
8 ounces mango coulis
1 ounce raspberry sauce
1 pint fresh raspberries
6 sprigs of fresh mint

Combine first 8 ingredients in bowl; beat until smooth. Chill, covered, for 2 hours. Place 3 tablespoonfuls at a time in heated nonstick 8-inch skillet over medium heat. Cook for 2 minutes or until batter appears dry; turn. Cook for 1 minute longer. Remove and drape over wire rack; cool for 15 to 20 minutes. Spread yogurt over half of each baked shell. Alternate 5 slices kiwifruit and 5 slices strawberry on yogurt. Fold shells over to form tacos. Spread mango coulis in 3x4-inch ovals on bottom halves of 6 plates. Pipe raspberry sauce in 2 stripes across coulis. Swirl through sauces with knife. Place 1 taco beside coulis on each plate. Garnish each plate with raspberries and mint. Yield: 6 servings.

Desert Inn Hotel
Chef Michael Ty

The Stars'
DESERT INN
Hotel & Country Club   Las Vegas

CASEROLETTE NOTTINGHAM

3 ounces chicken breast chunks
Butter
Minced garlic to taste
2 ounces fresh white mushroom
  halves
1 teaspoon fresh thyme

3 ounces fresh lobster meat
2 ounces white wine
1½ ounces Lobster Sauce
1½ ounces Curry Sauce
1 ounce cream
1 pastry casserolette

Rinse chicken and pat dry. Sauté in butter in sauté pan. Add garlic, mushrooms, thyme and lobster. Cook over high heat for 5 minutes. Add wine. Cook until reduced to desired consistency. Bring to a simmer. Add Lobster Sauce, Curry Sauce and cream; mix well. Simmer for 5 minutes. Spoon into casserolette; garnish with parsley. Serve with black fettucini and vegetable of choice. Yield: 1 serving.

Lobster Sauce: Sauté one 2-pound Maine lobster and 1 cup chopped celery, carrots and onion in 1 tablespoon butter in large saucepan until lobster is red. Add 1 ounce lobster base, ¼ cup tomato purée, pinch of Spanish paprika, 1 tablespoon curry powder, 1 bay leaf, 1 teaspoon pickling spice, ½ teaspoon thyme, pinch of cayenne pepper, salt and pepper to taste, 1 quart fish stock and 2 ounces sherry. Simmer for 45 minutes. Stir in ½ cup roux. Simmer for 25 minutes longer. Strain sauce, reserving lobster meat. Combine sauce with 1 cup heavy cream in medium saucepan. Bring to a simmer.

Curry Sauce: Sauté ¼ cup each chopped onion, celery, carrot and apple in 1 tablespoon butter in heavy saucepan. Add ¼ cup Madras curry powder, 2 bay leaves and 1 teaspoon thyme. Add 1 cup white wine, stirring to deglaze. Bring to a boil. Add 1 quart chicken stock, ¼ cup chopped banana and pinch of nutmeg. Simmer for 30 minutes. Stir in ½ cup roux and salt and pepper to taste. Simmer for 30 to 35 minutes longer. Strain sauce.

Excalibur Hotel and Casino
Executive Chef Lucio Arancibia

LINGUINE PORTO FINO

1¹/₂ pounds uncooked linguine
4 quarts boiling water
16 each shrimp and scallops
2 tablespoons chopped fresh garlic
1 ounce oil
8 ounces clam juice
4 ounces white wine

16 ounces marinara sauce
¹/₂ teaspoon crushed red pepper
1 tablespoon chopped basil
1 tablespoon chopped oregano
2 tablespoons butter
1 16-ounce jar baby clams
Salt to taste

Cook pasta in boiling water in large saucepan until tender; drain. Sauté shrimp, scallops, and garlic in oil in skillet. Add next 7 ingredients. Cook until reduced to desired consistency. Add clams and salt. Remove shrimp and scallops with slotted spoon. Add pasta to sauce in skillet; toss to mix well. Cook until heated through. Spoon onto serving plates; arrange shrimp and scallops around pasta. Yield: 4 servings.

SAUCY BREAD PUDDING

6 eggs
6 egg yolks
2¹/₂ cups sugar
2 cups half and half
2 quarts milk
1 cup dark rum

1 tablespoon vanilla extract
1¹/₂ 8-inch loaves French bread,
  torn
1¹/₄ cups sugar
2 cups water
3 cups cream

Combine eggs, egg yolks, and 2¹/₂ cups sugar in mixer bowl; beat until thick and lemon-colored. Add half and half, milk, rum and vanilla; mix well. Pour over bread in 9x10-inch baking pan. Bake at 375 degrees for 1 hour. Combine 1¹/₄ cups sugar with water in saucepan. Cook until golden brown. Add cream. Simmer over low heat until thickened to desired consistency. Serve over warm bread pudding. Top with whipped cream. Yield: 10 servings.

Greens Supper Club
Chef George Sanchez

Supper Club

CIOPPINO

Chopped shallots and garlic to taste
Basil, thyme, oregano, dill, rosemary and parsley to taste
1 ounce clarified butter
2 (12-count) shrimp
2 (10-count) scallops
2 littleneck clams
2 ounces snow crab
2 black mussels

2 ounces salmon, cubed
2 ounces swordfish, cubed
2 ounces white wine
1 ounce cubed Roma tomato
4 ounces lobster stock
4 ounces tomato juice
Salt and pepper to taste
Butter to taste
Parsley
1 sourdough crouton

Sauté shallots, garlic and herbs in clarified butter in saucepan for 1 minute. Add shrimp, scallops, clams, crab, mussels, salmon and swordfish. Sauté for 2 minutes. Add wine to saucepan, stirring to deglaze. Add tomato, lobster stock, tomato juice, salt, pepper and butter. Steam, covered, until done to taste. Garnish with parsley and crouton. Yield: 1 large serving.

Jerome's Restaurant
Chef Chris Sbrascia

J E R O M E ' S

ESCARGOT JEROME

6 snails
Chopped shallots and garlic to
  taste
1 ounce clarified butter
Basil, thyme, oregano, rosemary
  and dill to taste
1 ounce pine nuts

2 ounces white wine
1 ounce Gorgonzola cheese
2 ounces demi-glaze
1 ounce unsalted butter
Salt and pepper to taste
3 round croutons

Sauté snails, shallots and garlic in clarified butter in medium saucepan for 1 minute. Add herbs and pine nuts. Sauté for 1 minute. Add wine to saucepan, stirring to deglaze. Add cheese and demi-glaze. Simmer for several minutes. Add 1 ounce butter, salt and pepper. Arrange croutons on serving plate. Place 2 snails on each crouton; drizzle with sauce. Yield: 1 serving.

Jerome's Restaurant
Chef Chris Sbrascia

J E R O M E ' S

GRILLED SWORDFISH AND BARBECUED SHRIMP WITH HONEY-MUSTARD VINAIGRETTE AND SWEET ONIONS

1 teaspoon Dijon mustard
1 teaspoon corn oil
1 teaspoon rice wine
1 teaspoon honey
1   6-ounce swordfish filet, 1 inch thick
1 ounce olive oil

Salt and pepper to taste
3 (15-count) shrimp
1½ ounces barbecue sauce
1 small sweet onion, sliced ½ inch thick
Parsley sprigs

Combine mustard, corn oil, rice wine and honey in bowl; mix well. Rub swordfish with olive oil; sprinkle with salt and pepper. Rub shrimp with 1 ounce barbecue sauce. Arrange swordfish in 1 end of broiler pan; arrange shrimp in other end of broiler pan. Place sliced onion between seafood. Place on top rack of broiler preheated to 450 degrees. Broil for 4 minutes on each side. Spoon honey-mustard on 1 side of serving plate; place onions on other side of plate. Arrange swordfish in honey-mustard; arrange shrimp on onions. Drizzle shrimp with remaining ½ ounce barbecue sauce. Garnish with parsley sprigs. Yield: 1 serving.

Kokomo's
The Mirage
Chef Robert A. Camerota

KOKOMO'S

ARTICHOKE WITH GOAT CHEESE WRAPPED IN PHYLLO DOUGH

1 artichoke bottom
1 ounce white wine
1/4 ounce basil
1/4 ounce chives

2 ounces phyllo dough
1 ounce butter, softened
1 ounce goat cheese, crumbled

Sauté artichoke bottom in heated nonstick sauté pan. Add wine, basil and chives. Cool to room temperature. Spread phyllo dough with butter; put together by overlapping edges. Place small amount of phyllo dough in center; place artichoke bottom on center portion. Sprinkle with mixture of cheese and sautéed herbs. Fold dough to enclose artichoke. Place in baking pan. Bake in moderate oven for 12 minutes or until golden brown. Yield: 1 serving.

Las Vegas Hilton
Assistant Executive Chef John Guyer

)(Las Vegas Hilton
It's all in the style.®

AMARETTO CUSTARD

5 ounces sugar
10 egg yolks
2 ounces Amaretto
1 teaspoon vanilla extract

1 capful almond extract
Salt to taste
2¹/₂ ounces almond paste
1 quart half and half, scalded

Combine sugar, egg yolks, liqueur, flavorings and salt in mixer bowl; whip until smooth. Blend almond paste with a small amount of warm half and half in small saucepan. Add 2 cups half and half gradually, mixing well. Bring to a simmer. Stir in remaining half and half; remove from heat. Stir a small amount of warm mixture into egg mixture; stir egg mixture into warm mixture. Strain into buttered and sugared molds. Bake at 350 degrees for 45 minutes. Unmold onto serving plates. Yield: 9 servings.

Andiamo
Las Vegas Hilton
Stanton Ho, Executive Pastry Chef

AUSTRIAN CARAMEL PECAN TARTS

18 ounces bread flour
1/2 ounce baking powder
10 3/4 ounces butter, softened
5 1/4 ounces sugar
Grated rind of 1/2 lemon
1 egg
1 egg white

1 pound plus 2 ounces sugar
12 ounces almond paste
5 ounces milk
1 cup whipping cream
Chopped pecans to taste
Apricot glaze

Sift bread flour and baking powder together. Cream butter and 5 1/4 ounces sugar in mixer bowl until light and fluffy. Add lemon rind, egg and egg white; mix well. Add sifted flour mixture; mix well. Press mixture into fifteen 4-inch tart pans. Bake at 380 degrees for 10 minutes. Sprinkle 1 pound and 2 ounces sugar in saucepan. Cook over medium heat until sugar is caramelized. Blend almond paste with milk in bowl. Add to caramelized sugar; mix well with wooden spoon. Add cream gradually. Stir in pecans. Spoon into prepared pastry shells. Bake at 380 degrees for 30 minutes. Cool on wire rack. Brush with apricot glaze. Serve with vanilla ice cream or crème Anglaise. Yield: 15 servings.

Andiamo
Las Vegas Hilton
Stanton Ho, Executive Pastry Chef

GINGER CRÈME BRÛLÉE

20 egg yolks
³/₄ cup sugar
6 cups whipping cream
1 tablespoon vanilla extract

¹/₂ teaspoon ground ginger
2 tablespoons chopped preserved
  ginger
1 teaspoon preserved ginger syrup

Whisk egg yolks and sugar in double boiler until smooth. Cook over hot water until thickened, stirring constantly; remove from heat. Add whipping cream very gradually, stirring constantly. Cook until thickened, whisking frequently. Stir in vanilla; remove from heat. Add ground ginger, preserved ginger and preserved ginger syrup; mix well. Spoon into 9 individual ramekins. Chill for 6 hours. Yield: 9 servings.

Mayflower Cuisinier
Chef Ming See Woo

GRILLED SEA BASS WITH
FRESH TOMATO CURRY SAUCE

2 tablespoons canola oil
Juice of ½ lemon
1 tablespoon red wine vinegar
Kosher salt and freshly ground
  pepper to taste
2 8-ounce Chilean sea bass filets
1 tablespoon chopped garlic
1 tablespoon chopped shallot

1 tablespoon canola oil
4 Roma tomatoes, chopped
Juice of ½ lemon
2 ounces Chablis
4 ounces tomato juice
½ teaspoon curry powder
2 tablespoons basil leaf chiffonade
2 tablespoons mint leaves

Combine 2 tablespoons oil, juice of ½ lemon, vinegar, salt and pepper in bowl. Add bass. Marinate in refrigerator for 1 hour. Grill for 5 to 8 minutes or until fish flakes easily; keep warm. Sauté garlic and shallot in 1 tablespoon heated oil in nonstick sauté pan until golden brown. Add tomatoes. Sauté for 1 minute. Add juice of ½ lemon, wine, tomato juice and curry powder. Simmer for 2 minutes. Add basil chiffonade and mint. Simmer for 1 minute; adjust seasonings. Place fish on serving plates; spoon sauce over top. May reduce sauce more for thicker consistency. Yield: 2 servings.

The Mirage
Assistant Executive Chef Christopher Young

RACK OF LAMB LAFAYETTE

4 racks of lamb
4 cloves of garlic, chopped
Fresh mint to taste
1 teaspoon thyme
1 teaspoon rosemary
2 bay leaves

¹/₄ cup olive oil
Salt and pepper to taste
¹/₄ cup Dijon mustard
1 tablespoon white wine
Bread crumbs

Ask butcher to remove spine bones from racks of lamb. Cut out meat halfway down between rib bones, discarding fat from tops of racks. Rub lamb with garlic, mint, thyme, rosemary and bay leaves. Combine with olive oil in bowl. Marinate in refrigerator for 2 days or longer. Season lamb with salt and pepper. Cut each rack into halves and wrap rib bones with buttered paper to prevent burning. Place in roasting pan. Roast at 400 to 450 degrees for 30 minutes. Reduce oven temperature to 350 degrees. Combine mustard and wine in small bowl; mix well. Remove buttered paper from rib bones. Brush outside of racks with mustard mixture; dip in bread crumbs. Stand lamb in same roasting pan and fold rib bones between each other. Roast at 350 degrees for 10 minutes or until crumbs are brown. Serve standing on platter; garnish with additional mint. Yield: 4 servings.

MGM Grand Hotel, Inc.
Chef Bruno Wehren

WORLD'S LARGEST HOTEL, CASINO & THEME PARK

RASPBERRY VELVET TART

3/4 cup cake flour
3/4 cup all-purpose flour
1/4 cup sugar
1/2 cup unsalted butter, chopped
1 egg yolk
1 tablespoon whipping cream

1 tablespoon cold water
2 cups raspberries
12 ounces white chocolate, chopped
1/2 cup whipping cream, heated
1/4 cup unsalted butter, softened

Mix cake flour, all-purpose flour and sugar in large bowl. Cut in 1/2 cup butter until crumbly. Beat egg yolk with 1 tablespoon cream in small bowl. Add to flour mixture; mix to form dough, adding water if needed to bind. Shape into ball; press into disc. Chill, wrapped in plastic wrap, for 30 minutes. Roll 1/8 inch thick on lightly floured surface. Fit into 9-inch tart pan with removable bottom; trim edge. Chill for 30 minutes. Line pastry with foil or baking parchment and fill with dried beans or pie weights. Bake at 350 degrees for 15 minutes. Remove beans and foil. Bake for 15 minutes longer or until golden brown. Cool on wire rack. Reserve several raspberries for garnish. Distribute remaining raspberries evenly in cooled crust. Melt white chocolate in double boiler over simmering water, stirring until smooth. Stir in 1/2 cup hot cream and 1/4 cup butter. Spoon over raspberries. Chill, covered, for 1 hour to 1 day. Place on serving plate; remove side of pan. Garnish with reserved raspberries. Yield: 8 servings.

MGM Grand Hotel, Inc.
Chef Bruno Wehren

WORLD'S LARGEST HOTEL, CASINO & THEME PARK

LOBSTER VENTI

2 ounces lobster tail
Salt and pepper to taste
1 ounce flour
1 ounce olive oil
1 ounce shallots
2 ounces white wine
2 ounces lobster sauce
1 ounce whipping cream

$^1/_2$ teaspoon each chopped fresh
  basil and parsley
Chopped chives to taste
Crushed red pepper to taste
$1^1/_2$ ounces cooked capellini
1 tomato rose
3 Belgian endive leaves
1 tablespoon finely chopped tomato

Cut lobster tail into 3 pieces. Sprinkle with salt and pepper; coat with flour. Heat olive oil in skillet until smoking hot. Add lobster. Sauté until golden brown. Add shallots and wine. Cook until wine is reduced to desired consistency. Remove lobster to heated platter with slotted spoon and keep warm. Combine lobster sauce with cream, basil, parsley, chives and red pepper in saucepan. Bring to a boil. Add lobster; remove from heat. Place pasta in center of serving plate. Top with tomato rose. Alternate endive leaves and lobster meat around pasta. Spoon chopped tomato into tip of each endive leaf. Spoon sauce over lobster. Yield: 1 serving.

Le Montrachet
Las Vegas Hilton
Chef David Ventimiglia

PIGNOLI STRIPED BASS

2 ounces pine nuts, crushed	¹/₄ cup flour
1 ounce parsley, chopped	1 ounce clarified butter
1 egg	1 ounce champagne sauce
2 tablespoons water	¹/₄ teaspoon Sevruga caviar
1 3-ounce striped bass filet	1 tomato rose
Salt and white pepper to taste	2 sprigs of parsley

Mix pine nuts and chopped parsley in bowl; set aside. Beat egg with water in shallow bowl. Sprinkle fish with salt and pepper; coat with flour. Dip into egg mixture; roll in pine nut mixture, coating well. Place in baking dish; drizzle with butter. Bake at 350 degrees for 5 minutes or until fish flakes easily. Combine champagne sauce with caviar in small bowl. Pour into 7-inch serving plate; place fish in sauce. Garnish with tomato rose and parsley sprigs at top of plate. Yield: 1 serving.

Le Montrachet
Las Vegas Hilton
Chef David Ventimiglia

PHYLLO WITH FRESH BERRIES

2 cups fresh raspberries
2 cups fresh strawberries
2 cups fresh blackberries
2 ounces Grand Marnier

6 sheets of phyllo dough
1 tablespoon butter, softened
1 tablespoon confectioners' sugar

Combine raspberries, strawberries, blackberries and liqueur in bowl; mix gently and set aside. Place 1 sheet of phyllo dough on work surface; brush with softened butter. Cut sheet into halves. Crinkle up each half of the dough and place 1 half on top of the other on baking sheet. Repeat with remaining dough. Bake at 325 degrees for 4 minutes or until light brown. Place phyllo on 6 serving plates. Spoon berries over top; sprinkle with confectioners' sugar. May use any fresh berries in season for this refreshing and different dessert. Yield: 6 servings.

Palace Court Restaurant
Caesars Palace Hotel
Chef Arnauld Briand

SPRINGTIME CHICKEN SALAD

½ cup virgin olive oil
½ cup balsamic vinegar
2 tablespoons lemon juice
Salt and pepper to taste
3   8-ounce chicken breasts,
   skinned

8 cups Sonoma mixed greens
1 red endive
4 long chives, cut into strips
1 plum tomato, julienned

Combine olive oil, vinegar, lemon juice, salt and pepper in bowl. Rinse chicken and pat dry. Combine with ¼ of the olive oil mixture in bowl. Marinate for 15 minutes. Place chicken on rack in broiler pan. Broil just until cooked through; do not overcook. Combine remaining olive oil mixture with mixed greens in bowl; toss gently. Place on 6 serving plates. Arrange endive flower on top of each plate. Slice chicken and arrange over salad. Garnish with strips of chive and tomato. This tasty dish is especially good for spring and summer. Yield: 6 servings.

Palace Court Restaurant
Caesars Palace Hotel
Chef Arnauld Briand

ROSEMARY CHICKEN

1 cup extra-virgin olive oil
1¼ teaspoons ground garlic
¼ cup white wine
¼ cup chicken broth
1 ounce rosemary
½ ounce cracked pepper
4   20-ounce chickens

8 red potatoes
1 teaspoon minced garlic
½ ounce rosemary
1 tablespoon white wine
1 tablespoon chicken broth
¼ teaspoon butter

Combine olive oil, 1¼ teaspoons garlic, ¼ cup wine, ¼ cup chicken broth, 1 ounce rosemary and pepper in bowl. Rinse chickens and pat dry. Add to marinade. Marinate in refrigerator for 12 hours; drain. Combine chicken with potatoes in baking dish. Bake in moderate oven for 30 minutes or until cooked through. Drain pan drippings into sauté pan. Add 1 teaspoon garlic and ½ ounce rosemary. Sauté until golden brown. Add 1 tablespoon wine and 1 tablespoon chicken broth, stirring to deglaze skillet. Stir in butter. Place chicken and potatoes on serving plate; spoon sauce over top.
Yield: 4 servings.

Palace Station
Chef Walter Worotylko

CHAMPAGNE FETTUCINI

1 medium onion, coarsely chopped	2 cups coarsely chopped asparagus
1/4 tablespoon whole cloves	2 tablespoons olive oil
1/4 tablespoon olive oil	1 teaspoon minced garlic
8 ounces champagne	1/4 cup chopped fresh basil
1/4 cup fish broth	4 ounces butter
1 quart cream	Salt and pepper to taste
16 medium shrimp, cleaned, deveined	1 pound fettucini, cooked
	1 cup chopped fresh tomato

Sauté onion with cloves in 1/4 tablespoon olive oil in saucepan just until onion is tender but not browned. Stir in champagne, fish broth and cream. Simmer for 30 minutes, stirring frequently. Strain and set aside. Cut shrimp into halves lengthwise. Sauté shrimp and asparagus lightly in 2 tablespoons olive oil in saucepan. Add garlic. Sauté until golden brown. Add 16 ounces of the strained champagne sauce, basil, butter, salt and pepper. Simmer for 5 minutes or until slightly thickened. Add fettucini and tomato; toss lightly. Yield: 4 servings.

Palace Station
Chef Walter Worotylko

PALACE STATION
HOTEL · CASINO

TUACA TIRAMISU

6 ounces dry ladyfingers	3 tablespoons sugar
3/4 cup brewed espresso	1 pound mascarpone cheese
2 tablespoons Tuaca (Italian liqueur)	3 egg whites
3 egg yolks	1/4 cup unsweetened baking cocoa

Arrange ladyfingers on large baking sheet. Pour mixture of espresso and liqueur over ladyfingers; set aside. Beat egg yolks with sugar in mixer bowl for 4 to 5 minutes or until thick and lemon-colored. Add cheese, beating at low speed until smooth. Beat egg whites in large mixer bowl for 2 to 3 minutes or until soft peaks form. Fold into cheese mixture with rubber spatula. Line bottom of 2-quart glass soufflé dish with ladyfingers. Spread with half the cheese mixture and sift half the cocoa over cheese. Repeat layers with remaining ingredients. Chill, covered, overnight.
Yield: 6 servings.

Pegasus
Alexis Park Resort
Chef John Ciborski

BLACK PEPPER BEEF

12 ounces flank steak, cubed
1/4 cup oil
2 ounces fresh mushrooms
2 ounces white onion, chopped
2 ounces green onion bulbs,
  chopped
Minced garlic to taste
1/4 teaspoon pepper

1/4 cup water
1/2 teaspoon sugar
1/4 teaspoon instant chicken
  bouillon
1 teaspoon oyster sauce
1 teaspoon soy sauce
1 teaspoon cornstarch

Cook steak cubes in oil in skillet until medium brown; remove with slotted spoon. Stir mushrooms, onion, green onions, garlic, pepper and 1/4 cup water into skillet. Cook for several minutes. Add beef, sugar, chicken bouillon, oyster sauce and soy sauce to skillet. Blend cornstarch with a small amount of water in small bowl. Add to skillet. Cook until thickened, stirring constantly. Yield: 1 serving.

Rik'shaw
Riviera Hotel and Casino
Chef Mai Shao

APRICOT CHICKEN

1¹/₂ chicken breasts, skinned	1 ounce apricot brandy
Flour	3 apricot halves
2 ounces clarified butter	2 ounces apricot juice
1 teaspoon apricot preserves	¹/₂ ounce Bordelaise sauce
2¹/₄ ounces butter	Chopped parsley

Cut larger piece of chicken into 2 portions. Rinse chicken and pat dry. Coat well with flour, shaking off excess. Sauté in clarified butter in hot sauté pan until golden brown. Add apricot preserves and ¹/₄ ounce butter. Cook until preserves melt. Add brandy and ignite. Add remaining 2 ounces butter, apricot halves and apricot juice. Stir in Bordelaise sauce. Cook until heated through. Place chicken on serving plate. Place 1 apricot half on each piece of chicken; spoon sauce over top. Garnish with parsley. Yield: 1 serving.

Redwood Bar & Grill
Sam Boyd's California Hotel Casino
Chef Eric Kornbluh

LOBSTER THERMIDOR

1 10-ounce Australian lobster tail
1 pinch each garlic, shallots and
   thyme
2 ounces clarified butter
2 ounces mushrooms, sliced
2 tablespoons each sherry and
   white wine

1 tablespoon lemon juice
5 tablespoons whipping cream
2 ounces butter
2 ounces Parmesan cheese, grated
Salt and pepper to taste

Remove lobster meat from shell, reserving shell. Place shell in roasting pan. Roast until shell is bright red; set aside. Chop lobster into bite-sized pieces. Sauté with garlic, shallots and thyme in clarified butter in hot sauté pan. Add mushrooms. Sauté for several minutes. Add sherry, white wine and lemon juice. Cook until reduced to desired consistency. Stir in cream, 2 ounces butter, cheese, salt and pepper. Cook until slightly thickened. Place lobster shell on serving plate. Spoon lobster meat into shell. Spoon some of the sauce over lobster; serve remaining sauce in bowl. Yield: 1 serving.

Redwood Bar & Grill
Sam Boyd's California Hotel Casino
Chef Mark Piludo

SEAFOOD NEAPOLITAN

3 large scallops
3 (10-count) shrimp
3 fresh clams
1/2 each yellow and red bell
  pepper, chopped
1/2 onion, chopped
2 mushrooms
1 tablespoon minced fresh garlic

1 tablespoon minced shallots
1 teaspoon each oregano and basil
Salt and white pepper to taste
2 tablespoons sherry
6 tablespoons clam juice
3 ounces crushed tomatoes
1 tablespoon butter

Sauté scallops, shrimp and clams in hot skillet. Add bell peppers and onion. Cook until onion is translucent. Add mushrooms, garlic, shallots, oregano, basil, salt and pepper. Add sherry, stirring to deglaze skillet. Stir in clam juice and tomatoes. Cook for 5 minutes or until reduced to desired consistency. Stir in butter. Yield: 1 serving.

Ristorante Italiano
Riviera Hotel
Executive Chef Rene Werner

RISOTTO CON SALMONE AND FINOCCHIO

1 teaspoon chopped fresh garlic
1 tablespoon butter
6 ounces uncooked rice
2 tablespoons dry vermouth
17 ounces fish stock, heated
1 medium fresh fennel, thinly
 sliced
8 ounces fresh salmon

Salt and pepper to taste
1 tablespoon butter
2 tablespoons dry vermouth
1/2 teaspoon chopped fresh parsley
1 1/2 ounces Parmesan cheese,
 grated
1/4 cup dill leaves

Sauté garlic in 1 tablespoon butter in saucepan until light brown. Add rice. Cook until evenly coated, stirring constantly with wooden spoon. Add 2 tablespoons wine. Simmer for 1 minute. Add hot fish stock gradually. Simmer for 8 minutes. Stir in fennel. Simmer until rice is almost tender; do not overcook. Cover and set aside. Cut salmon into 1/2-inch pieces; sprinkle with salt and pepper. Sauté in 1/2 tablespoon butter in heated nonstick sauté pan for 2 minutes or until nearly cooked. Add 2 tablespoons wine. Cook for 30 seconds or until fish flakes easily. Fold into rice with remaining 1/2 tablespoon butter, parsley, cheese and 1 tablespoon dill. Spoon into 2 serving bowls. Garnish with remaining 3 tablespoons dill. Yield: 2 servings.

Ristorante Riva
The Mirage
Chef Tom Janarone

RISTORANTE
R I V A

SMOKED TURKEY SALAD

2 pounds smoked turkey
8 ounces Jarlsberg cheese
2 cups seedless green grapes
2 cups seedless red grapes
1 cup thinly sliced celery
1 cup salted cashews

1½ cups mayonnaise
¼ cup medium-dry sherry
2 tablespoons Dijon mustard
Green leaf lettuce
Salad greens

Cut turkey into 1-inch cubes; cut cheese into ¼x1½-inch strips. Combine turkey, cheese, grapes, celery and cashews in bowl. Combine mayonnaise, wine and mustard in small bowl; mix until smooth. Add to turkey mixture; mix well. Chill until serving time. Arrange lettuce and salad greens in serving bowl. Spoon turkey salad into center. Yield: 12 servings.

Socorro Springs Cafe
Las Vegas Hilton
Sous Chef Ken Bozzo

SALAD WITH LIME VINAIGRETTE

1 tablespoon white wine
2 tablespoons fresh lime juice
1/2 tablespoon grated lime zest
6 tablespoons olive oil
2 tablespoons chopped cilantro
2 ounces chopped iceberg lettuce
2 ounces chopped romaine lettuce
1 radish, thinly sliced
1 ounce broccoli flowerets
1 ounce cauliflowerets

1/2 ounce sliced red onion
1 1/2 ounces shredded carrot
1 green leaf
4 ounces orange roughy, steamed, flaked
Croutons
2 cherry tomatoes
1 lime slice
1 1/2 ounces sliced cucumber

Combine wine, lime juice, lime zest, olive oil and cilantro in small bowl; mix well. Combine lettuce, radish, broccoli, cauliflower, onion and carrot in medium bowl; toss to mix well. Arrange on green leaf in serving bowl. Top with flaked fish and croutons. Decorate with cherry tomatoes on 1 side, lime slice in center and cucumber slices. Serve with lime vinaigrette.
Yield: 1 serving.

Socorro Springs Cafe
Las Vegas Hilton
Sous Chef Ken Bozzo

BEEF SATÉ WITH SPICY SZECHUAN SAUCE

12 ounces New York or filet steak, trimmed
1/2 cup soy sauce
1 tablespoon honey
1 teaspoon chili flakes
1/2 teaspoon each cumin and turmeric
1 green onion, finely chopped

1 tablespoon chopped blanched garlic
2 tablespoons unsalted butter
1 cup brown veal or chicken stock
1/4 cup soy sauce
1 teaspoon chili flakes
1/4 cup unsalted butter

Soak twenty-four 6-inch bamboo skewers in cold water in refrigerator for 1 hour; drain. Cut steak into twenty-four 1x3-inch strips. Thread each strip lengthwise onto skewers; arrange on large platter. Combine 1/2 cup soy sauce, honey, 1 teaspoon chili flakes, cumin and turmeric in bowl; mix well. Pour over skewered steak. Marinate at room temperature for 15 minutes. Sauté green onion and garlic in 2 tablespoons butter in small skillet over medium-high heat for 2 minutes or until tender. Add veal stock, 1/4 cup soy sauce and 1 teaspoon chili flakes. Cook for 1 to 2 minutes longer. Strain into clean saucepan. Whisk in 1/4 cup butter; keep warm. Arrange skewered steak on grill or broiler pan. Grill or broil for 30 to 40 seconds on each side or until medium rare, taking care not to burn ends of skewers. Pour sauce into small bowl and place in center of large serving platter. Arrange skewers around bowl. Serve immediately. May marinate earlier in day and grill or broil just before serving. Yield: 2 servings.

Spago
Chef Wolfgang Puck

Wolfgang Puck's

Spago

Las Vegas

TILLERMAN'S PORTO FINO

1 tablespoon olive oil
1/2 tablespoon freshly chopped garlic
3 ounces fresh fish, cut into bite-sized pieces
1 scallop
2 large peeled shrimp
5 mussels
5 clams

2 large tomatoes, chopped
6 tablespoons tomato purée
1/2 tablespoon chopped fresh oregano
1/2 tablespoon chopped fresh basil
4 ounces chicken stock
1 tablespoon grated Reggianito cheese
4 ounces linguine, cooked

Heat oil in medium saucepan. Sauté garlic in saucepan until tender but not browned. Add fish, scallop, shrimp, mussels and clams. Sauté for 1 minute. Add tomatoes, tomato purée, oregano, basil, chicken stock and cheese. Bring to a boil; reduce heat. Add cooked linguine. Simmer for 3 minutes, stirring constantly. Remove to serving plate, arranging clams and mussels around edge of plate. Yield: 1 serving.

The Tillerman Restaurant
Chef Miguel Magana

SAMOAN SEAFOOD SALAD

1 pound chicken breast filets
Flour
1 cup margarine
4 ounces garlic, minced
3/4 cup sherry
1 cup soy sauce
1 cup honey
16 ounces salmon filet
16 ounces (16 to 20-count) shrimp

8 ounces (10-count) sea scallops
2 heads romaine lettuce, chopped
1 head iceberg lettuce, chopped
3 tomatoes, cut into wedges
1 6-ounce jar stuffed green olives
4 ounces fresh mushrooms, sliced
Croutons
Salad dressing

Rinse chicken and pat dry; cut into strips. Coat with flour. Sauté chicken in 1/4 cup margarine in sauté pan. Stir in garlic, wine, soy sauce and honey. Bring to a boil. Spoon into bowl. Cut salmon into 1/4-inch slices. Coat salmon, shrimp and scallops with flour. Sauté each seafood separately in 1/4 cup margarine in sauté pan, adding each to bowl with chicken to marinate. Cool chicken and seafood. Combine lettuces, tomatoes, green olives and mushrooms in salad bowl; toss gently. Arrange chicken and seafood on salad; garnish with croutons. Serve with choice of salad dressing.
Yield: 4 to 6 servings.

Tropicana Resort and Casino
Chef Kerry Slagle

TROPICANA
Resort & Casino

GARLIC SMASHED POTATOES

15 pounds red potatoes with skins
1 cup butter
6 cups half and half
2 cups heavy cream

1¹/₂ cups mashed roasted garlic
3 tablespoons mixed salt and
** white pepper**

Boil potatoes in skins in water to cover in saucepan until tender. Combine butter, half and half and cream in glass bowl. Microwave on High until butter melts. Drain potatoes. Mash with potato masher, leaving a few lumps. Add warmed half and half mixture, garlic paste, salt and pepper; mix well. Yield: 30 servings

Vine Street Cafe
Chef Sammy Pollack

BREAD PUDDING

3 quarts whipping cream
6 cups sugar
48 eggs
Salt and cinnamon to taste

1 ounce vanilla extract
2 large baking dishes of torn dry
    bread or Danish pastry

Combine cream, sugar and eggs in mixer bowl; mix at low speed for 1 minute. Add salt, cinnamon and vanilla; mix well. Pour over bread in 2 large baking dishes. Let stand for 1 hour. Bake in moderate oven for 35 minutes or until golden brown. Yield: 40 servings.

World's Fare Buffet
Riviera Hotel and Casino
Pastry Chef Tom Martinez

APPETIZERS & BEVERAGES

BRUSCHETTA

This simple appetizer is a special treat during the height of the summer season, when both vine-ripened tomatoes and fresh basil are at their peak. For an authentic Italian taste, toast the bread over a grill; in Italy a wood fire is used.

20 ½-inch slices Italian bread
1 small clove of garlic, cut into
  halves
¼ cup extra-virgin olive oil

1 to 1½ cups chopped tomatoes
1 tablespoon minced red onion
20 small basil leaves or torn
  pieces of larger leaves

Rub 1 side of each bread slice with cut side of garlic; brush each slice lightly with ½ teaspoon olive oil. Grill or toast for 1 to 2 minutes or until lightly browned on both sides. Combine remaining olive oil with tomatoes and onion in small bowl. Arrange bread on serving plate. Place a small basil leaf on each slice; top with 1 spoonful of tomato mixture. Serve with small dish of coarse salt. Use the best Italian bread available, preferably whole wheat, the sweetest plum tomatoes and a flavorful extra-virgin olive oil in this recipe. Yield: 20 servings.

Approx Per Serving: Cal 113; Prot 3 g; Carbo 18 g; Fiber 1 g;
  T Fat 3 g; 24% Calories from Fat; Chol 0 mg; Sod 178 mg.

CALIFORNIA-STYLE CAPONATA

¼ cup golden raisins
1 tablespoon dry sherry
2 small eggplant, chopped
1 large onion, chopped
5 tablespoons olive oil
6 ripe plum tomatoes, peeled,
  chopped

1 tablespoon tomato paste
2 tablespoons red wine vinegar
¼ cup chopped black olives
1 tablespoon capers
¼ cup coarsely chopped toasted
  walnuts
Salt and pepper to taste

Plump raisins in wine in small bowl. Sauté eggplant and onion in olive oil in skillet for 6 minutes. Add tomatoes, tomato paste, vinegar, olives, capers, walnuts, raisins, salt and pepper; mix well. Simmer over low heat for 15 minutes, stirring frequently. Spoon into mound in center of serving plate. Serve warm or cooled with toasted baguette slices or water crackers. Yield: 16 servings.

Approx Per Serving: Cal 78; Prot 1 g; Carbo 6 g; Fiber 2 g;
  T Fat 6 g; 66% Calories from Fat; Chol 0 mg; Sod 27 mg.
  Nutritional information does not include capers.

HERBED CHEESE TARTS

These tarts look very festive for the holidays when garnished in red and green.

1/3 cup seasoned dry bread crumbs	1/4 teaspoon dried basil, crushed
8 ounces cream cheese, softened	1/4 teaspoon garlic powder
3/4 cup ricotta cheese	2 eggs
1/2 cup shredded Gruyère cheese	1 cup sour cream
1 tablespoon flour	

Spray twenty-four 1³/₄-inch muffin cups with nonstick cooking spray. Sprinkle bread crumbs over bottoms and sides, coating well. Shake out excess crumbs. Combine cream cheese, ricotta cheese, Gruyère cheese, flour, basil and garlic powder in small bowl; beat until fluffy. Add eggs; mix just until smooth. Spoon into prepared muffin cups. Bake at 375 degrees for 15 minutes or until centers appear set. Cool in pan on wire rack for 10 minutes. Remove from pan to wire rack to cool completely; centers will fall. Top each tart with 1 teaspoon sour cream Garnish with choice of sliced black or green olives, minced green onion tops, red caviar, minced red peppers or pimento cut-outs. Yield: 24 servings.

Approx Per Serving: Cal 90; Prot 3 g; Carbo 2 g; Fiber <1 g; T Fat 8 g; 76% Calories from Fat; Chol 39 mg; Sod 63 mg.

HONEY CHICKEN WINGS

1 cup honey	2 teaspoons oil
1/2 cup catsup	2 large cloves of garlic, minced
1/2 cup soy sauce	3 pounds chicken wings

Combine honey, catsup, soy sauce, oil and garlic in medium bowl; mix well. Cut each chicken wing into 3 portions, discarding tip portions. Rinse chicken and pat dry. Dip into sauce; arrange in shallow baking dish. Drizzle with remaining sauce. Bake at 375 degrees for 45 minutes; turn chicken. Bake for 30 to 45 minutes longer or until brown. Yield: 30 servings.

Approx Per Serving: Cal 144; Prot 9 g; Carbo 11 g; Fiber <1 g; T Fat 7 g; 44% Calories from Fat; Chol 29 mg; Sod 350 mg.

 *Appetizers*

HOT CLAM DIP WITH GREEN CHILIES

8 ounces cream cheese, softened
8 ounces sour cream
2 7-ounce cans minced clams, drained
4 green onions with tops, chopped

1 4-ounce can chopped green chilies
Salt and pepper to taste
1 round loaf sourdough bread

Combine cream cheese, sour cream, clams, green onions, green chilies, salt and pepper in bowl; mix well. Cut off top of bread and scoop out center; tear bread center into bite-sized pieces. Spoon clam mixture into bread indentation. Place dip-filled bread loaf shell and torn bread pieces on baking sheet. Bake at 350 degrees for 1½ hours. May bake at 250 degrees for a longer period if preferred. Yield: 12 servings.

Approx Per Serving: Cal 260; Prot 15 g; Carbo 23 g; Fiber <1 g; T Fat 13 g; 43% Calories from Fat; Chol 51 mg; Sod 400 mg.

CRAB DIP WITH SAUTERNE

16 ounces cream cheese, softened
⅓ cup homemade mayonnaise
3 tablespoons Sauterne
4 teaspoons confectioners' sugar
1 tablespoon minced green onions

1 teaspoon dry mustard
¼ teaspoon garlic salt
½ teaspoon salt
1 cup cooked fresh crab meat, flaked

Combine cream cheese, mayonnaise, wine, confectioners' sugar, green onions, dry mustard, garlic salt and salt in double boiler; mix well. Cook over hot water until smooth, stirring to mix well. Stir in crab meat. Spoon into baking dish. Bake at 350 degrees until bubbly. Serve with crackers. May substitute two 6½-ounce cans crab meat or shrimp for fresh crab meat if preferred. Yield: 12 servings.

Approx Per Serving: Cal 194; Prot 5 g; Carbo 2 g; Fiber <1 g; T Fat 18 g; 85% Calories from Fat; Chol 56 mg; Sod 310 mg.

Appetizers

GRUYÈRE FONDUE

1 clove of garlic
1 pound Swiss cheese, shredded
3 ounces Gruyère cheese, cut into
  cubes
3 tablespoons flour

2 cups white wine
Lemon juice or lemon powder to
  taste
3 tablespoons Kirsch
Nutmeg to taste

Cut garlic into halves; rub bowl with cut sides of garlic. Combine cheeses in bowl. Toss with flour 1 tablespoon at a time, coating well. Combine wine and lemon juice in heavy saucepan. Cook over medium-high heat until small foamy bubbles appear over surface, but do not allow to boil. Add cheese gradually, stirring constantly. Add Kirsch, stirring vigorously. Stir in nutmeg. Spoon into fondue pot; mixture will continue to thicken. Serve with 1-inch cubes of bread and long forks for dipping. May substitute Cognac or sherry for Kirsch. Yield: 8 servings.

Approx Per Serving: Cal 321; Prot 20 g; Carbo 7 g; Fiber <1 g; T Fat 19 g; 53% Calories from Fat; Chol 64 mg; Sod 186 mg.

EASY GUACAMOLE

This recipe can be used either as a dip with tortilla chips or as a topping for fajitas. It is especially good with Margaritas and cold Mexican beers.

15 ripe avocados, pitted, peeled
1¹/₂ cups medium-hot salsa

2 tablespoons buttermilk-recipe
  ranch-style salad dressing mix

Mash avocados coarsely in large bowl. Stir in salsa and salad dressing mix. Cover with plastic wrap, placing wrap directly on surface. Chill for up to 2 hours. Serve with tortilla chips. Yield: 24 servings.

Approx Per Serving: Cal 211; Prot 2 g; Carbo 11 g; Fiber 12 g; T Fat 19 g; 76% Calories from Fat; Chol 0 mg; Sod 213 mg.

We only grow when we push ourselves beyond what we already know.

—from *Live and Learn and Pass It On*

EGGPLANT DIP

1 large eggplant
1/3 cup lemon juice
1/3 cup sesame oil

1 large clove of garlic, minced
1/2 teaspoon salt
1 teaspoon olive oil

Cut stem from eggplant; place eggplant in baking dish. Bake at 400 degrees for 1 hour or until very tender. Scoop pulp from skin into bowl; mash or sieve until smooth. Beat in lemon juice alternately with sesame oil. Stir in garlic and salt. Spoon into serving bowl; sprinkle with olive oil. Garnish with chopped parsley and a row of pomegranate seed. Serve with pita bread, radishes and scallions. Yield: 12 servings.

Approx Per Serving: Cal 66; Prot <1 g; Carbo 2 g; Fiber 1 g;
T Fat 6 g; 84% Calories from Fat; Chol 0 mg; Sod 90 mg.

JOSEPHINES

1 pound mozzarella cheese,
shredded
1 4-ounce can chopped green
chilies

2 or 3 tablespoons mayonnaise
1 loaf French bread

Combine cheese and green chilies in bowl. Add enough mayonnaise to bind mixture; mix well. Cut bread into halves horizontally. Spread cut halves with cheese mixture. Place on baking sheet. Broil until cheese melts. Slice and serve immediately. May spread on party rounds if preferred. Yield: 20 servings.

Approx Per Serving: Cal 145; Prot 7 g; Carbo 12 g; Fiber <1 g;
T Fat 7 g; 46% Calories from Fat; Chol 19 mg; Sod 268 mg.

Love is the only thing we can carry with us when we go...
—Louisa May Alcott, *Little Women*

COCKTAIL MEATBALLS

1 pound ground chuck	1/2 teaspoon pepper
1 egg	3 cups catsup
1/2 teaspoon garlic salt	1/2 8-ounce jar grape jelly
1 teaspoon salt	Juice of 1 lemon

Combine ground chuck, egg, garlic salt, salt and pepper in bowl; mix well. Shape into 1/2-inch meatballs. Brown on all sides in large skillet; drain. Combine catsup, jelly and lemon juice in saucepan; mix well. Add meatballs. Simmer for 20 minutes. Serve warm. May substitute ground turkey for ground chuck. Yield: 12 servings.

Approx Per Serving: Cal 183; Prot 9 g; Carbo 24 g; Fiber 1 g; T Fat 6 g; 29% Calories from Fat; Chol 42 mg; Sod 1004 mg.

BOURBON DOGS

2 pounds hot dogs	1 cup bourbon
1 cup catsup	1 cup packed brown sugar

Cut hot dogs into quarters. Combine with catsup, bourbon and brown sugar in bowl; mix well. Spoon into 9x13-inch baking dish. Bake at 325 degrees for 2 hours; basting every 20 minutes. Serve hot with wooden picks. Yield: 20 servings.

Approx Per Serving: Cal 212; Prot 5 g; Carbo 11 g; Fiber <1 g; T Fat 13 g; 56% Calories from Fat; Chol 23 mg; Sod 653 mg.

FESTIVE STUFFED PEA PODS

2 cups water	1/2 cup shredded Cheddar cheese
50 pea pods	1/2 teaspoon coarsely ground
8 ounces cream cheese, softened	pepper

Bring 2 cups water to a boil in 2-quart saucepan. Add pea pods. Cook for 1 minute; drain. Place in ice water; drain well. Remove stems. Cut seam on 1 side of each pod; open to form pocket. Combine cream cheese, Cheddar cheese and pepper in small mixer bowl; beat at medium speed for 1 to 2 minutes or until smooth. Spoon or pipe mixture into pea pods. Arrange on serving plate. Chill until serving time. Yield: 50 servings.

Approx Per Serving: Cal 22; Prot 1 g; Carbo <1 g; Fiber <1 g; T Fat 2 g; 78% Calories from Fat; Chol 6 mg; Sod 21 mg.

PICO DE GALLO

This is a fresh salsa best eaten within a few hours of preparation.

6 cups drained chopped tomatoes
3 medium onions, minced
1¹/₂ cups chopped fresh cilantro

6 jalapeño peppers, seeded,
  minced
Salt and pepper to taste

Combine tomatoes, onions, cilantro, jalapeño peppers, salt and pepper in large bowl; mix well. Serve immediately or chill for up to 3 hours. Let stand, covered, until at room temperature. Yield: 40 servings.

Approx Per Serving: Cal 11; Prot <1 g; Carbo 2 g; Fiber 1 g;
  T Fat <1 g; 7% Calories from Fat; Chol 0 mg; Sod 3 mg.

PICKLED SHRIMP

3 cloves of garlic, chopped
2 onions, coarsely chopped
¹/₄ cup olive oil
2 pounds shrimp, peeled, cleaned
2 onions, thinly sliced
2 jalapeño peppers, chopped

¹/₂ cup vinegar
¹/₄ cup olive oil
¹/₄ teaspoon dry mustard
1¹/₂ teaspoons salt
¹/₂ teaspoon pepper

Sauté garlic and chopped onion in ¹/₄ cup olive oil in skillet for 10 minutes. Add shrimp. Sauté for 7 minutes. Cool for 15 minutes. Combine sliced onions, peppers, vinegar, ¹/₄ cup olive oil, dry mustard, salt and pepper in bowl; mix well. Add shrimp mixture; mix well. Marinate in refrigerator for 24 hours. Serve cold. May substitute ¹/₄ teaspoon ground dried chili peppers for jalapeño peppers. Yield: 12 servings.

Approx Per Serving: Cal 155; Prot 12 g; Carbo 5 g; Fiber 1 g;
  T Fat 10 g; 56% Calories from Fat; Chol 105 mg; Sod 389 mg.

I've learned that regardless of how little you have, you can always give comfort and encouragement.

—from *Live and Learn and Pass It On*

SHRIMP DIP WITH HORSERADISH

8 ounces cream cheese, softened
1 tablespoon mayonnaise
1 teaspoon lemon juice
2 tablespoons horseradish

¹/₄ teaspoon seasoning salt
1   4¹/₂-ounce can shrimp, drained
2 tablespoons chopped onion
¹/₂ cup chopped celery

Combine cream cheese, mayonnaise, lemon juice, horseradish and seasoning salt in bowl; mix until smooth. Add shrimp, onion and celery; mix well. Spoon into serving bowl. May substitute clams or crab meat for shrimp. Yield: 8 servings.

Approx Per Serving: Cal 134; Prot 6 g; Carbo 2 g; Fiber <1 g;
    T Fat 12 g; 77% Calories from Fat; Chol 60 mg; Sod 171 mg.

PARMESAN-MOZZARELLA ARTICHOKE SPREAD

2   16-ounce cans water-pack
    artichoke hearts, drained
1 cup mayonnaise
1¹/₂ cups shredded mozzarella
    cheese

1 cup grated Parmesan cheese
1   4-ounce can chopped green
    chilies
¹/₄ teaspoon garlic powder

Chop artichokes. Combine with mayonnaise, mozzarella cheese, Parmesan cheese, green chilies and garlic powder in bowl; mix well. Spoon into 12-inch round baking dish; sprinkle with paprika. Bake at 350 degrees for 25 minutes. May use more green chilies for a spicier taste. Yield: 6 servings.

Approx Per Serving: Cal 463; Prot 14 g; Carbo 11 g; Fiber 0 g;
    T Fat 40 g; 78% Calories from Fat; Chol 54 mg; Sod 1078 mg.

I've learned that a good feeling gets even better when it is shared.

—from *Live and Learn and Pass It On*

 *Appetizers*

FAST AND FESTIVE SEVEN-LAYER TACO DIP

Men love this appetizer.

1 cup sour cream
1 envelope taco seasoning mix
2 16-ounce cans bean dip
2 cups avocado dip
2 cups finely shredded Cheddar
  cheese
2 cups finely shredded Monterey
  Jack cheese

1 large tomato, seeded, chopped
6 bunches green onions with part
  of tops, chopped
1 4-ounce can chopped black
  olives

Combine sour cream and taco seasoning mix in bowl; mix well. Layer bean dip, sour cream mixture and avocado dip in shallow 14-inch round dish. Layer Cheddar cheese, Monterey Jack cheese, tomato, green onions and olives over top in order listed. Serve with corn chips. May vary amounts of ingredients to suit tastes or size of guest list. Yield: 16 servings.

Approx Per Serving: Cal 290; Prot 13 g; Carbo 14 g; Fiber 1 g;
  T Fat 20 g; 63% Calories from Fat; Chol 36 mg; Sod 991 mg.

TOSTADA GRANDE

12 ounces ground beef
1 16-ounce can whole tomatoes,
  drained, chopped
1 teaspoon cumin
3/4 teaspoon salt
8 6 to 8-inch flour tortillas

1 cup picante sauce
1 1/2 cups shredded Monterey Jack
  cheese
2 cups shredded lettuce
1 medium fresh tomato, chopped
1 avocado, sliced

Brown ground beef in skillet, stirring until crumbly; drain. Stir in canned tomatoes, cumin and salt. Simmer, covered, for 5 minutes. Arrange tortillas over bottom and side of 12-inch pizza pan, overlapping edges. Spread with picante sauce. Top with ground beef mixture. Bake at 350 degrees for 20 minutes. Sprinkle with cheese, lettuce, fresh tomato and avocado. Cut into wedges to serve. May substitute ground pork or turkey for beef, thick and chunky salsa for picante sauce or Cheddar cheese for Monterey Jack cheese. Yield: 6 servings.

Approx Per Serving: Cal 454; Prot 23 g; Carbo 36 g; Fiber 6 g;
  T Fat 26 g; 49% Calories from Fat; Chol 63 mg; Sod 972 mg.

ZUCCHINI APPETIZERS

3 cups thinly sliced zucchini
1 cup baking mix
1/2 cup finely chopped onion
1/2 cup grated Parmesan cheese
1/2 cup oil

4 eggs, slightly beaten
2 tablespoons chopped parsley
1/2 teaspoon basil
Garlic powder to taste
1/2 teaspoon salt

Combine zucchini, baking mix, onion, Parmesan cheese, oil, eggs, parsley, basil, garlic powder and salt in bowl; mix well. Spread in greased 9x13-inch baking dish. Bake at 350 degrees for 25 minutes or until golden brown. Cut into 1x2-inch pieces. Cool for 15 minutes. Serve warm. Yield: 54 servings.

Approx Per Serving: Cal 39; Prot 1 g; Carbo 2 g; Fiber <1 g;
T Fat 3 g; 69% Calories from Fat; Chol 16 mg; Sod 69 mg.

FIDDLE FADDLE

4 quarts popped popcorn
1 cup chopped peanuts
Salt to taste
1 cup margarine

1 1/3 cups sugar
1/2 cup light corn syrup
1 teaspoon vanilla extract

Spread popcorn and peanuts on baking sheet; salt lightly. Combine margarine, sugar and corn syrup in saucepan. Cook for 10 minutes or until mixture comes to a boil, stirring constantly; remove from heat. Stir in vanilla. Pour over popcorn and peanuts; mix well. Let stand until cool. Store in airtight container. May substitute 1/4 cup honey for 1/4 cup corn syrup. Yield: 16 servings.

Approx Per Serving: Cal 268; Prot 3 g; Carbo 32 g; Fiber 2 g;
T Fat 15 g; 50% Calories from Fat; Chol 0 mg; Sod 140 mg.

Joy is often the ability to be happy in small ways.
—from *Live and Learn and Pass It On*

NUT SNACK

1 cup dried garbanzos	1 tablespoon garlic powder
3 cups water	1 teaspoon oregano
1 tablespoon soy sauce	1/4 to 1/2 teaspoon cayenne pepper
2 tablespoons nutritional yeast	1 cup almonds
2 tablespoons cornmeal	1 cup pumpkin seed
1/2 teaspoon oil	1 cup sunflower seed

Soak garbanzos in 3 cups water in saucepan overnight. Cook over low heat for 2 hours or until tender; drain. Combine with soy sauce, yeast, cornmeal, oil, garlic powder, oregano and cayenne pepper in bowl; mix well. Spread in shallow baking pan. Bake at 300 degrees until golden brown. Cool completely. Combine with almonds, pumpkin seed and sunflower seed in airtight container. May use raw or dry-roasted almonds, pumpkin seed and sunflower seed. Yield: 8 servings.

Approx Per Serving: Cal 409; Prot 18 g; Carbo 28 g; Fiber 10 g; T Fat 28 g; 58% Calories from Fat; Chol 0 mg; Sod 143 mg.

Karon Kate Blackwell

PEOPLE PUPPY CHOW

1/2 cup margarine	9 cups rice Chex
1/2 cup creamy peanut butter	1/2 1-pound package
1 cup semisweet chocolate chips	confectioners' sugar

Combine margarine, peanut butter and chocolate chips in large saucepan. Cook over low heat until melted, stirring to mix well. Stir in cereal. Cool until mixture is sticky. Place confectioners' sugar in large bowl with tight-fitting lid. Add cereal mixture; shake to mix well. Yield: 12 servings.

Approx Per Serving: Cal 374; Prot 5 g; Carbo 51 g; Fiber 1 g; T Fat 18 g; 42% Calories from Fat; Chol 0 mg; Sod 390 mg.

APRICOT BRANDY SLUSH

2 cups water
4 tea bags
2 cups sugar
7 cups hot water
1 12-ounce can frozen orange
  juice concentrate

1 12-ounce can frozen lemonade
  concentrate
2 cups apricot brandy
14 cups 7-Up

Bring 2 cups water to a boil in saucepan. Add tea bags. Let steep for several minutes; discard tea bags. Stir in sugar until dissolved. Add 7 cups water, orange juice concentrate, lemonade concentrate and brandy; mix well. Pour into plastic freezer containers. Freeze overnight. Fill 4 to 6-ounce glasses half full with slush. Add 7-Up to fill glasses. Yield: 48 servings.

Approx Per Serving: Cal 108; Prot <1 g; Carbo 25 g; Fiber <1 g; T Fat <1 g; 0% Calories from Fat; Chol 0 mg; Sod 9 mg.

HOLIDAY EGGNOG

6 eggs
1/4 cup sugar
1/4 teaspoon each cinnamon,
  ginger and cloves
8 cups orange juice, chilled

1/2 cup lemon juice, chilled
1 quart vanilla ice cream
4 cups ginger ale, chilled
Nutmeg to taste

Beat eggs in mixer bowl. Add sugar, cinnamon, ginger and cloves; mix well. Stir in orange juice and lemon juice. Cut ice cream into chunks; place in punch bowl. Add ginger ale gradually. Stir in egg mixture gently; sprinkle with nutmeg. May substitute 1½ cups egg substitute for uncooked eggs. Yield: 20 servings.

Approx Per Serving: Cal 150; Prot 4 g; Carbo 24 g; Fiber <1 g; T Fat 5 g; 28% Calories from Fat; Chol 76 mg; Sod 48 mg.

 *Beverages*

MARGARITAS

1 12-ounce can frozen limeade
  concentrate
9 ounces Tequila

1 ounce Triple Sec
Crushed ice

Combine limeade, Tequila and Triple Sec in shaker; shake to mix well. Fill blender with crushed ice. Fill ⅔ full with Margarita mixture. Process until slushy. Yield: 2 servings.

Approx Per Serving: Cal 650; Prot <1 g; Carbo 90 g; Fiber 1 g;
  T Fat <1 g; 0% Calories from Fat; Chol 0 mg; Sod 1 mg.

ICE CREAM PUNCH

1½ cups sugar
2 cups water
2 quarts lemonade
6 ounces white grapefruit juice
1 46-ounce can pineapple juice

½ gallon vanilla ice cream,
  softened
½ gallon pineapple sherbet,
  softened
2 quarts ginger ale, chilled

Dissolve sugar in water in pitcher. Combine with lemonade, grapefruit juice and pineapple juice in punch bowl; mix well. Add ice cream and sherbet; mix gently. Add ginger ale; mix gently. Yield: 40 servings.

Approx Per Serving: Cal 193; Prot 2 g; Carbo 40 g; Fiber <1 g;
  T Fat 4 g; 17% Calories from Fat; Chol 15 mg; Sod 45 mg.

PINEAPPLE WASSAIL

4 cups unsweetened pineapple
  juice
1 12-ounce can apricot nectar
2 cups cider

1 cup orange juice
1 6-inch cinnamon stick, broken
1 teaspoon whole cloves
4 cardamom seed, crushed

Combine pineapple, apricot nectar, cider, orange juice, cinnamon, cloves and cardamom in saucepan; mix well. Bring to a boil; reduce heat. Simmer for 15 to 20 minutes. Strain into pitcher. Serve hot. May add brandy or whiskey if desired. Yield: 16 servings.

Approx Per Serving: Cal 68; Prot <1 g; Carbo 17 g; Fiber <1 g;
  T Fat <1 g; 2% Calories from Fat; Chol 0 mg; Sod 2 mg.

SOUPS & SALADS

BROCCOLI-CAULIFLOWER SOUP

1 quart chicken broth
1 10-ounce package frozen
    broccoli
1 10-ounce package frozen
    cauliflower

¹/₄ cup quick-cooking rice
8 ounces cream cheese, softened
¹/₂ cup grated Parmesan cheese
1¹/₄ cups milk
Salt and pepper to taste

Combine chicken broth, broccoli, cauliflower and rice in large saucepan. Cook over medium heat until vegetables and rice are tender. Add cream cheese and Parmesan cheese, stirring until melted. Stir in milk until of desired consistency. Season with salt and pepper. Yield: 6 servings.

Approx Per Serving: Cal 257; Prot 13 g; Carbo 12 g; Fiber 2 g;
   T Fat 18 g; 62% Calories from Fat; Chol 54 mg; Sod 796 mg.

VERMONT CHEDDAR BISQUE

1 cup chopped, peeled potatoes
1¹/₂ cups chicken stock
1 cup coarsely chopped onion
5 tablespoons unsalted butter
3 tablespoons flour
2 cups warm milk

1¹/₂ cups shredded sharp Cheddar
   cheese
1 teaspoon Dijon mustard
Salt, black pepper and cayenne
   pepper to taste

Simmer potatoes in chicken stock in covered saucepan until tender. Mash with the chicken stock; set aside. Sauté onion in butter in large saucepan until tender but not browned. Add flour. Cook over low heat for several minutes, stirring often. Add warm milk 1 cup at a time, whisking constantly. Cook for 3 to 4 minutes or until thickened. Add potato mixture. Cook over low heat for 2 to 3 minutes, stirring constantly. Add cheese, mustard, salt, black pepper and cayenne pepper. Heat until soup begins to boil. Remove from heat and serve hot. Yield: 4 servings.

Approx Per Serving: Cal 453; Prot 19 g; Carbo 21 g; Fiber 1 g;
   T Fat 33 g; 66% Calories from Fat; Chol 100 mg; Sod 643 mg.

EASY BACON-CLAM CHOWDER

8 ounces bacon, chopped
3 potatoes, cubed
1 onion, chopped
1/4 cup margarine

2 to 3   6-ounce cans minced clams
Creole pepper, parsley and celery
   salt to taste
4 cups half and half

Fry bacon in skillet until crispy; drain and set aside. Sauté potatoes and onion in margarine in saucepan until tender. Add clams and clam juice; season with pepper, parsley and celery salt. Add half and half. Cook over low heat until heated through, stirring frequently. Yield: 4 servings.

Approx Per Serving: Cal 803; Prot 47 g; Carbo 40 g; Fiber 2 g;
   T Fat 50 g; 56% Calories from Fat; Chol 189 mg; Sod 652 mg.

FIRESTARTER CHILI

1 large onion, chopped
2 cloves of garlic, finely chopped
1 pound ground beef
2   10-ounce cans beef consommé
1 consommé can water
1   4-ounce can chopped green
   chilies, drained

1/4 cup tomato paste
2   16-ounce cans kidney beans,
   drained
1 teaspoon oregano
2 teaspoons ground cumin
1 to 3 tablespoons chili powder

Sauté onion and garlic in large saucepan until tender. Brown ground beef in skillet, stirring until crumbly; drain. Add to saucepan. Stir in consommé, water, chilies, tomato paste, kidney beans, oregano, cumin and chili powder. Simmer for 1 hour, stirring occasionally. Yield: 6 servings.

Approx Per Serving: Cal 335; Prot 27 g; Carbo 31 g; Fiber 13 g;
   T Fat 12 g; 31% Calories from Fat; Chol 49 mg; Sod 1240 mg.

Take time to laugh each day.

—from *Life Lessons For Women*

TWO-BEAN CHILI CON CARNE

2 pounds ground beef
1 tablespoon oil
3 cloves of garlic, minced
3 stalks celery, finely chopped
2 to 3 large onions, finely chopped
1 16-ounce can tomatoes
3 tablespoons brown sugar
2 bay leaves
2 4-ounce cans chopped green
  chilies, drained

2 tablespoons chili powder
1 teaspoon oregano
1/4 teaspoon cumin
6 whole allspice
1 15-ounce can pinto beans
3 8-ounce cans tomato sauce
1 15-ounce can kidney beans,
  drained
2 8-ounce cans seasoned tomato
  juice

Brown ground beef in oil in heavy deep saucepan, stirring until crumbly; drain. Add garlic, celery and onions. Sauté for 10 minutes. Add next 8 ingredients; mix well. Stir in undrained pinto beans, tomato sauce, kidney beans and tomato juice. Bring to a boil; reduce heat. Simmer for 30 minutes or until of desired consistency, stirring often. Remove bay leaves before serving. Yield: 12 servings.

Approx Per Serving: Cal 288; Prot 20 g; Carbo 26 g; Fiber 5 g;
  T Fat 13 g; 38% Calories from Fat; Chol 49 mg; Sod 1013 mg.

RANCH HOUSE CHILI

4 slices bacon, chopped
1 pound lean ground beef
Salt and pepper to taste
2 15-ounce cans red pinto beans,
  partially drained
1 28-ounce can whole tomatoes,
  chopped
1 8-ounce can tomato sauce
2 stalks celery, chopped
2 medium onions, chopped

1 green bell pepper, chopped
1 green chili pepper, seeded,
  finely chopped
1/4 to 1/2 cup dry red wine
2 tablespoons chili powder
1 teaspoon oregano
1 teaspoon white vinegar
2 cloves of garlic, chopped
3 drops of Tabasco sauce

Fry bacon in large kettle until crisp. Add ground beef. Brown in pan drippings, stirring until crumbly. Season with salt and pepper. Add pinto beans, undrained tomatoes, tomato sauce, celery, onions, bell pepper, chili pepper, wine, chili powder, oregano, vinegar, garlic and Tabasco sauce; stir well. Simmer for 30 minutes, stirring occasionally. Yield: 10 servings.

Approx Per Serving: Cal 225; Prot 15 g; Carbo 22 g; Fiber 3 g;
  T Fat 9 g; 34% Calories from Fat; Chol 32 mg; Sod 710 mg.

WHITE CHILI

1 16-ounce package dried large
   white beans
6 cups chicken broth
2 cloves of garlic, minced
2 onions, chopped
1 tablespoon canola oil
2 4-ounce cans chopped green
   chilies, drained

2 teaspoons ground cumin
1¹/₂ teaspoons dried oregano
¹/₄ teaspoon ground cloves
¹/₄ teaspoon cayenne pepper
4 cups cooked chopped chicken
   breasts
3 cups shredded Monterey Jack
   cheese

Soak beans in water to cover overnight; drain. Combine with chicken broth, garlic and half the onions in large kettle. Bring to a boil; reduce heat. Simmer for 3 hours or until beans are tender, stirring occasionally. Sauté remaining onions in oil in large skillet until tender. Add next 5 ingredients; mix well. Stir into bean mixture. Add chicken. Simmer for 1 hour longer, stirring occasionally. Serve topped with cheese. Yield: 8 servings.

Approx Per Serving: Cal 531; Prot 49 g; Carbo 41 g; Fiber 2 g; T Fat 19 g; 32% Calories from Fat; Chol 99 mg; Sod 1071 mg.

Marty Allen

FILÉ GUMBO

8 ounces unpeeled whole shrimp
10 cups water
1¹/₂ teaspoons salt
¹/₂ cup butter
1 10-ounce package frozen okra
¹/₂ cup chopped celery
¹/₂ cup chopped onion

1 tablespoon chopped parsley
¹/₄ cup flour
6 ounces ham, chopped
6 ounces smoked sausage, chopped
1 cup cooked crab meat
¹/₂ teaspoon each salt and pepper
1 tablespoon filé powder

Place shrimp in stockpot with water and 1¹/₂ teaspoons salt. Boil for 30 minutes or until liquid is reduced to 8 cups. Strain and reserve stock; clean shrimp, discarding heads and shells. Melt butter in heavy kettle. Sauté okra, celery, onion and parsley for 5 minutes; reduce heat. Simmer for 15 to 20 minutes. Add flour. Cook for 15 to 20 minutes or until golden brown, stirring frequently. Add ham and sausage. Pour in reserved shrimp stock gradually. Simmer for 30 minutes, stirring occasionally. Stir in shrimp and remaining ingredients. Heat to serving temperature. Yield: 12 servings.

Approx Per Serving: Cal 196; Prot 11 g; Carbo 5 g; Fiber <1 g; T Fat 25 g; 68% Calories from Fat; Chol 81 mg; Sod 807 mg.

 *Soups*

LOUISIANA GUMBO

This recipe originated in South Louisiana.

1¹/₂ pounds hot sausage, skin
   removed
2 onions, finely chopped
6 cloves of garlic, finely chopped
¹/₂ cup bacon grease
2 to 3 tablespoons flour
4 sprigs of thyme
1¹/₂ to 2 quarts water

6 tomatoes, chopped
¹/₂ teaspoon sugar
1 bay leaf
1 pound peeled shrimp
1 pound crab meat
24 oysters
Cayenne pepper, filé powder, salt
   and black pepper to taste

Brown sausage in skillet until cooked through; set aside. Sauté onions and garlic in pan drippings until tender; drain. Melt bacon grease in large heavy saucepan. Add flour. Cook until browned to make roux, stirring frequently. Add onions, garlic, thyme, water, tomatoes, sugar and bay leaf; mix well. Bring to a boil. Cook for 15 minutes. Add shrimp, crab meat, oysters, sausage, cayenne pepper, filé powder, salt and black pepper. Cook on low for 45 minutes, stirring frequently. Remove bay leaf. Serve over cooked rice. Yield: 8 servings.

Approx Per Serving: Cal 433; Prot 32 g; Carbo 11 g; Fiber 3 g;
   T Fat 36 g; 66% Calories from Fat; Chol 299 mg; Sod 941 mg.

Jeanne R. Jones
Board of Trustees

POTATO AND LEEK SOUP

3 large leeks
3 tablespoons margarine
3 10-ounce cans double-strength
   chicken broth

3 soup cans water
3 cups instant potato flakes
Salt and white pepper to taste

Trim leeks, leaving 2 to 3 inches of green tops. Slice into halves lengthwise. Rinse well and pat dry. Slice thinly. Sauté in margarine in large saucepan for 5 minutes or until tender. Add chicken broth and water. Bring to a boil. Add potato flakes. Cook for 15 minutes longer or until of desired consistency, stirring frequently. Season with salt and white pepper. May add chopped ham, smoked sausage or sliced hot dogs. Yield: 8 servings.

Approx Per Serving: Cal 350; Prot 9 g; Carbo 68 g; Fiber 5 g;
   T Fat 5 g; 14% Calories from Fat; Chol <1 mg; Sod 499 mg.

Soups

LAS VEGAS LENTIL SOUP

1¹/₂ cups dried lentils, rinsed
1 small onion, chopped
1 carrot, chopped
1 stalk celery, chopped
1¹/₂ cups uncooked rigatoni
2 cloves of garlic, minced

10 cups water
2 vegetable bouillon cubes with sea salt
1 teaspoon Tabasco sauce
¹/₂ teaspoon Worcestershire sauce

Combine lentils, onion, carrot, celery, rigatoni, garlic and water in large saucepan. Add bouillon cubes, Tabasco sauce and Worcestershire sauce; mix well. Bring to a boil; reduce heat. Simmer for 1¹/₂ hours. Yield: 8 servings.

Approx Per Serving: Cal 174; Prot 12 g; Carbo 31 g; Fiber 5 g;
  T Fat 1 g; 3% Calories from Fat; Chol <1 mg; Sod 305 mg.

Alan Duncan
Board of Trustees

MUSHROOM SOUP WITH WHITE WINE

A wonder soup for a first course for company. Keep in the freezer to serve when entertaining.

6 scallions, trimmed, finely chopped
¹/₄ cup butter
16 ounces mushrooms, finely chopped
3 tablespoons flour

¹/₂ teaspoon ground cumin
1 teaspoon salt
¹/₂ teaspoon pepper
2¹/₂ cups scalded milk
1 cup dry white wine

Sauté scallions in butter in large saucepan for 7 minutes or until tender. Add mushrooms. Cook for 5 minutes, stirring frequently. Add flour, cumin, salt and pepper. Cook for 5 minutes or until thickened, stirring constantly. Add milk gradually, stirring constantly. Stir in wine. Bring to a boil; reduce heat. Simmer for 5 minutes. May purée 2 cups at a time in blender for smooth soup. Yield: 6 servings.

Approx Per Serving: Cal 193; Prot 6 g; Carbo 12 g; Fiber 2 g;
  T Fat 11 g; 53% Calories from Fat; Chol 35 mg; Sod 468 mg.

PEA SOUP

8 ounces bacon, chopped
3 green onions, chopped
2 sprigs of fresh rosemary

2 quarts fresh chicken stock
3 pounds green peas
Salt and pepper to taste

Sauté bacon in saucepan until nearly crisp. Add green onions and rosemary; drain. Add chicken stock. Bring to a boil. Stir in peas. Bring to a boil; remove to large pan of ice water. Let stand until cool. Stir in salt and pepper. Process in blender until smooth; strain into saucepan. May add some of the strained pulp if needed for desired consistency. Reheat to serve. Yield: 6 servings.

Approx Per Serving: Cal 302; Prot 23 g; Carbo 34 g; Fiber 11 g;
  T Fat 8 g; 25% Calories from Fat; Chol 11 mg; Sod 1227 mg.

Arnauld Briand
Palace Court Restaurant at Caesars Palace Hotel

"PENICILLIN" SOUP WITH NOODLES

This recipe is over 90 years old.

1 3-pound whole chicken,
   skinned
1/2 teaspoon salt
8 cups water
4 large stalks celery, sliced

6 carrots, sliced
Fresh parsley and dill to taste
1 8-ounce package thin noodles,
   cooked

Rinse chicken; remove gizzards and neck and reserve. Place breast side down in boiling salted water in stockpot. Boil for 10 minutes; turn. Boil for 10 minutes longer. Add neck and gizzards. Simmer until liquid is reduced by half, skimming surface. Remove chicken, discarding neck and gizzards. Cool. Shred meat, discarding bones. Place shredded chicken, celery, carrots, parsley and dill in stock. Simmer for 45 minutes to 1 hour or until vegetables are tender. Add cooked noodles just before serving. May also add 1 cup barley, 1 cup cooked rice or matzo balls. Yield: 8 servings.

Approx Per Serving: Cal 297; Prot 29 g; Carbo 26 g; Fiber 2 g;
  T Fat 8 g; 24% Calories from Fat; Chol 126 mg; Sod 247 mg.

SOUTHWEST CHOWDER

3 jalapeño peppers, seeded, cut
  into strips
3 tablespoons oil
2 teaspoons cumin
1 tablespoon ground coriander
2 large tomatoes, peeled, seeded
1 small onion
3 cups corn kernels
2 cups milk

1¹/₂ cups chicken stock
5 medium red potatoes, chopped
¹/₄ cup shredded Monterey Jack
  cheese
2 carrots, peeled, grated
2 cups corn kernels
Salt and freshly ground pepper to
  taste
¹/₂ cup chopped coriander leaves

Sauté peppers in hot oil in 4-quart saucepan over low heat for 3 minutes or just until tender. Stir in cumin and ground coriander. Process tomatoes and onion in blender until smooth. Add to peppers. Cook for 5 minutes. Purée 3 cups corn with milk in blender or food processor. Strain into saucepan. Add stock. Bring to a boil. Add potatoes. Simmer, covered, for 6 to 8 minutes or until potatoes are tender. Add cheese, carrots and 2 cups corn. Cook for 3 minutes or until heated through. Season with salt and pepper. Top servings with coriander leaves. Yield: 10 servings.

Approx Per Serving: Cal 224; Prot 7 g; Carbo 35 g; Fiber 5 g;
  T Fat 8 g; 30% Calories from Fat; Chol 9 mg; Sod 175 mg.

TOMATO AND GIN SOUP

3 ounces chopped onion
¹/₄ ounce chopped garlic
2 ounces butter
2 ounces bacon, chopped
12 ounces fresh tomatoes, peeled,
  seeded, chopped
¹/₄ ounce mixed chopped basil
  and oregano

¹/₂ ounce parsley, chopped
24 ounces tomato juice
1 tablespoon sugar
¹/₂ ounce chicken bouillon paste
Salt and pepper to taste
4 ounces mushrooms, sliced
3 ounces gin

Sauté onion and garlic in butter in saucepan until onion is tender. Add bacon. Sauté for 2 to 3 minutes. Add tomatoes, basil, oregano and parsley. Stir in tomato juice, sugar, bouillon paste, salt and pepper. Bring to a boil. Add mushrooms. Cook for 1 minute; remove from heat. Stir in gin and serve immediately. May substitute olive oil for butter. Yield: 4 servings.

Approx Per Serving: Cal 256; Prot 5 g; Carbo 19 g; Fiber 4 g;
  T Fat 14 g; 50% Calories from Fat; Chol 35 mg; Sod 1605 mg.

Chef Bruno Wehren, MGM Grand Hotel, Inc.

SOPA DE TORTILLA (Tortilla Soup)

3 cloves of garlic, roasted, minced
1 large red onion, chopped
1 4-ounce can chopped green
  chilies, drained
3 tablespoons oil
1 teaspoon red chili powder
2 large tomatoes, chopped

1¹/₂ cups tomato sauce
1 teaspoon ground cumin
6 cups chicken broth
6 corn tortillas, cut into 8 wedges
Oil for frying
1 cup shredded Monterey Jack
  cheese

Sauté garlic, onion and green chilies in oil in saucepan until tender. Stir in chili powder. Cook for 5 minutes. Add tomatoes, tomato sauce, cumin and chicken broth. Bring to a boil; reduce heat. Simmer for 45 minutes. Fry tortillas in small amount of oil until crisp; drain on paper towels. Place tortilla wedges in serving bowls. Pour soup over wedges; top with cheese. May place under broiler to melt cheese. Garnish with cilantro. Yield: 10 servings.

Approx Per Serving: Cal 166; Prot 8 g; Carbo 14 g; Fiber 3 g;
  T Fat 9 g; 48% Calories from Fat; Chol 11 mg; Sod 832 mg.

MONTEREY TORTILLA SOUP

A last-minute soup for cold nights!

1 large onion, chopped
1 large green bell pepper, chopped
2 large stalks celery, chopped
1 large tomato, chopped
2 tablespoons minced parsley
2 8-ounce cans tomato sauce
3³/₄ cups chicken broth

¹/₄ teaspoon thyme
¹/₂ teaspoon salt
Pepper and Tabasco sauce to taste
4 ounces tortilla chips
2 cups shredded Monterey Jack
  cheese

Combine onion, green pepper, celery, tomato, parsley, tomato sauce, chicken broth, thyme, salt, pepper and Tabasco sauce in large saucepan. Bring to a boil; reduce heat. Simmer for 20 minutes, stirring occasionally. Place equal amount of tortilla chips and cheese in individual serving bowls. Pour soup over chips and cheese. Yield: 4 servings.

Approx Per Serving: Cal 449; Prot 24 g; Carbo 32 g; Fiber 5 g;
  T Fat 26 g; 52% Calories from Fat; Chol 53 mg; Sod 2145 mg.

FRESH VEGETABLE SOUP

2 tablespoons olive oil
1 cup chopped carrot
1 cup sliced fresh green beans
1 cup sliced asparagus
1 cup chopped red potatoes
1/2 cup chopped leek (white part only)
1/2 cup chopped red onion
1/2 cup sliced celery
1/2 cup green peas
8 cups unsalted chicken broth
2 cups packed shredded escarole
1/4 teaspoon salt
Freshly ground pepper to taste
2 tablespoons grated Parmesan cheese

Heat olive oil in large saucepan. Add carrot, green beans, asparagus, potatoes, leek, red onion, celery and peas. Cook over medium-low heat for 10 minutes or until vegetables are tender-crisp, stirring occasionally. Add chicken broth and escarole. Simmer for 20 minutes. Season with salt and pepper. Ladle into individual serving bowls; top with Parmesan cheese. Garnish with garlic crostini. Yield: 6 servings.

Approx Per Serving: Cal 137; Prot 7 g; Carbo 15 g; Fiber 3 g;
T Fat 6 g; 39% Calories from Fat; Chol 1 mg; Sod 220 mg.

HEARTY TURKEY-VEGETABLE SOUP

This is a low-fat, healthy soup. Great as a balanced main-dish meal served with fresh baked bread.

1 pound lean ground turkey
2 onions, chopped
1 teaspoon oregano
1 teaspoon Italian seasoning
2 14-ounce cans Italian tomatoes
4 to 5 carrots, thinly sliced
2 potatoes, peeled, chopped
1 12-ounce can tomato juice
3 10-ounce cans double-strength beef broth
4 soup cans water
1 tablespoon Worcestershire sauce
2 cups uncooked pasta spirals
3 zucchini, quartered and sliced
1 teaspoon Tabasco sauce

Spray large soup pot with nonstick cooking spray. Cook turkey with onions, oregano and Italian seasoning in prepared pot for 5 minutes, stirring until turkey is crumbly. Add next 7 ingredients. Bring to a boil; reduce heat. Simmer, covered, for 20 minutes, stirring occasionally. Add pasta. Cook, covered, for 5 minutes. Add zucchini. Cook for 5 minutes longer. Stir in Tabasco sauce. Yield: 8 servings.

Approx Per Serving: Cal 259; Prot 18 g; Carbo 34 g; Fiber 6 g;
T Fat 7 g; 22% Calories from Fat; Chol 36 mg; Sod 752 mg.

SPICY AVOCADO SALAD

1 teaspoon salt
1 clove of garlic, minced
1 teaspoon Worcestershire sauce
1/2 teaspoon Tabasco sauce
Juice of 1/3 lemon
3 tablespoons olive oil
3 ripe tomatoes, diced
2 ripe avocados, diced
Freshly ground pepper to taste

1 green chili, seeded, minced
3 tablespoons cilantro, minced
3 tablespoons (heaping) diced
  Monterey Jack cheese
3 tablespoons (heaping) crumbled
  crisp-fried bacon
2 tablespoons (heaping) minced
  onion
1/2 green bell pepper, diced

Mash salt and garlic in bowl with fork until smooth paste forms. Whisk in Worcestershire sauce, Tabasco sauce, lemon juice and olive oil until well blended. Pour over mixture of tomatoes, avocados, pepper, green chili, cilantro, cheese, bacon, onion and green pepper in bowl; mix well. Marinate in refrigerator for 30 minutes. Serve on bed of mixed salad greens. Yield: 4 servings.

Approx Per Serving: Cal 306; Prot 5 g; Carbo 15 g; Fiber 12 g;
  T Fat 28 g; 76% Calories from Fat; Chol 6 mg; Sod 631 mg.

SUNFLOWER-BROCCOLI SALAD

1 small bunch broccoli
1/4 red onion, chopped
1/4 cup sunflower seed kernels
1/4 cup raisins
1/4 cup sliced mushrooms

4 ounces bacon, crisp-fried,
  crumbled
1/2 cup mayonnaise
2 tablespoons sugar
1 tablespoon vinegar

Blanch broccoli in simmering water in saucepan; drain and cool. Break into bite-sized pieces. Combine with onion, sunflower seed kernels, raisins, mushrooms and bacon in bowl; mix well. Chill until serving time. Mix mayonnaise, sugar and vinegar in small bowl. Pour over broccoli mixture, stirring to coat. Yield: 6 servings.

Approx Per Serving: Cal 254; Prot 5 g; Carbo 15 g; Fiber 3 g;
  T Fat 21 g; 69% Calories from Fat; Chol 16 mg; Sod 212 mg.

FRUITED CHICKEN SALAD WITH CURRIED GINGER DRESSING

4 chopped cooked chicken breasts
1 cup chopped celery
1 large red or green Delicious apple, cubed
1 cup seedless grapes, cut into halves

1 cup stuffed green olives
1/3 cup slivered almonds
1   8-ounce can chopped water chestnuts
Curried Ginger Dressing

Combine chicken, celery, apple, grapes, olives, almonds and water chestnuts in bowl; mix well. Pour Curried Ginger Dressing over chicken mixture, stirring to coat. Let stand for 30 minutes before serving. Yield: 6 servings.

Curried Ginger Dressing

2/3 cup mayonnaise
1/3 cup mayonnaise-type salad dressing
1/4 cup whipped cream

1 teaspoon lemon juice
1/4 teaspoon curry powder
1/4 teaspoon ginger
Salt and pepper to taste

Mix mayonnaise, salad dressing, whipped cream, lemon juice, curry powder, ginger, salt and pepper in small bowl. Yield: 6 servings.

Approx Per Serving: Cal 459; Prot 21 g; Carbo 21 g; Fiber 4 g;
T Fat 34 g; 65% Calories from Fat; Chol 73 mg; Sod 638 mg.

Find a way to serve others and your life will have meaning.
—from *Life Lessons For Women*

 *Salads*

CHICKEN SALAD AÏOLI

Aïoli is a garlic mayonnaise usually served with vegetables, meats and soups.
Here it gives the chicken salad pizzazz.

4 chicken breast filets
1 cup chicken stock
1/4 teaspoon thyme
1/4 teaspoon red pepper flakes
1 clove of garlic, crushed
1/2 cup mayonnaise

2 tablespoons olive oil
1/4 teaspoon lemon juice
2 tablespoons capers, rinsed,
   drained
Salt to taste
Ground black pepper to taste

Rinse chicken. Combine with chicken stock, thyme and red pepper flakes in heavy saucepan. Cook, covered, over low heat for 12 minutes or until chicken is tender. Cool chicken in stock; drain. Cut chicken into large pieces. Mix garlic and mayonnaise in bowl. Beat in olive oil gradually until blended. Add lemon juice, capers, salt, pepper and chicken; mix well. Serve on bed of leaf lettuce. Garnish with radishes or cherry tomatoes. Yield: 4 servings.

Approx Per Serving: Cal 408; Prot 28 g; Carbo 1 g; Fiber <1 g;
   T Fat 32 g; 71% Calories from Fat; Chol 89 mg; Sod 414 mg.
   Nutritional information does not include capers.

TERIYAKI-CHICKEN SALAD

1 cup oil
6 tablespoons rice vinegar
5 packets sugar substitute
1 teaspoon pepper
2 packages Ramen oriental soup
   seasoning
3 chicken breast filets, cut into
   bite-sized pieces

1 cup teriyaki sauce
10 tablespoons slivered almonds
10 tablespoons sesame seed
16 ounces chopped cabbage
8 green onions, finely chopped
2 packages Ramen noodles,
   broken up

Mix first 5 ingredients in small bowl. Chill while preparing salad. Cook chicken with teriyaki sauce in skillet for 15 to 20 minutes or until browned. Remove and set aside. Bake almonds and sesame seed on baking sheet at 350 degrees for 5 minutes or until toasted. Combine chicken, almonds, sesame seed, cabbage, green onions and noodles in bowl; mix well. Add rice vinegar mixture, stirring gently. Yield: 6 servings.

Approx Per Serving: Cal 751; Prot 31 g; Carbo 35 g; Fiber 5 g;
   T Fat 54 g; 65% Calories from Fat; Chol 54 mg; Sod 2273 mg.
   Nutritional information does not include Ramen oriental
   soup seasoning.

74

CRANBERRY-BORSCHT SALAD

1 16-ounce can sliced pickled
  beets
3/4 cup water
2 cups cranberry juice
1/4 teaspoon salt
1/8 teaspoon pepper
1 bay leaf
2 3-ounce packages lemon gelatin
2 tablespoons lemon juice

2 tablespoons minced green onions
3 tablespoons finely chopped
  celery
1 cup sour cream
2 tablespoons milk
1 tablespoon prepared horseradish
1/4 teaspoon salt
1 teaspoon sugar

Drain beets, reserving juice. Chop beets and set aside. Combine beet juice, water, cranberry juice, 1/4 teaspoon salt, pepper and bay leaf in small saucepan. Cook over medium heat until mixture begins to simmer, stirring often. Add gelatin and lemon juice, stirring until gelatin is dissolved; remove bay leaf. Chill until mixture is syrupy. Stir in green onions, celery and beets. Pour into 8-cup mold. Chill until firm. Mix sour cream, milk, horseradish, 1/4 teaspoon salt and sugar in small bowl. Unmold beet mixture onto serving plate. Serve with sour cream dressing. Yield: 16 servings.

Approx Per Serving: Cal 110; Prot 2 g; Carbo 20 g; Fiber 1 g;
  T Fat 3 g; 25% Calories from Fat; Chol 7 mg; Sod 187 mg.

CRANBERRY FLUFF SALAD

2 cups freshly ground
  cranberries
3 cups miniature marshmallows
3/4 cup sugar
2 cups chopped tart unpeeled
  apples

1/2 to 1 cup seedless green grapes
1/4 teaspoon salt
1/4 cup chopped walnuts
1 cup whipping cream, whipped

Combine ground cranberries, marshmallows and sugar in bowl; mix well. Chill overnight. Add apples, grapes, salt and walnuts, stirring gently. Fold in whipped cream. Chill until serving time. Yield: 8 servings.

Approx Per Serving: Cal 322; Prot 2 g; Carbo 52 g; Fiber 3 g;
  T Fat 14 g; 36% Calories from Fat; Chol 41 mg; Sod 98 mg.

FRESH MUSHROOM SALAD

2 stuffed green olives, chopped
1/2 green bell pepper, chopped
1 pimento, chopped
1 tablespoon finely chopped red
  onion
1 tablespoon finely chopped
  parsley

16 ounces fresh mushrooms,
  thinly sliced
Salt and pepper to taste
French Dressing

Combine olives, green pepper, pimento, onion, parsley, mushrooms, salt and pepper in bowl, tossing to mix. Pour French Dressing over mushroom mixture, stirring gently to mix. Marinate in refrigerator for 1 to 3 hours. Yield: 4 servings.

French Dressing

1 clove of garlic, minced
Salt and pepper to taste
1/4 teaspoon oregano
1 teaspoon Worcestershire sauce

1/2 teaspoon Dijon mustard
1/2 cup olive oil
1 tablespoon wine vinegar
Juice of 1 lemon

Crush garlic in small bowl with salt and pepper. Stir in oregano, Worcestershire sauce and mustard. Add oil gradually, beating constantly until smooth. Add wine vinegar and lemon juice, beating well. Yield: 4 servings.

Approx Per Serving: Cal 283; Prot 3 g; Carbo 9 g; Fiber 3 g; T Fat 28 g; 85% Calories from Fat; Chol 0 mg; Sod 81 mg.

Think big thoughts, but relish small pleasures.
    —from *Life's Little Instruction Book* by H. Jackson Brown, Jr.

Salads

FRESH MUSHROOM SALAD WITH CHILIES

2 cloves of garlic, minced
1 teaspoon salt
1 teaspoon Worcestershire sauce
Juice of 2 lemons
1 cup olive oil
Freshly ground pepper to taste
Salt to taste
20 to 25 mushrooms, stems
 removed, thinly sliced

2 tablespoons chopped parsley
1 to 3 tablespoons diced chilies
1 green bell pepper, diced
3 whole pimentos, sliced into thin
 strips
1 red onion, thinly sliced
Oregano to taste

Mash garlic and 1 teaspoon salt in bowl with fork until smooth paste forms. Add Worcestershire sauce and lemon juice; mix well. Stir in enough olive oil to make of desired consistency and taste. Add pepper and salt to taste; mix well. Combine mushrooms, parsley, chilies, green pepper, pimentos, onion and oregano in bowl. Pour just enough dressing over mixture to moisten. Marinate in refrigerator for 1 hour. Mushrooms will discolor after 4 hours. Yield: 6 servings.

Approx Per Serving: Cal 365; Prot 2 g; Carbo 10 g; Fiber 3 g;
 T Fat 37 g; 87% Calories from Fat; Chol 0 mg; Sod 368 mg.

COLORFUL PASTA SALAD

1 large clove of garlic, minced
1/4 teaspoon salt
1/3 cup white wine vinegar
2 tablespoons water
2 teaspoons salt
1/2 teaspoon sugar
2 teaspoons minced fresh tarragon
1/2 cup olive oil

1 1-pound package medium
 pasta shells, cooked, rinsed
2 cups quartered cherry tomatoes
2 cups julienne yellow bell
 peppers
1/2 cup minced fresh basil
Pepper to taste
1 1/2 cups green peas

Mash garlic and 1/4 teaspoon salt in bowl until soft paste forms. Combine garlic mixture with vinegar, water, 2 teaspoons salt, sugar, tarragon and olive oil in jar, shaking until blended. Pour over mixture of pasta, tomatoes, bell peppers, basil and pepper in bowl; mix well. Store in refrigerator. Add peas just before serving. Pasta should be cooked *al dente*. Yield: 12 servings.

Approx Per Serving: Cal 247; Prot 7 g; Carbo 34 g; Fiber 4 g;
 T Fat 10 g; 36% Calories from Fat; Chol 0 mg; Sod 406 mg.

PASTA SALAD WITH SMOKED SALMON

¹/₄ cup mayonnaise
¹/₂ cup whipping cream
¹/₄ cup lemon juice
3 tablespoons prepared
  horseradish
Salt and pepper to taste
1 small red onion, chopped

¹/₂ cup chopped chives
12 ounces small pasta shells,
  cooked
8 ounces smoked salmon, cut into
  strips
1 tomato, peeled, seeded, coarsely
  chopped

Combine mayonnaise, cream, lemon juice, horseradish, salt and pepper in serving bowl; mix well. Add onion, chives, pasta, salmon and tomato; mix gently. Chill until serving time. Yield: 4 servings.

Approx Per Serving: Cal 607; Prot 23 g; Carbo 71 g; Fiber 5 g;
  T Fat 26 g; 38% Calories from Fat; Chol 62 mg; Sod 549 mg.

FRESH PASTA AND VEGETABLE SALAD

1   16-ounce package medium
  shell pasta
1 large bunch broccoli, cut into
  bite-sized pieces
4 zucchini, cut into bite-sized
  pieces
3 carrots, finely chopped

3 yellow squash, cut into bite-
  sized pieces
2¹/₈ cups mayonnaise
1¹/₂ cups buttermilk
1 envelope buttermilk-recipe
  ranch-style dressing mix
Salt and pepper to taste

Cook pasta in boiling water using package directions; rinse under cold water. Combine with broccoli, zucchini, carrots and squash in large bowl, tossing to mix. Mix mayonnaise, buttermilk, dressing mix, salt and pepper in small bowl, beating with wire whisk. Pour over pasta mixture, stirring to coat. Yield: 8 servings.

Approx Per Serving: Cal 717; Prot 14 g; Carbo 62 g; Fiber 8 g;
  T Fat 48 g; 59% Calories from Fat; Chol 36 mg; Sod 651 mg.

Never underestimate the power of a kind word or deed.
  —from *Life's Little Instruction Book* by H. Jackson Brown, Jr.

CREAMY POTATO SALAD

9 potatoes
3 hard-boiled eggs
2/3 cup mayonnaise
1 teaspoon prepared mustard
3/4 cup sour cream
1 teaspoon salt
1/4 teaspoon pepper

11 slices bacon, crisp-fried, crumbled
1/2 cup chopped green onions
1/2 cup chopped celery
1/4 cup prepared Italian salad dressing

Cook potatoes in boiling water for 30 minutes or until tender. Peel and cut into 3/4-inch cubes. Remove yolks from eggs and mash in small bowl. Chop whites and set aside. Add mayonnaise, mustard, sour cream, salt and pepper to yolks, mixing well; set aside. Combine chopped egg whites, bacon, potatoes, green onions, celery and Italian dressing in large bowl. Add mayonnaise mixture, stirring gently to coat. Chill for 2 hours or longer before serving. Yield: 12 servings.

Approx Per Serving: Cal 286; Prot 6 g; Carbo 23 g; Fiber 2 g;
T Fat 20 g; 61% Calories from Fat; Chol 72 mg; Sod 402 mg.

INDONESIAN RICE SALAD

2 cups cooked brown rice
1/2 cup raisins
2 scallions, chopped
1/4 cup toasted sesame seed
1/2 cup thinly sliced water chestnuts
1 cup fresh mung bean sprouts
1/4 cup toasted cashews
1 or 2 stalks celery, chopped

Freshly chopped parsley to taste
3/4 cup orange juice
1/2 cup safflower oil
1 tablespoon sesame oil
3/4 tablespoon tamari
2 tablespoons dry sherry
Juice of 1 lemon
1 clove of garlic, minced
1/2 teaspoon grated ginger

Combine rice, raisins, scallions, sesame seed, water chestnuts, bean sprouts, cashews, celery and parsley in bowl; mix well. Combine orange juice, safflower oil, sesame oil, tamari, sherry, lemon juice, garlic and ginger in small bowl, beating with wire whisk. Add to salad; mix gently. May also add 1/2 cup bamboo shoots, fresh snow peas or fresh pineapple. Yield: 4 servings.

Approx Per Serving: Cal 606; Prot 9 g; Carbo 55 g; Fiber 6 g;
T Fat 41 g; 59% Calories from Fat; Chol 0 mg; Sod 30 mg.

FROZEN COLESLAW

A great salad to pull out of the freezer for last-minute dinner guests.

1 head cabbage, chopped
1 teaspoon salt
2 large carrots, finely grated
1 large green bell pepper, finely chopped
1 small red onion, chopped

1 cup apple cider vinegar
1/4 cup water
2 cups sugar
1 teaspoon celery seed
1 teaspoon mustard seed

Place cabbage in colander; sprinkle with salt. Let stand for 1 hour; drain. Combine with carrots, green pepper and onion in bowl. Mix vinegar, water, sugar, celery seed and mustard seed in saucepan. Bring to a boil. Cook for 1 minute or until syrupy, stirring often. Let stand until lukewarm. Pour over cabbage mixture, tossing to coat. Place in six 6-ounce containers in freezer until ready to use. Yield: 6 servings.

Approx Per Serving: Cal 292; Prot 1 g; Carbo 76 g; Fiber 2 g; T Fat <1 g; 1% Calories from Fat; Chol 0 mg; Sod 374 mg.

PEPPER SLAW

This recipe is from Nat Hart's cooking class at Caesars Palace.

1 large head cabbage, shredded
1 Bermuda onion, finely chopped
1 green bell pepper, chopped
1 cup cider vinegar
3/4 cup oil

1 tablespoon celery seed
1 tablespoon sugar
1 tablespoon salt
1 teaspoon dry mustard

Layer cabbage, onion and green pepper in bowl. Combine vinegar, oil, celery seed, sugar, salt and mustard in saucepan. Bring to a boil. Cook until sugar is dissolved, stirring frequently. Pour over cabbage mixture, but do not stir. Chill, covered, overnight. Toss before serving. May store in refrigerator for 2 weeks. Yield: 10 servings.

Approx Per Serving: Cal 170; Prot 1 g; Carbo 6 g; Fiber 1 g; T Fat 17 g; 85% Calories from Fat; Chol 0 mg; Sod 646 mg.

SPINACH SALAD WITH AVOCADO AND SHRIMP

1 bunch fresh spinach leaves
3 ounces cooked bay shrimp
1 tablespoon fresh lemon juice
1/2 cup sliced fresh mushrooms

1/2 cup chopped tomato
1 California avocado, sliced
1/3 cup honey-mustard dressing

Rinse spinach leaves and pat dry; chill. Sprinkle shrimp with lemon juice in bowl. Add mushrooms, tomato, avocado, spinach leaves and dressing, tossing to coat spinach with avocado. Yield: 2 servings.

Approx Per Serving: Cal 394; Prot 15 g; Carbo 27 g; Fiber 13 g; T Fat 28 g; 60% Calories from Fat; Chol 83 mg; Sod 571 mg.

TABOULI SALAD

2 cups boiling water
1 cup bulgur wheat
1 teaspoon salt
1 green bell pepper, chopped
2 medium tomatoes, chopped
1/3 cup vegetable oil
1/4 cup lemon juice

1 clove of garlic, minced
6 green onions, chopped
1 tablespoon chopped fresh mint
   leaves
1/2 cup fresh parsley, chopped
Pepper to taste
6 romaine lettuce leaves

Pour boiling water over bulgur wheat and salt in bowl. Let stand for 1 hour or until bulgur is softened and chewable. Toss green pepper, tomatoes, oil, lemon juice, garlic, green onions, mint, parsley and pepper with wheat in bowl. Refrigerate for several hours. Divide salad on lettuce leaves; roll to enclose filling. Wrap in foil or plastic wrap; chill. Yield: 6 servings.

Approx Per Serving: Cal 228; Prot 4 g; Carbo 26 g; Fiber 7 g; T Fat 13 g; 48% Calories from Fat; Chol 0 mg; Sod 364 mg.

GEORGIA MACCURTIN'S "ISADORA" SALAD WITH HONEY DRESSING

½ small cauliflower, chopped
¼ head red cabbage, shredded
2 stalks celery, diced
½ bunch watercress, diced
8 to 10 cherry tomatoes, diced

1 apple, diced
1 stalk fresh anise, minced
Honey Dressing
Romaine lettuce
¼ cup chopped walnuts

Combine cauliflower, cabbage, celery, watercress, tomatoes, apple and anise in bowl; mix well. Pour Honey Dressing over mixture; mix well. Spoon into lettuce-lined serving bowl; top with walnuts. Serve immediately.
Yield: 4 servings.

Honey Dressing

¼ cup apple cider vinegar
2 teaspoons honey
½ cup safflower oil

1 tablespoon mayonnaise
Garlic salt and pepper to taste
¼ teaspoon oregano

Combine vinegar, honey, safflower oil, mayonnaise, garlic salt, pepper and oregano in bowl; beat until smooth. Taste and adjust seasonings.
Yield: 4 servings.

Approx Per Serving: Cal 373; Prot 3 g; Carbo 16 g; Fiber 4 g; T Fat 35 g; 81% Calories from Fat; Chol 2 mg; Sod 52 mg.
Nutritional information does not include anise.

Being "glorified"—I know the meaning of that now. It's the time, after my death here, when I'll be dancing on my feet.
—Joni Eareckson Tada, paralyzed from the neck down in a diving accident

TUNA AND ARTICHOKE SALAD WITH VINAIGRETTE SAUCE

2 16-ounce cans artichokes,
   drained, cut into halves
5 to 6 large mushrooms, sliced
1 to 2 6-ounce cans tuna,
   drained, flaked

2 hard-boiled eggs, coarsely
   chopped
1/2 cup pine nuts, toasted
1 ripe avocado, chopped

Combine artichokes, mushrooms, tuna, eggs, pine nuts and avocado in bowl. Pour enough Vinaigrette Sauce over salad to moisten; mix well. Chill until serving time. Yield: 8 servings.

Vinaigrette Sauce

2/3 cup oil
1/3 cup white wine vinegar
1 clove of garlic, minced
2 tablespoons diced pimento
1 1/2 teaspoons salt
1/2 teaspoon freshly ground pepper

2 tablespoons chopped fresh
   parsley
1/2 teaspoon chervil
1/2 teaspoon tarragon
1 tablespoon minced onion
1 tablespoon pickle relish

Whisk oil and vinegar in bowl until blended. Add garlic, pimento, salt, pepper, parsley, chervil, tarragon, onion and pickle relish; mix well. Let stand for 15 to 20 minutes. Yield: 8 servings.

Approx Per Serving: Cal 375; Prot 18 g; Carbo 12 g; Fiber 4 g;
   T Fat 30 g; 69% Calories from Fat; Chol 77 mg; Sod 874 mg.
   Nutritional information includes entire amount of Vinaigrette Sauce.

"Goodbye," said the fox. "And now here is my secret, a very simple secret: It is only with the heart that one can see rightly; what is essential is invisible to the eye."
   —Antoine De Saint-Exupery, *"The Little Prince"*

TUNA-RICE SALAD WITH GRUYÈRE

2 cups rice
Salt to taste
1 6-ounce can tuna, drained, flaked
4 to 5 ounces Gruyère cheese, diced
4 tomatoes, peeled, coarsely chopped
2 carrots, chopped
1 celery heart, chopped
¼ cup chopped green olives
Chopped parsley to taste
Chopped basil leaves to taste
2 hard-boiled eggs, chopped
2 tablespoons olive oil
Juice of 1 lemon
Salt and freshly ground pepper to taste
1 hard-boiled egg, sliced

Cook rice al dente in lightly salted water using package directions; drain. Combine rice, tuna, cheese, tomatoes, carrots, chopped celery heart, green olives, parsley, basil and 2 chopped eggs in bowl; mix well. Add olive oil; mix well. Add lemon juice, salt and pepper, tossing until salad is coated. Top with 1 sliced egg. Yield: 6 servings.

Approx Per Serving: Cal 474; Prot 24 g; Carbo 57 g; Fiber 3 g;
   T Fat 17 g; 32% Calories from Fat; Chol 148 mg; Sod 407 mg.

MARINATED SLICED TOMATOES

4 large tomatoes, peeled, sliced
¼ cup oil
1 tablespoon lemon juice
½ teaspoon minced garlic
½ teaspoon salt
½ teaspoon oregano leaves

Arrange tomato slices in shallow dish. Combine oil, lemon juice, garlic, salt and oregano in small bowl; mix well. Pour over tomatoes. Chill, covered, for 1 hour. Yield: 6 servings.

Approx Per Serving: Cal 98; Prot 1 g; Carbo 4 g; Fiber 1 g;
   T Fat 9 g; 82% Calories from Fat; Chol 0 mg; Sod 184 mg.

MEAT ENTREES

BULKOKI (Barbecued Korean Beef)

1 teaspoon sesame oil
1/2 cup sweet sake
1/4 to 1/2 cup soy sauce
2 cloves of garlic, cut into halves, flattened

1/4 cup finely chopped onion
1/2 tablespoon salt
1 teaspoon pepper
3 tablespoons sugar
3 pounds lean beef, thinly sliced

Combine sesame oil, sake, soy sauce, garlic, onion, salt, pepper and sugar in small bowl; mix well. Pour over beef in shallow dish. Marinate, covered, in refrigerator overnight, turning occasionally. Drain, reserving marinade. Grill beef over hot coals, basting occasionally with reserved marinade. Garnish with sesame seed. Serve with short grain rice, green salad and sake. May substitute regular sake mixed with 1 tablespoon sugar and 1 teaspoon oil for sweet sake. Yield: 6 servings.

Approx Per Serving: Cal 378; Prot 44 g; Carbo 11 g; Fiber <1 g;
T Fat 13 g; 32% Calories from Fat; Chol 128 mg; Sod 1977 mg.

BARBECUED BRISKET OF BEEF

1   4-pound beef brisket
Garlic salt, onion salt and celery salt to taste
Worcestershire sauce to taste
Pepper to taste
1 cup catsup

1 cup water
1 teaspoon salt
1 teaspoon chili powder
3 tablespoons Worcestershire sauce
2 drops of Tabasco sauce

Sprinkle brisket with garlic salt, onion salt and celery salt. Place in glass baking dish. Sprinkle with Worcestershire sauce to taste. Marinate, covered, overnight. Sprinkle with pepper. Bake, covered, at 250 degrees for 5 hours. Remove to platter to cool, discarding pan juices. Slice brisket partially through. Return to baking dish. Combine catsup, water, salt, chili powder, 3 tablespoons Worcestershire sauce and Tabasco sauce in small bowl; mix well. Pour over brisket. Bake, covered, at 250 degrees for 30 minutes. Remove cover. Bake for 10 to 15 minutes longer. Yield: 8 servings.

Approx Per Serving: Cal 338; Prot 43 g; Carbo 10 g; Fiber 1 g;
T Fat 13 g; 36% Calories from Fat; Chol 128 mg; Sod 747 mg.

EIN GEDEMPFTER RINDER RUST (Pot Roast)

1   4-pound beef brisket
2 teaspoons butter
Salt, pepper, garlic powder and
   paprika to taste
1 medium onion, chopped
1   6-ounce can tomato sauce

1   6-ounce can water
2 bay leaves
1 cup red wine
1 cup water
10 gingersnaps

Brown brisket on both sides in butter in large saucepan; remove to platter. Season with salt, pepper, garlic powder and paprika. Add onions, tomato sauce, 6 ounces water and bay leaves to saucepan. Simmer, covered, until onion is tender. Return brisket to saucepan. Add wine and 1 cup water. Cook over low heat for 3 to 4 hours or until brisket is tender. Remove brisket to platter; discard bay leaves. Add gingersnaps to cooking liquid, stirring to break up. Slice brisket thinly; add to sauce. Simmer until heated through. Serve with potato pancakes, applesauce, carrots and sweet red cabbage. Yield: 12 servings.

Approx Per Serving: Cal 252; Prot 29 g; Carbo 7 g; Fiber <1 g;
   T Fat 10 g; 35% Calories from Fat; Chol 87 mg; Sod 172 mg.

SWEET AND SOUR POT ROAST

1 tablespoon shortening
1   4-pound chuck or rump roast
2 onions, sliced
1/4 teaspoon pepper
1/4 teaspoon ground cloves

1/4 cup honey
1/4 cup sugar
Juice of 2 lemons
1 teaspoon salt

Heat shortening in Dutch oven. Add roast and onions. Cook until roast is browned, turning frequently. Add pepper, cloves, honey, sugar, lemon juice and salt. Bake, tightly covered, at 300 degrees for 3 to 3½ hours or until roast is tender. May thicken gravy and slice roast into gravy, keeping warm until serving time. Serve with brown or wild rice. May simmer roast on top of stove for 3 to 3½ hours if preferred. Yield: 6 servings.

Approx Per Serving: Cal 512; Prot 57 g; Carbo 25 g; Fiber 1 g;
   T Fat 20 g; 35% Calories from Fat; Chol 170 mg; Sod 450 mg.

HONEY-VINEGAR FLANK STEAK

1/4 cup soy sauce
3 tablespoons honey
2 tablespoons vinegar
1 1/2 teaspoons ginger

1/2 teaspoon garlic powder
3/4 cup oil
2 green onions, chopped
1 2-pound flank steak

Mix soy sauce, honey, vinegar, ginger, garlic powder, oil and green onions in bowl. Pour over flank steak in shallow dish. Marinate in refrigerator for 4 hours to overnight, turning occasionally; drain. Place on rack in broiler pan. Broil for 4 to 5 minutes on each side or until done to taste. Slice diagonally. Yield: 4 servings.

Approx Per Serving: Cal 719; Prot 43 g; Carbo 15 g; Fiber <1 g;
T Fat 54 g; 67% Calories from Fat; Chol 128 mg; Sod 1099 mg.

TERIYAKI FLANK STEAK

1 3-pound flank steak
1/4 cup sherry
1/4 cup soy sauce
1/4 cup olive oil

1 or 2 cloves of garlic, crushed
1/4 teaspoon ground ginger
Pepper to taste

Trim fat from steak and score both sides with 1/4-inch slashes in diamond pattern. Place in shallow dish. Combine sherry, soy sauce, olive oil, garlic, ginger and pepper in small bowl; mix well. Pour over steak. Marinate for 1 hour, turning occasionally. Drain, discarding marinade. Place on rack in broiler pan. Broil for 3 to 5 minutes on each side for rare or until done to taste. Slice diagonally to serve. Yield: 6 servings.

Approx Per Serving: Cal 396; Prot 43 g; Carbo 1 g; Fiber <1 g;
T Fat 22 g; 53% Calories from Fat; Chol 128 mg; Sod 756 mg.

Make friends with people who help you feel good about yourself.

—from *Life Lessons For Women*

Meat Entrées

NEW ENGLAND STEAK AND BEAN POT

1 pound round steak, pounded thin
1/4 cup dark molasses
2 tablespoons soy sauce
1 tablespoon lemon juice
1 medium onion, chopped

1/4 cup sweet pickle relish
4 slices bacon
1 tablespoon shortening
1   16-ounce can Boston-style pork
    and beans

Cut round steak into 4 equal portions. Combine molasses, soy sauce, lemon juice and onion in small bowl; mix well. Brush one side of round steak with mixture, reserving remaining mixture. Top each portion with 1 tablespoon pickle relish. Roll up to enclose pickle; wrap with bacon, securing with wooden picks. Brown in shortening in skillet. Stir remaining molasses mixture into beans in 1-quart baking dish. Arrange steak rolls over top. Bake, covered, at 375 degrees for 45 minutes. Yield: 4 servings.

Approx Per Serving: Cal 421; Prot 30 g; Carbo 44 g; Fiber 7 g;
    T Fat 15 g; 31% Calories from Fat; Chol 77 mg; Sod 1175 mg.

BEEF AND VEGETABLE STEW

3 pounds stew beef, cut into
    1-inch pieces
6 tablespoons oil
1 cup chopped green bell pepper
1 cup chopped onion
1 cup sliced celery
1/2 cup water
1   10-ounce can condensed beef
    broth
1   8-ounce can tomato sauce
2 teaspoons chopped parsley

1 clove of garlic, minced
1 tablespoon salt
1/4 teaspoon pepper
1 bay leaf
1/8 teaspoon dried thyme
6 small potatoes, peeled
6 medium carrots, sliced
6 small white onions, sliced
1 to 2 tablespoons flour
2 tablespoons water
1 tomato, cut into wedges

Brown beef in oil in large saucepan; remove to platter. Add green pepper, chopped onion and celery. Sauté for 8 minutes or until tender. Return beef to saucepan. Add next 9 ingredients. Bring to a boil; reduce heat. Simmer, covered, for 1¼ hours, stirring occasionally. Add potatoes, carrots and sliced onions. Simmer, covered, for 1 hour longer or until tender. Remove from heat; skim fat. Mix flour with 2 tablespoons water in small bowl. Stir into beef mixture. Place tomato wedges on top. Simmer, covered, for 10 minutes. Discard bay leaf. Yield: 8 servings.

Approx Per Serving: Cal 487; Prot 37 g; Carbo 38 g; Fiber 6 g;
    T Fat 21 g; 39% Calories from Fat; Chol 96 mg; Sod 1297 mg.

STONED STEW

1/4 cup flour
1/2 teaspoon salt
1/2 teaspoon pepper
3 pounds stew beef, cut into
   bite-sized pieces
1/4 cup oil
2 large onions, thinly sliced
1   10-ounce can sliced mushrooms

1   10-ounce can beef broth
1   12-ounce bottle of beer
2 tablespoons vinegar
2 teaspoons sugar
2 cloves of garlic, minced
1 teaspoon thyme
3 bay leaves
2 tablespoons dried parsley

Combine flour, salt and pepper in plastic bag. Add beef, shaking to coat. Brown in hot oil in large saucepan. Add onions, undrained mushrooms, beef broth, beef, vinegar, sugar, garlic, thyme and bay leaves. Simmer, covered, for 2 hours, stirring occasionally. Add water if necessary. Stir in parsley. Remove bay leaves before serving. Serve over hot buttered noodles. Yield: 8 servings.

Approx Per Serving: Cal 345; Prot 34 g; Carbo 11 g; Fiber 2 g;
   T Fat 17 g; 46% Calories from Fat; Chol 96 mg; Sod 455 mg.

BEEF STROGANOFF

1 pound beef tenderloin, sliced
   1/4 inch thick
1 clove of garlic, cut into halves
3 tablespoons flour
1 1/2 teaspoons salt
1/4 teaspoon pepper
1/4 cup butter

1/2 cup minced onion
1/4 cup water
1   10-ounce can cream of chicken
   soup
16 ounces mushrooms, sliced
1 cup sour cream

Rub beef with garlic; sprinkle both sides with mixture of flour, salt and pepper. Pound with meat mallet. Cut into 1x1 1/2-inch strips. Brown in hot butter in skillet, turning often. Add onions. Sauté until onions are tender. Stir in water, soup and mushrooms. Cook over low heat for 20 minutes or until sauce is thickened and meat is tender, stirring occasionally. Stir in sour cream just before serving. Serve over rice, noodles or mashed potatoes. Garnish with chopped parsley, chives or dill. Yield: 6 servings.

Approx Per Serving: Cal 331; Prot 19 g; Carbo 13 g; Fiber 2 g;
   T Fat 23 g; 62% Calories from Fat; Chol 84 mg; Sod 1016 mg.

Meat Entrées

STEAK DIANE

1 8-ounce filet mignon
Black peppercorns to taste
1/2 ounce green peppercorns
2 ounces Dijon mustard
2 tablespoons clarified butter

Minced garlic and shallots to taste
Salt and pepper to taste
1 ounce brandy
2 ounces Quick Bordalaise Sauce
(page 156)

Cut steak into 3 portions. Coat with black and green peppercorns; spread with mustard. Sauté in clarified butter in hot sauté pan until done to taste. Add garlic, shallots, salt, pepper and brandy; ignite. Stir in Quick Bordalaise Sauce. Place steak on platter; spoon sauce over top. Yield: 1 serving.

Approx Per Serving: Cal 634; Prot 42 g; Carbo 14 g; Fiber 0 g; T Fat 43 g; 63% Calories from Fat; Chol 175 mg; Sod 1696 mg. Nutritional information does not include Quick Bordalaise Sauce.

Chef Eric Kornbluh
Redwood Bar & Grill

COGNAC BEEFBURGERS

2 pounds lean ground beef
2 eggs, slightly beaten
1/4 cup dry bread crumbs

Freshly cracked pepper
Chopped parsley or chives to taste
1/2 cup Cognac

Combine ground beef, eggs and bread crumbs in bowl; mix well. Shape into 6 patties; sprinkle with pepper and parsley. Sprinkle both sides with small amount of Cognac, reserving remaining Cognac. Let stand for 15 to 30 minutes. Grill or broil for 6 minutes on each side for medium-rare or until done to taste. Place on warmed serving platter. Heat remaining Cognac in saucepan. Flame and pour over patties. Serve immediately. Yield: 6 servings.

Approx Per Serving: Cal 395; Prot 31 g; Carbo 10 g; Fiber <1 g; T Fat 23 g; 56% Calories from Fat; Chol 170 mg; Sod 141 mg.

Muriel Stevens
Board of Trustees

BEEF CUPS

1 medium onion, finely chopped
2 tablespoons shortening
1 pound ground beef
2 medium potatoes, peeled, grated
1/4 teaspoon minced garlic

1/2 teaspoon salt
1/4 pepper
2 eggs, beaten
12 slices lean bacon

Sauté onion in shortening in skillet until tender. Combine with ground beef, potatoes, garlic, salt, pepper and eggs in bowl; mix well. Line muffin cups with bacon slices. Fill with ground beef mixture; fold bacon over ground beef mixture, securing with wooden picks. Bake at 350 degrees for 20 minutes. Cool in pan for 10 minutes. Remove to wire rack to drain. Serve hot or cold. Yield: 12 servings.

Approx Per Serving: Cal 178; Prot 11 g; Carbo 7 g; Fiber 1 g;
  T Fat 13 g; 62% Calories from Fat; Chol 70 mg; Sod 373 mg.

DON'S STUFFED HAMBURGERS

1 1/2 pounds ground beef
2 or 3 green onions, chopped

1 cup shredded Cheddar cheese

Shape ground beef into 8 patties. Sprinkle green onions and cheese in center of 4 patties; top with remaining patties, sealing edges. Grill over hot colas for 3 minutes on each side or until done to taste. May also fill with chopped green bell pepper, mushrooms, crumbled bacon and various cheeses. Yield: 4 servings.

Approx Per Serving: Cal 461; Prot 39 g; Carbo 1 g; Fiber <1 g;
  T Fat 33 g; 65% Calories from Fat; Chol 141 mg; Sod 273 mg.

GREEN CHILI AND CHEESE CASSEROLE

1 pound ground beef
1 cup sliced green onions
2 4-ounce cans chopped green
chilies, drained
2 12-ounce cans Mexicorn,
drained
16 ounces Monterey Jack cheese,
shredded

2 teaspoons salt
1/2 teaspoon pepper
21/2 cups milk
6 eggs
11/2 cups buttermilk baking mix

Brown ground beef in skillet, stirring until crumbly; drain. Remove with slotted spoon to large bowl; cool slightly. Add green onions, green chilies, Mexicorn, cheese, salt and pepper; mix well. Beat milk, eggs and baking mix with wire whisk in medium bowl until smooth. Layer ground beef mixture and egg mixture 1/2 at a time in greased 8x8-inch baking dish. Bake at 400 degrees for 35 minutes. Yield: 6 servings.

Approx Per Serving: Cal 815; Prot 47 g; Carbo 50 g; Fiber <1 g;
T Fat 47 g; 52% Calories from Fat; Chol 345 mg; Sod 2301 mg.

ITALIAN NOODLE BAKE

11/2 pounds ground beef
1/2 yellow onion, chopped
Salt and pepper to taste
1 15-ounce jar spaghetti sauce

1 8-ounce package egg noodles
3 ounces cream cheese, softened
1 cup sour cream
4 to 5 green onions, minced

Brown ground beef and onion in skillet, stirring until ground beef is crumbly; drain. Stir in spaghetti sauce. Simmer for 30 minutes, stirring occasionally. Cook noodles using package directions; drain. Place noodles in 9x13-inch baking dish. Mix cream cheese, sour cream and green onions in small bowl. Spread over noodles. Top with ground beef mixture. Bake at 350 degrees for 30 minutes. Garnish with grated cheese. Yield: 8 servings.

Approx Per Serving: Cal 444; Prot 23 g; Carbo 31 g; Fiber 1 g;
T Fat 26 g; 52% Calories from Fat; Chol 130 mg; Sod 364 mg.

 *Meat Entrées*

LAUNDRY DAY BAKED DINNER

3 medium potatoes, sliced
3 medium carrots, sliced
1/4 cup uncooked rice
1 medium onion, sliced

1 pound ground beef
1 16-ounce can whole tomatoes
Salt and pepper to taste

Layer potatoes, carrots, rice, onion, ground beef and tomatoes in 1½-quart casserole. Sprinkle with salt and pepper. Bake, covered, at 350 degrees for 1 hour. Serve with salad and fresh bread. This recipe dates from the days when laundry took an entire day and dinner took care of itself. Yield: 6 servings.

Approx Per Serving: Cal 279; Prot 17 g; Carbo 29 g; Fiber 3 g;
T Fat 11 g; 35% Calories from Fat; Chol 49 mg; Sod 183 mg.

SWEDISH MEATBALLS

2 medium onions, chopped
3 tablespoons butter
3 slices fresh bread
1/2 cup milk
1½ pounds lean ground beef
2 eggs, beaten

1 tablespoon salt
1/2 teaspoon freshly ground pepper
1 tablespoon flour
1 cup beef bouillon
1/2 cup milk
2 tablespoons sherry

Sauté onions in butter in skillet until golden brown. Soak bread in ½ cup milk in bowl. Add onions, ground beef, eggs, salt and pepper; mix well. Shape into 1-inch balls. Sauté in drippings in skillet until evenly browned. Remove with slotted spoon. Add flour to pan drippings, stirring until smooth. Add bouillon and ½ cup milk. Cook over medium heat until sauce is smooth and thickened, stirring constantly. Stir in sherry. Add meatballs. Simmer, covered, for 15 minutes. Yield: 6 servings.

Approx Per Serving: Cal 401; Prot 27 g; Carbo 14 g; Fiber 1 g;
T Fat 26 g; 59% Calories from Fat; Chol 166 mg; Sod 1423 mg.

SWEET AND SOUR MEAT LOAF

1¹/₂ pounds ground beef
1 cup dry bread crumbs
1 teaspoon salt
¹/₄ teaspoon pepper
2 eggs, beaten
1 teaspoon minced onion flakes

1 15-ounce can tomato sauce
2 tablespoons brown sugar
2 tablespoons vinegar
¹/₂ cup sugar
2 teaspoons prepared mustard

Combine ground beef, bread crumbs, salt, pepper and eggs in bowl; mix well. Stir in onion flakes and half the tomato sauce. Shape into loaf. Place in 5x9-inch baking pan. Bake at 350 degrees for 50 minutes. Combine remaining tomato sauce, brown sugar, vinegar, sugar and mustard in saucepan. Bring to a boil, stirring constantly. Pour over meat loaf. Bake for 10 minutes longer. Yield: 6 servings.

Approx Per Serving: Cal 427; Prot 26 g; Carbo 39 g; Fiber 2 g;
T Fat 19 g; 39% Calories from Fat; Chol 146 mg; Sod 1019 mg.

TAGLIARINI

1 8-ounce package noodles
1¹/₂ pounds ground beef
1 onion, chopped
1 clove of garlic, finely chopped
1 20-ounce can whole kernel
    corn, drained
1 4-ounce can mushrooms,
    drained

1 10-ounce can mushroom soup
1 4-ounce can black olives,
    drained
1 20-ounce can tomatoes,
    drained, chopped
8 ounces Velveeta cheese, cubed
¹/₂ green bell pepper, chopped

Cook noodles using package directions; drain. Brown ground beef, onion and garlic in skillet, stirring until ground beef is crumbly; drain. Combine with noodles, corn, mushrooms, mushroom soup, olives, tomatoes, cheese and green pepper in bowl; mix well. Spoon into baking dish. Bake at 350 degrees for 1¹/₂ hours. May double recipe for large crowd. Yield: 8 servings.

Approx Per Serving: Cal 530; Prot 30 g; Carbo 42 g; Fiber 3 g;
T Fat 29 g; 48% Calories from Fat; Chol 133 mg; Sod 1193 mg.

 *Meat Entrées*

SPOON BREAD TAMALE BAKE

1¹/₂ pounds ground chuck
¹/₄ cup olive oil
1 cup chopped onion
1 clove of garlic, crushed
¹/₂ cup chopped green pepper
1 20-ounce can tomatoes, drained, chopped

1 13-ounce can whole kernel corn, drained
Salt to taste
1 cup pitted black olives
1¹/₂ tablespoons chili powder
¹/₄ teaspoon pepper
Spoon Bread Batter

Brown ground chuck in olive oil in skillet, stirring until crumbly. Add onion, garlic and green pepper. Cook until onion is golden brown; drain. Stir in tomatoes, corn, salt, olives, chili powder and pepper. Spoon into 3-quart casserole. Pour Spoon Bread Batter over ground chuck mixture. Bake at 350 degrees for 30 to 40 minutes or until browned. Yield: 8 servings.

Spoon Bread Batter

1 cup cornmeal
1 cup water
1¹/₂ cups milk
1 teaspoon salt

2 tablespoons margarine
4 ounces Cheddar cheese, shredded
2 eggs, beaten

Mix cornmeal and water in small bowl. Heat milk, salt and margarine in saucepan. Add cornmeal mixture ¹/₂ cup at a time. Cook over low heat until thickened, stirring frequently; remove from heat. Stir in cheese and eggs. Yield: 8 servings.

Approx Per Serving: Cal 507; Prot 26 g; Carbo 31 g; Fiber 4 g; T Fat 33 g; 57% Calories from Fat; Chol 130 mg; Sod 790 mg.

Cherish your memories. Recall those that make you smile.

SUMMER SAUSAGE

3 pounds ground beef
1 cup water
1/2 teaspoon pepper
1/2 teaspoon garlic powder

1/2 teaspoon mustard seed
2 teaspoons liquid smoke
3 tablespoons Tender-Quick salt

Combine ground beef, water, pepper, garlic powder, mustard seed, liquid smoke and salt in bowl; mix well. Shape into logs or balls. Wrap tightly in foil. Chill for 24 hours. Cut slits in foil. Place in roasting pan. Bake at 325 degrees for 1 1/4 hours or until cooked through. May also add 1/4 to 1/2 teaspoon oregano and 1 teaspoon whole peppercorns. May substitute ground pork, turkey or venison for ground beef. Yield: 24 servings.

Approx Per Serving: Cal 115; Prot 11 g; Carbo 0 g; Fiber 0 g;
T Fat 8 g; 63% Calories from Fat; Chol 37 mg; Sod 832 mg.
Nutritional information does not include liquid smoke.

HAM 'N CHEESE QUICHE

1 1/2 cups cooked cubed ham
1 1/2 cups shredded Cheddar cheese
1/4 cup chopped onion
3 tablespoons chopped green bell
pepper
1 cup pancake mix

1/4 teaspoon salt
1/2 teaspoon pepper
2 cups milk
5 eggs
1/2 cup crushed cornflakes
1/4 cup melted butter

Sprinkle ham, cheese, onion and green pepper evenly in 8x12-inch baking dish. Beat pancake mix, salt, pepper, milk and eggs in mixer bowl at medium speed for 3 minutes. Pour over ham mixture. Sprinkle cornflakes over top; drizzle with melted butter. Bake at 350 degrees for 50 to 60 minutes or until golden brown. Yield: 6 servings.

Approx Per Serving: Cal 465; Prot 27 g; Carbo 27 g; Fiber <1 g;
T Fat 27 g; 53% Calories from Fat; Chol 258 mg; Sod 1241 mg.

 *Meat Entrées*

LOUISIANA RED BEANS AND RICE

16 ounces dried red beans
8 cups water
1 pound ham, cubed
1 to 3 teaspoons red pepper

Salt to taste
1 bay leaf
1 pound sausage
2 cups rice

Soak beans in water in large saucepan overnight. Add ham, red pepper, salt and bay leaf. Bring to a boil; reduce heat. Simmer for 2 hours, stirring occasionally. Crumble sausage into mixture. Simmer for 20 to 30 minutes longer or until beans are tender, mashing with spoon to thicken. Remove bay leaf. Cook rice using package directions. Serve bean mixture over rice. Yield: 10 servings.

Approx Per Serving: Cal 435; Prot 29 g; Carbo 57 g; Fiber 10 g;
T Fat 10 g; 20% Calories from Fat; Chol 42 mg; Sod 890 mg.

POTATO AND HAM SKILLET TORTA

6 large eggs
1/2 cup milk
1 tablespoon freshly chopped parsley
1/2 teaspoon salt
1/4 teaspoon freshly ground black pepper
1/8 teaspoon ground red pepper

1 tablespoon olive oil
1 pound baking potatoes, peeled, cut into 1/4-inch cubes
1 cup chopped onions
1 cup chopped red bell pepper
1 teaspoon minced garlic
8 ounces ham, cut into 1/2-inch pieces

Whisk eggs, milk, parsley, salt, black pepper and red pepper in bowl; set aside. Heat oil in 10-inch cast-iron skillet. Add potatoes, onions and bell pepper. Cook over medium heat for 15 minutes or until potatoes are tender, stirring frequently. Add garlic and ham. Cook for 1 minute, stirring often; remove from heat. Pour egg mixture over potato mixture. Cover with foil. Bake at 350 degrees for 15 minutes; remove foil. Bake for 5 minutes longer or until set. Yield: 6 servings.

Approx Per Serving: Cal 250; Prot 18 g; Carbo 20 g; Fiber 2 g;
T Fat 11 g; 39% Calories from Fat; Chol 237 mg; Sod 762 mg.

LEG OF LAMB WITH GARLIC AND LIMES

1 6-pound leg of lamb	5 slices of bacon, cut into ½ inch
5 cloves of garlic, cut into	pieces
halves	Ground pepper and rosemary to
2 limes, cut into ½ inch pieces	taste

Remove excess fat from lamb. Cut several deep slits in surface. Wrap garlic cloves and limes in bacon pieces. Insert into slits in lamb. Rub with pepper and rosemary. Place on rack in roasting pan. Roast at 350 degrees for 1½ hours or until done to taste. Yield: 12 servings.

Approx Per Serving: Cal 282; Prot 38 g; Carbo 2 g; Fiber <1 g; T Fat 13 g; 41% Calories from Fat; Chol 124 mg; Sod 135 mg.

PORK CHOPS FLORENTINE

6 pork chops, ½ inch thick	1 carrot, sliced
¼ cup flour	½ bay leaf
Salt and pepper to taste	6 tablespoons butter
3 10-ounce packages frozen	6 tablespoons flour
chopped spinach	1¾ cups milk
1 10-ounce can chicken broth	2 egg yolks, beaten
1 onion, sliced	1 cup shredded Swiss cheese

Coat pork chops with ¼ cup flour; sprinkle with salt and pepper. Brown in nonstick skillet; reduce heat. Cook over very low heat for 30 minutes or until tender. Cook spinach using package directions; drain. Spread spinach in shallow baking dish. Arrange pork chops on top. Simmer chicken broth, onion, carrot and bay leaf in saucepan for 10 minutes. Strain, reserving broth. Melt butter in saucepan. Blend in 6 tablespoons flour. Cook until bubbly. Stir in reserved broth and milk. Cook over low heat until thickened, stirring constantly. Add a small amount of hot mixture to egg yolks, beating well. Stir egg yolks into hot mixture, beating constantly. Pour sauce over pork chops. Sprinkle with cheese. Bake at 375 degrees for 15 minutes or until cheese is melted and lightly browned. Yield: 6 servings.

Approx Per Serving: Cal 575; Prot 48 g; Carbo 25 g; Fiber 5 g; T Fat 32 g; 50% Calories from Fat; Chol 227 mg; Sod 532 mg.

EASY OVEN-BARBECUED PORK CHOPS

1¹/₂ pounds shoulder cut pork
  chops, trimmed
1 tablespoon garlic powder
2 medium onions, sliced

2 lemons, sliced
2 cups catsup
1 cup water
1 cup packed brown sugar

Place pork chops in 10x14-inch baking dish. Rub with garlic powder. Top with onions and lemon slices. Mix catsup, water and brown sugar in bowl. Pour over pork chops. Bake at 325 degrees for 1 to 1¹/₂ hours or until cooked through and tender. Serve over rice. Yield: 6 servings.

Approx Per Serving: Cal 459; Prot 25 g; Carbo 74 g; Fiber 3 g;
  T Fat 8 g; 15% Calories from Fat; Chol 69 mg; Sod 1025 mg.

SAVORY STUFFED PORK CHOPS

¹/₃ cup chopped onion
¹/₂ cup chopped celery
2 tablespoons margarine
1¹/₂ cups bread cubes
¹/₄ cup dark raisins
2 tablespoons chopped parsley

1 teaspoon salt
¹/₈ teaspoon pepper
¹/₂ teaspoon marjoram
3 tablespoons apple juice
4 rib pork chops, 2 inches thick
1 teaspoon seasoned salt

Sauté onion and celery in margarine in skillet until tender. Add bread cubes. Cook until slightly browned; remove from heat. Add next 6 ingredients; mix well. Slit pork chops to form pocket. Sprinkle with seasoned salt. Spoon stuffing mixture into each pork chop. Stand on rib bones on rack in shallow roasting pan. Add water to fill pan ¹/₂ inch. Cover with foil. Bake at 350 degrees for 45 minutes; remove foil. Bake for 45 to 55 minutes longer or until tender and browned. Yield: 4 servings.

Approx Per Serving: Cal 354; Prot 33 g; Carbo 17 g; Fiber 1 g;
  T Fat 17 g; 43% Calories from Fat; Chol 98 mg; Sod 1076 mg.

CHAR SUE (Paper Clip Pork)

¹/₄ cup honey
¹/₄ cup dry sherry
Pepper to taste
1 tablespoon salt
1 teaspoon finely chopped or
  grated gingerroot
3 cloves of garlic, coarsely
  chopped

4 to 5 tablespoons hoisen sauce
1 tablespoon soy sauce
1 tablespoon chopped chives
2 teaspoons Chinese red food
  coloring
1 3-pound boneless pork loin,
  trimmed
6 to 8 large paper clips

Combine honey, sherry, pepper, salt, gingerroot, garlic, hoisen sauce, soy sauce, chives and food coloring in bowl; mix well. Pour into oblong pan. Cut pork into halves. Place in sauce, turning to coat. Marinate, covered, in refrigerator overnight, turning occasionally. Place 1 oven rack to highest position in oven and 1 rack at lowest position. Place foil covered baking sheet on lowest rack. Open paper clips to "S" shape. Insert paper clips 1 inch into pork, using 2 or 3 for each portion. Hang pork from top rack in cold oven by other end of paper clips. Roast at 425 degrees for 15 minutes; reduce oven temperature to 325 degrees. Roast for 1¹/₄ hours longer. Remove from oven; discard paper clips. Slice pork and serve. Yield: 6 servings.

Approx Per Serving: Cal 398; Prot 45 g; Carbo 16 g; Fiber <1 g;
  T Fat 15 g; 35% Calories from Fat; Chol 139 mg; Sod 1389 mg.

Far away there in the sunshine are my highest aspirations.
I may not reach them, but I can look up and see their
beauty, believe in them and try to follow where they lead.
—Louisa May Alcott

ROAST PORK TENDERLOIN

2¹/₂ pounds pork tenderloin,
  trimmed
1 tablespoon butter, softened
1 cup coarsely chopped parsley
Salt, pepper and paprika to taste
3 tablespoons butter

2 medium onions, cut into wedges
1¹/₂ cups beef bouillon
6 whole peppercorns
3 tablespoons butter
3 tablespoons flour
1 cup light cream

Cut slits in pork at regular intervals. Combine 1 tablespoon butter and parsley in bowl. Stuff into slits. Season with salt, pepper and paprika. Heat 3 tablespoons butter in heavy ovenproof skillet until brown. Add pork. Brown well on all sides. Add onions, bouillon and peppercorns. Place in 350-degree oven. Roast for 20 to 30 minutes or until tender. Place pork on warm platter. Strain pan juices into glass measure, adding more bouillon or water to measure 1¹/₂ cups; reserve peppercorns and set aside. Melt 3 tablespoons butter in saucepan. Blend in flour. Cook until lightly browned. Add reserved pan juices and cream. Cook over low heat for 5 minutes or until thickened, stirring constantly. Adjust seasonings and add additional bouillon if necessary. Slice pork into thick slices. Garnish with sautéed peppercorns. Serve with sauce. Yield: 4 servings.

Approx Per Serving: Cal 721; Prot 61 g; Carbo 14 g; Fiber 2 g;
  T Fat 46 g; 58% Calories from Fat; Chol 250 mg; Sod 631 mg.

SWEET AND SOUR PORK

1¹/₂ pounds pork, cubed
2 teaspoons oil
¹/₄ cup vinegar
1 tablespoon soy sauce
¹/₂ cup chopped onion
³/₄ cup chopped green bell pepper
³/₄ cup chopped red bell pepper

¹/₂ teaspoon salt
1 16-ounce can chunked
  pineapple
1 16-ounce can sliced peaches
¹/₄ cup packed brown sugar
2 tablespoons cornstarch

Brown pork in hot oil in 16-inch skillet. Add vinegar, soy sauce, onion, green pepper, red pepper and salt. Simmer for 25 to 30 minutes or until tender. Drain pineapple and peaches, reserving juice. Add reserved juice and brown sugar to skillet, stirring to mix. Add pineapple and peaches. Cook until heated through. Stir in cornstarch. Cook until thickened, stirring constantly. Serve over rice. Yield: 6 servings.

Approx Per Serving: Cal 356; Prot 24 g; Carbo 47 g; Fiber 2 g;
  T Fat 9 g; 23% Calories from Fat; Chol 69 mg; Sod 416 mg.

◈Meat Entrées

LASAGNA ✓

2 pounds sweet Italian sausage, casing removed
1 large onion, chopped
2 cloves of garlic, minced
Garlic salt and Italian seasoning to taste
2 30-ounce jars spaghetti sauce with mushrooms

1 8-ounce package lasagna noodles
1¹/₂ pounds ricotta cheese
1 cup grated Parmesan cheese
16 ounces mozzarella cheese, shredded

Cook sausage in large saucepan, stirring until crumbly. Add onion, garlic, garlic salt and Italian seasoning. Cook until onion is tender. Add spaghetti sauce. Simmer for 2 to 3 hours, stirring occasionally. Cook noodles using package directions; drain. Layer half the noodles, ¹/₃ of the sauce, half the ricotta cheese, half the Parmesan cheese and half the mozzarella cheese in 9x13-inch baking dish. Repeat layers. Top with remaining sauce. Bake at 350 degrees for 45 minutes or until bubbly. Let stand for 15 minutes before serving. Yield: 12 servings.

Approx Per Serving: Cal 581; Prot 29 g; Carbo 41 g; Fiber 2 g;
T Fat 34 g; 52% Calories from Fat; Chol 91 mg; Sod 1347 mg.

ITALIAN SAUSAGE PASTA SAUCE

1 pound sweet Italian sausage, cut into bite-sized circles
¹/₄ cup olive oil
1 onion, chopped
1 clove of garlic, minced
1 20-ounce can stewed tomatoes
1 6-ounce can tomato paste
2 cups chicken broth

Salt and pepper to taste
1 tablespoon sugar
1 teaspoon allspice
1 teaspoon oregano
1 bay leaf
1 cup dry white wine
1 4-ounce can mushrooms, drained

Brown sausage in oil in skillet; remove to paper towels. Sauté onion and garlic in pan drippings until tender. Add sausage, tomatoes, tomato paste, chicken broth, salt, pepper, sugar, allspice, oregano and bay leaf; mix well. Simmer for 1¹/₂ hours, stirring occasionally. Stir in wine. Cook for 30 minutes longer. Stir in mushrooms. Remove bay leaf. Serve over pasta. Yield: 6 servings.

Approx Per Serving: Cal 309; Prot 12 g; Carbo 19 g; Fiber 2 g;
T Fat 19 g; 58% Calories from Fat; Chol 28 mg; Sod 991 mg.

SPAGHETTI SAUCE

1 gallon tomato sauce
1 tablespoon oregano
1¹/₂ teaspoons rosemary
1¹/₂ teaspoons thyme
1¹/₂ teaspoons celery flakes
2¹/₂ teaspoons onion salt
1 bay leaf
1 tablespoon sweet basil

1¹/₂ teaspoons marjoram
1¹/₂ teaspoons crushed fennel seed
3¹/₂ teaspoons minced garlic
1 teaspoon brown sugar
8 ounces Italian sausage
8 ounces ground beef
8 ounces ground pork

Combine tomato sauce, oregano, rosemary, thyme, celery flakes, onion salt, bay leaf, basil, marjoram, fennel, garlic and brown sugar in large kettle. Bring to a boil; reduce heat. Simmer for 2 hours, stirring occasionally. Brown sausage, ground beef and ground pork in skillet, stirring until crumbly; drain well. Add to sauce mixture; mix well. Spoon into slow cooker. Cook for 2 to 3 hours, stirring occasionally. Yield: 16 servings.

Approx Per Serving: Cal 152; Prot 11 g; Carbo 19 g; Fiber 4 g;
   T Fat 5 g; 29% Calories from Fat; Chol 25 mg; Sod 1808 mg.

STUFFED FRANK BOATS

8 frankfurters
¹/₂ cup soft bread crumbs
¹/₄ cup chopped salted peanuts
¹/₄ cup chopped stuffed olives

1 tablespoon chopped pimento
¹/₄ cup catsup
1 egg, slightly beaten
1 cup shredded American cheese

Cut slit in each frankfurter; spread open. Combine bread crumbs, peanuts, olives, pimento, catsup, egg and half the cheese in bowl; mix well. Spoon mixture into frankfurters. Place on baking pan. Broil 7 inches from heat source for 3 to 5 minutes or until brown. Top with remaining cheese. Broil for 1 to 2 minutes longer or until cheese is melted. Yield: 8 servings.

Approx Per Serving: Cal 253; Prot 10 g; Carbo 6 g; Fiber 1 g;
   T Fat 21 g; 74% Calories from Fat; Chol 63 mg; Sod 962 mg.

Meat Entrées

SALTIMBOCCA

12 veal scallopini
1 tablespoon flour
Salt and pepper to taste
12 thin slices prosciutto
2 teaspoons crushed sage leaves

1/4 cup butter
1/4 cup olive oil
3/4 cup Marsala wine
1/4 cup brandy
3/4 cup white wine

Pound veal until thin. Dust with flour, salt and pepper. Layer with ham; sprinkle with sage. Roll up to enclose ham and sage; secure with wooden picks. Melt butter with oil in chafing dish. Add veal rolls. Sauté until golden brown. Pour in Marsala wine, brandy and white wine; ignite. Simmer for 3 to 4 minutes. Yield: 6 servings.

Approx Per Serving: Cal 510; Prot 48 g; Carbo 8 g; Fiber <1 g; T Fat 24 g; 43% Calories from Fat; Chol 189 mg; Sod 907 mg.

VEAL POJARSKY

4 slices white bread, crusts
  removed, torn
1/2 cup whipping cream
1 pound coarsely ground lean veal

Salt and white pepper to taste
1 egg, beaten
2 tablespoons flour
1/4 cup clarified butter

Soak bread in cream. Mix until smooth paste forms, adding additional cream if needed. Add veal, salt, pepper and egg, mixing well. Divide into 4 portions and shape as for veal chops. Dust with flour on both sides. Heat clarified butter in large skillet. Brown veal on each side. Place in baking dish. Bake in preheated 425-degree oven for 8 to 10 minutes or until brown, turning once. May substitute evaporated milk for cream. Note: To clarify butter, melt butter over low heat until milk solids sink to bottom. Remove clear butter carefully from top. May store in refrigerator for at least 2 weeks. Yield: 4 servings.

Approx Per Serving: Cal 445; Prot 32 g; Carbo 14 g; Fiber <1 g; T Fat 29 g; 58% Calories from Fat; Chol 242 mg; Sod 298 mg.

VEAL SCALLOPINI

1/4 cup olive oil
1/2 cup butter
2 tablespoons finely chopped salt
  pork
1 large onion, finely chopped
1 pound veal scallopini, 1/4 inch
  thick
2 tablespoons flour
Salt and pepper to taste

1 large tomato, thinly sliced
1 large green bell pepper, thinly
  sliced
4 ounces fresh mushrooms, thinly
  sliced
1/2 to 3/4 cup Chianti wine
2 large cloves of garlic
8 sprigs of fresh parsley

Heat oil and butter over medium heat in large skillet. Add salt pork. Cook
until pork is translucent. Add onion. Sauté until tender but not browned.
Pound veal to 1/8-inch thickness. Dust with flour, salt and pepper on both
sides. Brown in skillet on both sides. Add tomato, green pepper, mushrooms
and wine. Simmer, covered, over low heat for 20 to 30 minutes or until veal
is tender, stirring occasionally. Adjust seasonings. Mince garlic and parsley
together until paste forms. Add to skillet, stirring to mix. Simmer for 10
minutes longer; remove from heat. Let stand for 5 minutes before serving.
Serve with fresh pasta and Chianti. Yield: 4 servings.

Approx Per Serving: Cal 523; Prot 25 g; Carbo 11 g; Fiber 2 g;
  T Fat 40 g; 72% Calories from Fat; Chol 155 mg; Sod 280 mg.

*I don't know what your destiny will be, but one thing I
know; the only ones among you who will be really happy
are those who will have sought and found how to serve.*
—Dr. Albert Schweitzer

POULTRY & SEAFOOD

Poultry

HERB BROILED CHICKEN

1 cup oil
1/2 cup lemon juice
1/8 teaspoon oregano
1/2 teapoon marjoram
1 teaspoon salt

1 teaspooon seasoned salt
Pepper to taste
2 tablespoons finely chopped
parsley
3 2-pound chickens

Combine oil, lemon juice, oregano, marjoram, salt, seasoned salt, pepper and parsley in small bowl; mix well. Rinse chickens and pat dry. Split into halves. Brush with lemon mixture. Place skin side down on broiler rack. Broil 8 inches from heat source for 25 minutes, basting with lemon mixture 2 to 3 times. Turn chickens. Broil for 20 to 25 minutes longer or until chicken is cooked through. Yield: 6 servings.

Approx Per Serving: Cal 614; Prot 44 g; Carbo 2 g; Fiber <1 g;
T Fat 48 g; 70% Calories from Fat; Chol 135 mg; Sod 702 mg.

CHICKEN ALFREDO

4 chicken breast filets
1/2 cup flour
3 eggs, beaten
3 tablespoons water
1/2 cup grated Romano cheese
1/4 cup chopped parsley
1/2 teaspoon salt
1 cup bread crumbs

3 tablespoons butter
2 tablespoons oil
4 slices mozzarella cheese
1 cup sliced mushrooms
1 8-ounce jar artichoke hearts,
drained
1/2 cup white wine
1/2 cup chicken bouillon

Rinse chicken and pat dry. Coat with flour. Beat eggs, water, Romano cheese, parsley and salt in bowl. Dip chicken in egg mixture; roll in bread crumbs. Heat butter and oil in skillet. Brown chicken on both sides. Remove to baking dish. Top with mozzarella cheese. Sauté mushrooms in pan drippings. Add artichoke hearts, wine and bouillon. Simmer until heated through. Pour over chicken. Bake, covered, at 350 degrees for 40 minutes. Yield: 4 servings.

Approx Per Serving: Cal 667; Prot 47 g; Carbo 36 g; Fiber 2 g;
T Fat 34 g; 48% Calories from Fat; Chol 290 mg; Sod 1128 mg.

CHICKEN BREASTS AND ARTICHOKE HEARTS

4 chicken breast filets
Salt and pepper to taste
6 tablespoons butter
3 tablespoons sherry
1   9-ounce package frozen
   artichoke hearts, thawed
2 cups sliced fresh mushrooms

1 cup chicken broth
1/4 cup whipping cream
1 egg yolk
1 tablespoon water
1 tablespoon chopped fresh
   parsley
16 ounces fettucini, cooked

Rinse chicken and pat dry. Cut into 1-inch pieces. Rub with salt and pepper. Heat half the butter in skillet over low heat. Add chicken; sprinkle with 1 tablespoon sherry. Cook, covered, for 3 minutes or until cooked through. Remove to warm platter. Add remaining butter to skillet. Sauté artichoke hearts and mushrooms over medium heat for 2 minutes; remove to platter. Add chicken broth and remaining sherry to skillet. Simmer until reduced by 1/2, stirring frequently. Add cream. Simmer until reduced by 1/3, stirring constantly. Beat egg yolk with water in small bowl until foamy. Add to sauce gradually, whisking constantly; remove from heat. Stir in parsley. Arrange chicken and artichoke mixture over cooked fettucini; spoon sauce over top. Yield: 4 servings.

Approx Per Serving: Cal 772; Prot 48 g; Carbo 69 g; Fiber 5 g;
   T Fat 32 g; 38% Calories from Fat; Chol 294 mg; Sod 487 mg.

SOUR CREAM CHICKEN AND BROCCOLI

2 pounds fresh broccoli
Salt to taste
12 chicken breast halves, skinned
1/4 cup butter
Pepper to taste

2 cups sour cream
1 envelope onion soup mix
1 cup whipping cream, whipped
1/4 cup grated Parmesan cheese

Cook broccoli in boiling salted water until tender-crisp. Place in large buttered baking dish. Rinse chicken and pat dry. Brown on both sides in hot butter in large skillet; season with salt and pepper. Cook over low heat until tender; remove with slotted spoon. Cut into chunks and set aside. Stir sour cream and onion soup mix into pan drippings. Spread half the mixture over broccoli; top with chicken. Fold remaining mixture into whipped cream. Spread over chicken. Sprinkle with Parmesan cheese. Bake at 350 degrees for 20 minutes or until browned. Yield: 6 servings.

Approx Per Serving: Cal 710; Prot 62 g; Carbo 13 g; Fiber 5 g;
   T Fat 46 g; 58% Calories from Fat; Chol 256 mg; Sod 456 mg.

CHICKEN AND BROCCOLI

4 large chicken breasts
1/2 onion, sliced
4 stalks celery, sliced
Salt and pepper to taste
2   10-ounce packages frozen
  broccoli spears

1 cup butter, softened
2 teaspoons lemon juice
2   10-ounce cans cream of
  chicken soup
1/2 cup shredded Cheddar cheese
1/2 cup crushed butter crackers

Rinse chicken. Stew with onion, celery, salt and pepper until tender. Remove chicken with slotted spoon. Cut into large pieces, discarding skin and bones. Place in cooking broth. Chill overnight. Cook broccoli using package directions; drain. Arrange in baking dish. Drain chicken, discarding broth. Layer chicken over broccoli. Mix butter, lemon juice and soup in bowl. Pour over chicken. Sprinkle with cheese; cover with crushed crackers. Bake at 350 degrees for 15 to 20 minutes or until bubbly. Do not substitute margarine for butter in this recipe. Yield: 4 servings.

Approx Per Serving: Cal 834; Prot 40 g; Carbo 28 g; Fiber 5 g;
  T Fat 65 g; 68% Calories from Fat; Chol 223 mg; Sod 1812 mg.

CHICKEN DIABLO

6 chicken breast filets
1/4 cup margarine
1/2 cup honey

1/4 cup mustard
1 teaspoon salt
1 teaspoon curry powder

Rinse chicken and pat dry. Place in 12x14-inch baking dish. Melt margarine in saucepan. Stir in honey, mustard, salt and curry powder. Pour over chicken Bake at 350 degrees for 1 to 1 1/2 hours or until chicken is tender. Serve with rice. Yield: 6 servings.

Approx Per Serving: Cal 302; Prot 27 g; Carbo 24 g; Fiber <1 g;
  T Fat 11 g; 33% Calories from Fat; Chol 72 mg; Sod 640 mg.

We make a living by what we get, but we make a life by what we give.

—Norman Macewan

CRUSTED DIJON CHICKEN

6   6-ounce chicken breast filets
1 tablespoon Dijon mustard
1 tablespoon chopped chervil
1 tablespoon chopped flat-leaf
  parsley
1 tablespoon chopped chives
1/2 cup herb-seasoned stuffing
  mix, crushed
Salt and pepper to taste

Rinse chicken breasts and pat dry. Spread with mustard. Combine chervil, parsley, chives and stuffing mix in bowl. Coat chicken with stuffing mix crumbs. Add salt and pepper. Place in baking dish. Bake at 360 degrees for 30 minutes. Yield: 6 servings.

Approx Per Serving: Cal 236; Prot 41 g; Carbo 4 g; Fiber 0 g;
  T Fat 5 g; 20% Calories from Fat; Chol 108 mg; Sod 239 mg.

CHICKEN IN BLACK BEAN SAUCE

2 tablespoons dry sherry
4 teaspoons soy sauce
2 teaspoons cornstarch
2 cups chopped smoked chicken
4 to 6 fermented black beans,
  rinsed
4 teaspoons black bean sauce
6 cloves of garlic, minced
1 teaspoon brown sugar
1 1/2 cups chicken stock
2 tablespoons oil
24 fresh asparagus spears, sliced
  diagonally into 2 1/2-inch pieces
2 teaspoons cornstarch
2 tablespoons water

Combine sherry, soy sauce and 2 teaspoons cornstarch in bowl; mix well. Add chicken, stirring to coat. Marinate for 15 to 30 minutes, stirring frequently. Mash black beans in bowl. Stir in black bean sauce, garlic, brown sugar and chicken stock. Let stand for 15 minutes. Heat oil in wok. Add black bean mixture. Stir-fry for 1 minute. Add asparagus, stirring to coat. Bring to a boil. Add chicken and marinade, tossing well. Mix 2 teaspoons cornstarch with water. Stir into mixture. Stir-fry until sauce begins to glaze and asparagus is tender. Serve over rice. Fermented black beans and black bean sauce are available in oriental food stores. Yield: 4 servings.

Approx Per Serving: Cal 263; Prot 26 g; Carbo 9 g; Fiber 1 g;
  T Fat 13 g; 44% Calories from Fat; Chol 63 mg; Sod 697 mg.
  Nutritional information does not include fermented black beans
  and black bean sauce.

CREAMY CHICKEN 'N CHEESE ENCHILADAS

2 pounds chicken breast filets
2　10-ounce cans cream of
　chicken soup
1　4-ounce can chopped green
　chilies

2 cups sour cream
1¹/₂ pounds Monterey Jack cheese,
　shredded
12 flour tortillas

Cook chicken in boiling water until cooked through. Cool. Chop into bite-sized pieces. Combine soup, green chilies and sour cream in bowl; mix well. Spoon half the soup mixture into large bowl. Stir in chicken. Warm tortillas on Defrost in microwave. Spoon 2 heaping tablespoons soup mixture in center of each tortilla; sprinkle with cheese. Roll up to enclose filling. Place seam side down in 9x13-inch baking dish. Pour remaining soup mixture over tortillas. Top with remaining cheese. Bake at 300 degrees for 20 to 30 minutes or until bubbly. Yield: 12 servings.

Approx Per Serving: Cal 539; Prot 37 g; Carbo 25 g; Fiber 1 g;
　T Fat 33 g; 54% Calories from Fat; Chol 121 mg; Sod 939 mg.

CHICKEN ENCHILADAS WITH TOMATO SAUCE

1　16-ounce can tomatoes
1　4-ounce can green chili
　peppers, drained, seeded
¹/₂ teaspoon ground coriander
¹/₂ teaspoon salt
1 cup sour cream
2 cups finely chopped cooked
　chicken

3 ounces cream cheese, softened
¹/₄ cup finely chopped onion
³/₄ teaspoon salt
12 flour tortillas
1 tablespoon oil
1 cup shredded Monterey Jack
　cheese

Process tomatoes, chili peppers, coriander and ¹/₂ teaspoon salt in blender until smooth; set aside. Combine sour cream, chicken, cream cheese, onion and ³/₄ teaspoon salt in bowl; mix well. Fry tortillas in hot oil in skillet for 15 to 20 seconds or until soft. Drain on paper towels. Spoon chicken mixture into center of tortillas; roll up to enclose filling. Place seam side down in 7x12-inch baking dish. Pour tomato mixture over tortillas. Bake, covered with foil, at 350 degrees for 30 minutes; remove foil. Sprinkle with cheese. Bake for 5 minutes longer or until cheese is melted. Yield: 12 servings.

Approx Per Serving: Cal 271; Prot 13 g; Carbo 23 g; Fiber 1 g;
　T Fat 15 g; 48% Calories from Fat; Chol 46 mg; Sod 586 mg.

CHICKEN KASHMIR

4 whole chicken breasts, boned,
 split
3/4 cup flour
1 tablespoon curry powder
Chopped chervil and parsley to
 taste

Salt, pepper and garlic salt to taste
1/4 cup butter
1/4 cup oil
1/4 cup orange juice
1/4 cup packed brown sugar
1/2 cup dry white wine

Rinse chicken and pat dry. Mix flour with next 6 ingredients in small bowl. Coat chicken in flour mixture. Heat butter and oil in skillet until bubbly. Sauté chicken until golden brown and partially cooked. Drain all but 1 tablespoon pan drippings. Combine orange juice, brown sugar and wine in small bowl. Pour over chicken. Cook for 10 to 15 minutes longer or until liquid is reduced by half and chicken is glazed. Serve with brown rice, substituting orange juice for water when cooking rice. Yield: 4 servings.

Approx Per Serving: Cal 679; Prot 56 g; Carbo 36 g; Fiber 1 g;
 T Fat 31 g; 43% Calories from Fat; Chol 175 mg; Sod 233 mg.

Photograph for this recipe is on the Cover.

CHICKEN WITH MACADAMIA NUTS

6 chicken breast filets
1 ounce macadamia nuts, coarsely
 chopped
2 tablespoons butter
2 eggs, beaten
2 tablespoons peanut oil
2 tablespoons soy sauce
1 slice gingerroot, minced

2 tablespoons brandy
1 onion, minced
2 to 3 cloves of garlic, sliced
1/4 cup cold water
1/2 cup flour
1/4 cup cornstarch
Pepper to taste
1 tablespoon peanut oil

Rinse chicken and pat dry. Cut into halves lengthwise, then into 1/2-inch pieces. Place in shallow pan. Brown macadamia nuts in butter in skillet over low heat, shaking pan frequently to avoid scorching; set aside. Process next 11 ingredients in blender until well blended. Pour over chicken pieces, stirring to coat. Let stand for 20 minutes. Preheat electric skillet to 350 degrees. Add 1 tablespoon oil. Brown chicken on both sides for 10 minutes, stirring frequently. Remove to warm serving plate; sprinkle with macadamia nuts. Serve with dipping sauce made of equal parts soy sauce and plum sauce mixed with Chinese mustard to taste. Yield: 6 servings.

Approx Per Serving: Cal 377; Prot 31 g; Carbo 18 g; Fiber 1 g;
 T Fat 19 g; 47% Calories from Fat; Chol 154 mg; Sod 463 mg.

CHICKEN "MARGARITA"

2 cups Margarita mix
3/4 cup tequila
1/2 cup olive oil
Juice of 5 limes
4 cloves of garlic, crushed
1 large onion, finely chopped

5 chopped seeded jalapeño peppers
1/2 cup chopped cilantro
2 tomatoes, seeded, chopped
6 whole chicken breast filets, split
2 tablespoons cornstarch
Salt to taste

Combine Margarita mix, tequila, olive oil, lime juice, garlic, onion, jalapeño peppers, cilantro and tomatoes in bowl; mix well. Rinse chicken and pat dry. Place in shallow pan. Pour tequila mixture over chicken, turning to coat. Marinate in refrigerator overnight. Drain chicken, reserving marinade. Grill over medium-hot coals for 30 minutes or until cooked through, turning once. Place on warm serving plate. Pour reserved marinade into saucepan. Add cornstarch and salt. Bring to a boil; reduce heat. Cook until slightly thickened, stirring constantly. Pour over chicken. May adjust taste of marinade using lime juice, garlic, jalepeño peppers and cilantro to taste; may omit tomatoes. Add additional tequila or water to sauce for desired consistency; do not use oil. Yield: 6 servings.

Approx Per Serving: Cal 682; Prot 54 g; Carbo 43 g; Fiber 1 g; T Fat 24 g; 32% Calories from Fat; Chol 144 mg; Sod 223 mg.

Paul V. Carelli III

CHICKEN ORLEANS

1 3-pound chicken, cut into pieces
1/4 cup flour
1 teaspoon salt
1/8 teaspoon pepper
1/2 cup oil
1 large onion, chopped
2 cloves of garlic, minced

1 cup chopped celery
1 small green bell pepper, chopped
1 16-ounce can stewed tomatoes
1 cup uncooked rice
2 teaspoons Worcestershire sauce
2 1/2 teaspoons salt
2 1/2 cups water

Rinse chicken and pat dry. Coat with mixture of flour, salt and pepper. Brown in oil in skillet on both sides; remove with slotted spoon and set aside. Sauté onion, garlic, celery and green pepper in pan drippings until tender; drain. Add tomatoes, rice, Worcestershire sauce, salt and water. Top with chicken. Simmer, tightly covered, for 45 minutes. Yield: 4 servings.

Approx Per Serving: Cal 821; Prot 55 g; Carbo 58 g; Fiber 2 g; T Fat 40 g; 45% Calories from Fat; Chol 152 mg; Sod 2431 mg.

CHICKEN QUICK

2 tablespoons honey
2¹/₂ tablespoons Dijon mustard
1 tablespoon lemon juice
¹/₂ teaspoon dried tarragon

Pepper to taste
2 whole chicken breasts, skinned,
   split

Combine honey, mustard, lemon juice, tarragon and pepper in bowl; mix well. Rinse chicken and pat dry. Place on broiler pan bone side up. Broil 5 inches from heat source for 12 to 14 minutes. Brush with honey mixture; turn. Broil for 5 minutes longer. Baste with honey mixture. Broil 5 to 6 minutes longer or until cooked through. Yield: 4 servings.

Approx Per Serving: Cal 189; Prot 27 g; Carbo 10 g; Fiber <1 g; T Fat 4 g; 21% Calories from Fat; Chol 72 mg; Sod 314 mg.

Larry L. Spitler, Nevada State Assemblyman
Board of Trustees

CHICKEN SCARPARIELLO ALLA DOLCE VITA

3 chicken breasts, split, skinned
   and boned
2 chicken thighs, skinned, boned
2 chicken legs, skinned, boned
Salt and pepper to taste
¹/₂ cup flour
1 tablespoon olive oil

4 cloves of garlic, minced
1 tablespoon red wine vinegar
1 to 1¹/₂ cups chicken broth
1 tablespoon butter
Minced fresh parsley to taste
¹/₂ ounce dry Sauterne

Rinse chicken and pat dry. Cut into 3-inch pieces. Sprinkle with salt and pepper; coat with flour. Sauté in oil in skillet until golden brown; drain. Add garlic. Stir-fry until browned. Add wine vinegar and enough chicken broth to cover chicken halfway. Simmer, covered, for 15 minutes or until chicken is cooked through and liquid is reduced. Add butter, salt and pepper, parsley and wine, stirring until butter is melted. Serve immediately. Yield: 6 servings.

Approx Per Serving: Cal 221; Prot 25 g; Carbo 9 g; Fiber <1 g; T Fat 9 g; 37% Calories from Fat; Chol 72 mg; Sod 272 mg.

CHICKEN TAMALE CASSEROLE

4 cups sliced onions
2 cloves of garlic, minced
3 tablespoons oil
1 teaspoon cumin
4 cups chopped cooked chicken
2 cups canned tomatoes

3 cups chicken stock
2 teaspoons chili powder
Salt and pepper to taste
1½ cups shredded sharp Cheddar
   cheese
12 corn tortillas, dried

Sauté onions and garlic in oil with cumin in skillet until onions are golden brown. Combine with chicken in large bowl. Crush tomatoes and add to mixture with juice. Stir in chicken stock, chili powder, salt, pepper and ¼ cup cheese. Tear tortillas into 4 strips. Place half the tortillas in 2-quart casserole sprayed with nonstick cooking spray. Spoon in chicken mixture; top with remaining tortillas, pressing down firmly. Cover with remaining cheese. Bake at 350 degrees for 40 minutes or until browned and bubbly. May prepare and refrigerate ahead of time and bring to room temperature before baking. Yield: 8 servings.

Approx Per Serving: Cal 408; Prot 32 g; Carbo 27 g; Fiber 5 g;
   T Fat 20 g; 43% Calories from Fat; Chol 85 mg; Sod 583 mg.

ROASTED CHICKEN

1 3-pound chicken
½ teaspoon paprika
¼ teaspoon onion powder
¼ teaspoon garlic powder

¼ cup margarine
⅛ teaspoon sage
2 sprigs of fresh rosemary

Rinse chicken and pat dry. Place on rack in roasting pan breast side up. Combine paprika, onion powder, garlic powder, margarine, sage and rosemary in glass bowl. Microwave on High for 30 seconds; stir. Brush over chicken. Cover chicken breast with foil. Roast at 350 degrees for 1 hour. Baste with margarine mixture. Roast for 20 to 30 minutes longer or until chicken is cooked through. Place on lettuce-lined platter garnished with romaine lettuce and orange slices. Yield: 6 servings.

Approx Per Serving: Cal 283; Prot 33 g; Carbo <1 g; Fiber 0 g;
   T Fat 16 g; 52% Calories from Fat; Chol 101 mg; Sod 186 mg.

SOUTHERN FRIED CHICKEN WITH GRAVY

1 3-pound chicken, cut into
  serving pieces
1/2 cup flour
1 teaspoon salt
1/2 teaspoon paprika
1/4 teaspoon pepper

Oil for frying
3 tablespoons flour
3/4 cup milk
3/4 cup water
2 to 3 drops of Kitchen Bouquet

Rinse chicken and pat dry. Combine 1/2 cup flour, salt, paprika and pepper in shallow bowl. Coat chicken with mixture. Fry in hot oil in skillet over medium heat for 15 to 20 minutes; reduce heat. Simmer, covered, for 30 to 40 minutes longer or until chicken is cooked through, turning occasionally. Cook, uncovered, for 5 minutes longer. Remove chicken with slotted spoon to serving platter. Drain oil, leaving 3 tablespoons in skillet. Blend in 3 tablespoons flour. Cook over low heat until mixture is smooth and bubbly; remove from heat. Stir in milk and water. Bring to a boil. Cook for 1 minute, stirring constantly. Stir in Kitchen Bouquet and desired seasoning. Serve with chicken. Yield: 6 servings.

Approx Per Serving: Cal 286; Prot 35 g; Carbo 12 g; Fiber <1 g;
  T Fat 10 g; 31% Calories from Fat; Chol 105 mg; Sod 466 mg.
  Nutritional information does not include Kitchen Bouquet.

HONEY ROASTED CHICKEN

1 3-pound chicken
6 cloves of garlic

1 large orange
1/2 cup honey

Rinse chicken and pat dry. Place in roasting pan. Place garlic under skin and inside chicken. Squeeze orange lightly, reserving juice. Cut into 8 sections. Place orange sections under skin and inside chicken. Pour reserved juice and honey over chicken. Roast at 350 degrees for 1 to 1 1/2 hours or until cooked through, basting occasionally. Yield: 6 servings.

Approx Per Serving: Cal 316; Prot 33 g; Carbo 27 g; Fiber 1 g;
  T Fat 8 g; 24% Calories from Fat; Chol 101 mg; Sod 99 mg.

MAW MAW'S CHICKEN STEW

2 tablespoons salt	2 large green bell peppers,
2 teaspoons black pepper	chopped
1 tablespoon cayenne pepper	2 stalks celery, finely chopped
2 teaspoons white pepper	2 quarts chicken stock
5 pounds chicken pieces	2 cups sliced mushrooms
2 tablespoons oil	2 cups chopped green onions
5 cups medium-dark roux	1 cup chopped parsley
3 large yellow onions, chopped	

Combine salt, black pepper, cayenne pepper and white pepper in bowl. Rinse chicken and pat dry. Season with half the pepper mixture. Brown in oil in skillet; drain and set aside. Heat roux in saucepan until bubbly. Add half the onions, half the green peppers and half the celery; set aside. Heat chicken stock in stockpot. Add remaining onions, green peppers and celery. Bring to a boil; reduce heat to medium. Whisk in roux mixture and remaining pepper mixture. Simmer over low heat for 45 to 60 minutes, stirring occasionally. Add chicken. Simmer for 1½ to 2 hours or until chicken is tender; remove from heat. Let stand for 5 to 10 minutes. Skim off fat. Simmer over medium-high heat for several minutes. Add mushrooms, green onions and parsley. Simmer for 3 to 5 minutes longer. Serve with rice. Yield: 10 servings.

Approx Per Serving: Cal 303; Prot 39 g; Carbo 8 g; Fiber 2 g;
    T Fat 13 g; 38% Calories from Fat; Chol 102 mg; Sod 2009 mg.
    Nutritional information does not include roux.

ORANGE CHICKEN

1 3-pound chicken, cut into	1 cup orange marmalade
serving pieces	½ cup soy sauce
Juice of 1 lemon	

Rinse chicken and pat dry. Place in greased baking dish. Drizzle lemon juice over chicken. Mix marmalade and soy sauce in small bowl. Spoon over chicken, turning to coat. Bake, covered, at 350 degrees for 45 minutes; remove cover. Bake for 10 minutes longer. Yield: 6 servings.

Approx Per Serving: Cal 368; Prot 34 g; Carbo 40 g; Fiber 1 g;
    T Fat 8 g; 20% Calories from Fat; Chol 101 mg; Sod 1480 mg.

TERIYAKI CHICKEN

3 to 5 tablespoons brown sugar
1/4 cup sherry
3 tablespoons soy sauce
1 chicken bouillon cube
1 beef bouillon cube
1 teaspoon garlic
Pepper, lemon pepper and
    paprika to taste

1/4 teaspoon ground ginger
1 tablespoon vinegar
1 3-pound chicken, cut into
    serving pieces
3 tablespoons cornstarch
2 cups water

Combine brown sugar, sherry, soy sauce, bouillon cubes, garlic, pepper, lemon pepper, paprika, ginger and vinegar in bowl; mix well. Rinse chicken and pat dry. Place in shallow dish. Pour marinade over chicken, turning to coat. Marinate for 20 minutes; drain, reserving marinade. Cook over medium-hot coals until chicken is cooked through. Heat reserved marinade in saucepan to a gentle boil. Dissolve cornstarch in water. Stir into marinade; reduce heat. Cook until thickened, stirring constantly. Serve with chicken. Yield: 6 servings.

Approx Per Serving: Cal 293; Prot 34 g; Carbo 16 g; Fiber <1 g;
    T Fat 9 g; 28% Calories from Fat; Chol 101 mg; Sod 954 mg.

TURKEY TENDERLOIN

2 cups 7-Up
2 tablespoons prepared
    horseradish

1 cup soy sauce
1/2 cup oil
1 5-pound turkey breast

Combine 7-Up, horseradish, soy sauce and oil in bowl; mix well. Place turkey breast in deep pan. Cover with 7-Up mixture, turning to coat. Marinade for 12 hours to overnight, turning occasionally; drain. Grill over medium coals for 30 minutes. Yield: 6 servings.

Approx Per Serving: Cal 663; Prot 87 g; Carbo 13 g; Fiber <1 g;
    T Fat 27 g; 38% Calories from Fat; Chol 196 mg; Sod 2938 mg.

STEAMED ROASTED GOOSE

1 9 to 11-pound goose with giblets	1 large onion, chopped
Juice of 1 lemon	1 to 2 stalks celery, chopped
Salt to taste	2 to 3 cups white wine
1 large carrot, chopped	1/2 cup Port
	1 1/2 tablespoons cornstarch

Clean goose, removing excess fat. Clip tips from wings; reserve wing tips and giblets. Cut through wing joints and leg joints; secure with string and skewers. Prick through skin around breast and leg portions. Sprinkle cavity with lemon juice and salt. Place breast side up on rack in large roasting pan. Add 1 to 2 inches water; cover tightly. Bring to a boil; reduce heat. Steam for 45 minutes to 1 hour. Place reserved giblets and wing tips in saucepan with lighty salted water to cover. Simmer, covered, for 2 hours. Skim off fat and strain, reserving 2 cups stock. Chill in refrigerator. Preheat oven to 325 degrees. Remove goose to platter; drain off pan drippings. May stuff if desired. Place double layer of foil over rack in roasting pan. Place goose breast side down. Arrange carrot, onion and celery around edge of pan. Add white wine. Roast, covered, for 1 to 1 1/2 hours, basting occasionally with pan drippings; turn. Roast for 30 minutes longer or until tender, basting twice. Turn off oven and remove goose to carving board. Place in oven with door ajar until slightly cooled. Skim fat from pan drippings; strain into saucepan, discarding vegetables and fat. Add chilled goose stock, Port and cornstarch. Simmer until slightly thickened, skimming fat. Carve goose and serve with gravy. Yield: 10 servings.

Approx Per Serving: Cal 428; Prot 64 g; Carbo 6 g; Fiber 1 g;
T Fat 11 g; 22% Calories from Fat; Chol 449 mg; Sod 182 mg.

You will find as you look back upon your life that the moments when you have really lived are the moments when you have done things in the spirit of love.

—Henry Drummond

LIGHT AND EASY PICANTE FISH

1¹/₂ cups fresh mushrooms
1 green or red bell pepper, cut into 1-inch pieces
1 small onion, cut into halves and sliced
2 tablespoons chicken broth
4 4-ounce fish filets
¹/₂ teaspoon dried crushed oregano
1 cup picante sauce
2 tablespoons grated Parmesan cheese

Combine mushrooms, bell pepper, onion and chicken broth in microwave-safe bowl. Microwave, covered, on High for 5 to 6 minutes or until tender, stirring once. Arrange fish in 8x8-inch microwave-safe baking dish. Microwave, covered, for 4 to 5 minutes or until fish begins to flake; drain juices. Place vegetables over fish with slotted spoon; sprinkle with oregano. Spoon picante sauce over top. Microwave, uncovered, for 1 to 2 minutes or until heated through. Sprinkle with Parmesan cheese and serve. Yield: 4 servings.

Approx Per Serving: Cal 168; Prot 25 g; Carbo 10 g; Fiber 2 g; T Fat 3 g; 16% Calories from Fat; Chol 65 mg; Sod 489 mg.

CREOLE FLOUNDER

2 pounds flounder filets
1¹/₂ cups chopped tomatoes
¹/₂ cup chopped green bell pepper
¹/₃ cup lemon juice
1 tablespoon oil
2 teaspoons salt
¹/₄ teaspoon pepper
2 teaspoons minced onion
1 teaspoon basil leaves
4 drops of Tabasco sauce

Place filets in single layer in 9x13-inch baking dish. Combine tomatoes, green pepper, lemon juice, oil, salt, pepper, onion, basil and Tabasco sauce in small bowl; mix well. Spoon over filets. Bake at 500 degrees for 5 to 8 minutes or until fish flakes easily. Remove to warm platter. Garnish with green pepper rings. Yield: 6 servings.

Approx Per Serving: Cal 175; Prot 30 g; Carbo 4 g; Fiber 1 g; T Fat 4 g; 22% Calories from Fat; Chol 83 mg; Sod 842 mg.

BAKED GROUPER FILET

1 tablespoon lemon juice
Worcestershire sauce to taste
2 tablespoons white wine
Marjoram, thyme, salt and pepper
  to taste
4 6 to 8-ounce grouper filets
1 medium onion, chopped
2 cloves of garlic, finely chopped
2 medium tomatoes, chopped
1 each small red, green and
  yellow bell pepper, sliced
1/2 jalapeño pepper, finely chopped
2 tablespoons olive oil
2 tablespoons butter
2 tablespoons tomato paste
1/4 cup tomato juice
1/4 cup white wine

Combine first 7 ingredients in baking dish; mix well. Add fish, coating well. Marinate for several minutes. Bake at 350 degrees until fish flakes easily; keep warm. Sauté onion, garlic, tomatoes, bell peppers and jalapeño pepper in olive oil and butter in sauté pan until onion is tender. Stir in mixture of tomato paste, tomato juice and 1/4 cup wine. Cook until heated through. Spoon over fish. Serve with Pirate Rice (page 151). Yield: 4 servings.

Approx Per Serving: Cal 388; Prot 47 g; Carbo 11 g; Fiber 3 g;
  T Fat 15 g; 37% Calories from Fat; Chol 101 mg; Sod 243 mg.

Chef Bruno Wehren
MGM Grand Hotel, Inc.

SALMON WITH AVOCADO-CITRUS SALSA

2 oranges, peeled
2 small onions, chopped
2 cups chopped fresh pineapple
2 large tomatoes, peeled, seeded
  and chopped
1/2 cup oil
1/2 cup chopped fresh cilantro
6 small serrano chilies, minced
12 6-ounce 11/2-inch thick
  center-cut salmon filets with
  skin
3 cups pink grapefruit juice
1 avocado, cut into halves, pitted,
  chopped

Separate oranges into sections; cut sections into halves. Combine with onions, pineapple, tomatoes, oil, cilantro and chilies; mix well. Chill, covered, for 1 hour. Place salmon in shallow baking dish. Cover with grapefruit juice. Let stand for 1 hour at room temperature, turning occasionally; drain. Place skin side down on grill over medium-hot coals. Cook, covered, for 7 minutes or until fish flakes easily. Remove to warmed platter. Stir avocado into orange mixture. Spoon over salmon. Garnish with sprigs of cilantro. Yield: 12 servings.

Approx Per Serving: Cal 474; Prot 39 g; Carbo 19 g; Fiber 4 g;
  T Fat 27 g; 51% Calories from Fat; Chol 118 mg; Sod 97 mg.

SALMON AND SHELL PASTA

4 6-ounce salmon steaks
2 tablespoons lemon juice
2 tablespoons mayonnaise
Salt and pepper to taste
2 tablespoons finely chopped
  parsley
1 16-ounce package shell
  macaroni

2 10-ounce packages frozen peas
1/2 cup butter
Garlic powder, onion powder, salt
  and pepper to taste
6 to 8 large mushrooms, sliced
2 tablespoons butter
1/2 cup grated Romano cheese

Rinse salmon and pat dry. Place on double heavy foil-lined pan. Sprinkle with lemon juice; spread with mayonnaise. Season with salt, pepper and parsley. Broil with oven door closed for 12 to 15 minutes or until fish flakes easily. Cook shell macaroni using package directions; drain. Cook peas using package directions; drain. Melt 1/2 cup butter in saucepan. Add cooked shell macaroni; season with garlic powder, onion powder, salt and pepper. Toss to coat with butter. Stir in peas gently. Sauté mushrooms in 2 tablespoons butter in skillet. Arrange over shells; sprinkle with Romano cheese. Serve with salmon steaks. Yield: 4 servings.

Approx Per Serving: Cal 1180; Prot 64 g; Carbo 108 g; Fiber 13 g; T Fat 54 g; 42% Calories from Fat; Chol 212 mg; Sod 676 mg.

MICROWAVE SOLE AND BROCCOLI

2 tablespoons lemon juice
1 tablespoon olive oil
1 teaspoon capers, drained
1/2 teaspoon grated lemon peel

1/4 teaspoon salt
1/4 teaspoon pepper
1 pound sole filets
4 cups broccoli flowerets

Combine lemon juice, olive oil, capers, lemon peel, salt and pepper in small bowl; mix well. Arrange filets alternately with broccoli around 12-inch round microwave platter, leaving center open. Pour lemon mixture over filets and broccoli. Cover with plastic wrap, cutting vents. Microwave on High for 3 minutes; turn. Microwave for 3 minutes longer or until fish flakes easily. Let stand for 3 minutes before serving. Yield: 4 servings.

Approx Per Serving: Cal 161; Prot 25 g; Carbo 5 g; Fiber 3 g; T Fat 5 g; 28% Calories from Fat; Chol 62 mg; Sod 252 mg. Nutritional information does not include capers.

 *Seafood*

TROUT DELMONICO

1 ounce minced onion
1 ounce chopped green bell pepper
Thyme, sage and dill to taste
2 tablespoons butter
10 ounces crab meat
1/2 cup Béchamel sauce
1/2 teaspoon English mustard
4 whole 12-ounce trout, boned

Salt and white pepper to taste
Juice of 2 lemons
4 cups clam juice
1 cup Sauterne
2 bay leaves
2 ounces finely chopped carrot
2 ounces finely chopped celery
2 ounces chopped leeks

Sauté onion and green pepper with thyme, sage and dill in butter in saucepan until onion is tender. Mix in crab meat, Béchamel sauce and mustard. Remove from heat and cool. Open up trout; sprinkle with salt, pepper and lemon juice. Place 2 ounces of filling in center of each trout; fold over. Place in lightly greased oblong baking pan. Add clam juice, Sauterne, bay leaves, carrot, celery and leeks. Cover with heavy foil. Bake at 425 degrees for 22 to 25 minutes or until fish flakes easily, basting occasionally with pan juices. Remove to serving platter. Cut cucumbers and small potatoes into 1-inch barrel shapes. Garnish fish with cucumbers poached with dill and potatoes poached in salted water. Surround with lemon slices and sliced truffles. Yield: 4 servings.

Approx Per Serving: Cal 638; Prot 88 g; Carbo 10 g; Fiber 2 g;
 T Fat 20 g; 28% Calories from Fat; Chol 293 mg; Sod 1134 mg.

FISH CREOLE

1 onion, chopped
1 green bell pepper, chopped
2 tablespoons oil
2 cups vegetable juice cocktail
1/2 teaspoon salt

1/2 teaspoon pepper
1/4 teaspoon sage
1/4 teaspoon thyme
1 pound white fish, cut into
 chunks

Sauté onion and green pepper in oil in skillet for 3 minutes. Add vegetable juice cocktail, salt, pepper, sage and thyme. Simmer for 10 minutes, stirring occasionally. Place fish chunks in sauce. Steam, covered, over low heat for 10 minutes or until fish flakes easily. Serve over hot rice. Yield: 4 servings.

Approx Per Serving: Cal 207; Prot 23 g; Carbo 9 g; Fiber 2 g;
 T Fat 9 g; 37% Calories from Fat; Chol 62 mg; Sod 804 mg.

TUNA RING WITH CHEESE SAUCE

1 egg
2 7-ounce cans tuna, drained,
  flaked
1/2 cup chopped onion
1/2 cup shredded sharp Cheddar
  cheese

1/2 cup snipped parsley
1 teaspoon celery salt
1/4 teaspoon pepper
2 cups baking mix
1/2 cup cold water
Cheese Sauce

Beat egg slightly in bowl; reserve 2 tablespoons. Stir tuna, onion, cheese, parsley, celery salt and pepper into remaining egg. Combine baking mix with water, stirring to form soft dough. Knead 5 times on floured surface. Roll out to 10x15-inch rectangle. Spread with tuna mixture. Roll up from long side, sealing edge. Shape into a ring. Place on greased baking sheet, pinching ends to seal. Make cuts 2/3 of the way through the ring at 1-inch intervals. Turn each section to show filling. Brush with reserved egg. Bake at 375 degrees for 25 to 30 minutes or until browned. Serve tuna ring with Cheese Sauce. Yield: 6 servings.

Cheese Sauce

1/4 cup butter
1/4 cup baking mix
1/4 teaspoon salt
1/4 teaspoon pepper

2 cups milk
1 cup shredded Cheddar cheese
1/2 cup crumbled bleu cheese

Melt butter in saucepan over low heat. Stir in baking mix, salt and pepper. Cook over low heat until smooth and bubbly, stirring constantly.; remove from heat. Stir in milk. Bring to a boil. Boil for 1 minute, stirring constantly. Add cheeses, stirring until melted. Yield: 6 servings.

Approx Per Serving: Cal 575; Prot 36 g; Carbo 37 g; Fiber <1 g; T Fat 31 g; 48% Calories from Fat; Chol 141 mg; Sod 1589 mg.

When you were born, you cried and the world rejoiced. Live your life in such a manner that when you die the world cries and you rejoice.

—Old Indian Saying

FRESH CLAM SAUTÉ LA DOLCE VITA'S WAY

24 fresh clams in shells	Freshly ground pepper to taste
1 tablespoon olive oil	1 cup dry white wine
2 to 3 cloves of garlic, minced	Freshly chopped parsley to taste

Open clams and drain, reserving juice. Heat olive oil in large electric skillet. Sauté garlic in oil until lightly browned. Add pepper, wine, reserved clam juice and parsley. Place clams face side down in liquid. Simmer for 5 minutes. Garnish with lemon slices. Yield: 4 servings.

Approx Per Serving: Cal 113; Prot 7 g; Carbo 2 g; Fiber <1 g; T Fat 4 g; 31% Calories from Fat; Chol 18 mg; Sod 33 mg.

SPAGHETTI WITH CLAM SAUCE

3 tablespoons olive oil	2 6-ounce cans clams
3 tablespoons peanut oil	3 to 4 tablespoons grated
1 to 2 tablespoons butter	Parmesan cheese
3 cloves of garlic, minced	1 16-ounce package spaghetti,
Oregano, basil and parsley to taste	cooked

Heat olive oil, peanut oil and butter in saucepan. Add garlic, oregano, basil and parsley. Simmer for several minutes or until garlic is tender. Add undrained clams. Simmer until heated through. Stir in Parmesan cheese. Toss with cooked spaghetti. Yield: 4 servings.

Approx Per Serving: Cal 719; Prot 23 g; Carbo 89 g; Fiber 5 g; T Fat 35 g; 41% Calories from Fat; Chol 73 mg; Sod 181 mg.

I am only one: but still I am one. I cannot do everything, but still I can do something: I will not refuse to do the something I can do.

—Helen Keller

DEEP-SOUTH CRAB CAKES

3 eggs, beaten
3/4 teaspoon salt
1 teaspoon dry mustard
1/8 teaspoon garlic powder
1/8 teaspoon paprika
1 teaspoon Worcestershire sauce
3 tablespoons chopped parsley
3 tablespoons butter

3/4 cup finely chopped onion
1 cup bread crumbs
2 cups Alaskan King crab meat
1 tablespoon mayonnaise
1 to 2 tablespoons cream
1/2 cup flour
Oil for frying

Beat first 7 ingredients in bowl; set aside. Heat butter in skillet. Add onion. Sauté onion in butter until tender; remove from heat. Stir in bread crumbs and crab meat. Add egg mixture, mixing well. Add mayonnaise and enough cream to hold mixture together. Shape into 2½-inch patties. Coat with flour. Fry in oil in skillet on each side until golden brown; drain. Yield: 15 servings.

Approx Per Serving: Cal 109; Prot 6 g; Carbo 9 g; Fiber 1 g;
T Fat 5 g; 43% Calories from Fat; Chol 68 mg; Sod 249 mg.
Nutritional information does not include oil for frying.

ZESTY CRAB CAKES WITH SEAFOOD SAUCE

1/4 cup fat-free mayonnaise
1/4 cup nonfat sour cream
1/4 cup reduced-calorie catsup
1½ tablespoons finely chopped
green onions
2 tablespoons prepared
horseradish
1 teaspoon chopped fresh parsley
1½ teaspoons lemon juice
1 pound fresh crab meat, drained,
flaked

3/4 cup shredded carrot
1/2 cup fine dry bread crumbs
1/2 cup egg substitute
2 teaspoons chopped fresh parsley
1/2 teaspoon Italian seasoning
1/2 teaspoon dry mustard
1/4 teaspoon pepper
1/8 teaspoon garlic powder
2 teaspoons fat-free mayonnaise
1½ teaspoons low-sodium
Worcestershire sauce

Combine 1/4 cup mayonnaise, sour cream, catsup, green onions, horseradish, 1 teaspoon parsley and lemon juice in small bowl; mix well. Chill, covered, for 3 hours. Combine remaining ingredients in bowl; mix well. Shape into 6 patties. Chill, covered, for 1 hour. Coat large nonstick skillet with nonstick cooking spray. Fry patties over medium heat for 4 to 5 minutes on each side or until golden brown. Serve with seafood sauce. Yield: 6 servings.

Approx Per Serving: Cal 143; Prot 17 g; Carbo 13 g; Fiber 1 g;
T Fat 2 g; 15% Calories from Fat; Chol 61 mg; Sod 507 mg.

CRAB MEAT CRÊPES

2 teaspoons reduced-calorie
  margarine
1¹/₃ cups sliced fresh mushrooms
1 cup chopped green onions
1 teaspoon dried whole thyme
1 tablespoon flour
1 cup skim milk
1 pound fresh lump crab meat,
  drained

2 tablespoons chopped fresh
  parsley
2 teaspoons lemon juice
¹/₄ teaspoon salt
¹/₄ teaspoon dry mustard
¹/₈ teaspoon ground red pepper
16 Light Crêpes (see page 162)

Spray large nonstick skillet with nonstick cooking spray. Melt margarine over medium-high heat. Sauté mushrooms, green onions and thyme for 2 to 3 minutes or until vegetables are tender; reduce heat to low. Stir in flour. Cook for 1 minute, stirring constantly. Add milk gradually. Cook over medium heat until thickened and bubbly, stirring constantly; remove from heat. Stir in crab meat, parsley, lemon juice, salt, mustard and red pepper. Spoon 3 tablespoons crab meat mixture in center of each Light Crêpe; roll up to enclose filling. Place seam side down in two 9x13-inch baking dishes sprayed with nonstick cooking spray. Bake, covered, at 350 degrees for 15 to 18 minutes or until heated through; remove cover. Broil 5¹/₂ inches from heat source for 1 minute or until golden brown. Place 2 crêpes on each serving plate. Garnish with sprigs of thyme. Yield: 8 servings.

Approx Per Serving: Cal 142; Prot 17 g; Carbo 14 g; Fiber 1 g;
  T Fat 2 g; 13% Calories from Fat; Chol 58 mg; Sod 299 mg.

What is life? It is the flash of a firefly in the night. It is the breath of a buffalo in the wintertime. It is the little shadow which runs across the grass and loses itself in the sunset.

—Crowfoot, Canadian Indian

Seafood

CREOLE CRAB AND RICE

1 cup uncooked rice
2 tablespoons butter
1 small onion, minced
1 small green bell pepper, chopped
1   15-ounce can chopped tomatoes
1 teaspoon Cajun seasoning
1/4 teaspoon pepper
1/2 teaspoon brown sugar
1/2 teaspoon Worcestershire sauce
1 bay leaf
1/8 teaspoon ground cloves
1   6-ounce can crab meat,
   drained, flaked
3 tablespoons grated Parmesan
   cheese

Cook rice using package directions; set aside. Melt butter in skillet over medium heat. Sauté onion and green pepper for 2 to 3 minutes or until tender. Add undrained tomatoes, Cajun seasoning, pepper, brown sugar, Worcestershire sauce, bay leaf and cloves. Bring just to a boil; reduce heat to low. Cook for 10 minutes, stirring frequently. Discard bay leaf. Stir in rice and crab meat. Spoon into 1½-quart baking dish. Bake at 375 degrees for 10 minutes. Sprinkle with Parmesan cheese. Bake for 10 minutes longer. May add 6 ounces smoked Polish sausage and one 15-ounce can okra. Yield: 6 servings.

Approx Per Serving: Cal 210; Prot 10 g; Carbo 31 g; Fiber 2 g;
   T Fat 5 g; 23% Calories from Fat; Chol 38 mg; Sod 296 mg.

SPEEDY LOBSTER FRA DIAVOLO

3   16-ounce cans Marinara sauce
1 tablespoon chopped chives
1 onion, chopped
1/2 cup dry white wine
1/2 to 1 teaspoon crushed red
   pepper
1/4 teaspoon cayenne pepper
6   6-ounce lobster tails, cooked

Heat Marinara sauce in saucepan until mixture begins to simmer. Add chives, onion, wine and red pepper. Simmer until onion is tender. Add cayenne pepper. Remove lobster meat from shells; cut into bite-sized pieces. Add to sauce. Simmer until heated through. Serve over pasta. Yield: 6 servings.

Approx Per Serving: Cal 266; Prot 23 g; Carbo 26 g; Fiber <1 g;
   T Fat 8 g; 27% Calories from Fat; Chol 65 mg; Sod 1772 mg.

Larry L. Spitler, Nevada State Assemblyman
Board of Trustees

COQUILLES SAINT-JACQUES

1 cup water
1 teaspoon lemon juice
1/2 teaspoon salt
2 pounds scallops, rinsed, drained
1/4 cup butter
1/4 cup finely chopped onion
4 ounces mushrooms, sliced
1/3 cup flour
Pepper to taste

1 cup light cream
1/2 cup milk
1 cup grated Gruyère cheese
1/2 cup dry white wine
1 tablespoon lemon juice
1 tablespoon chopped parsley
1/2 cup dry bread crumbs
2 tablespoons melted butter

Combine water, 1 teaspoon lemon juice and salt in saucepan. Bring to a boil. Add scallops. Simmer for 6 minutes or until tender; drain on paper towels. Melt butter in large saucepan. Sauté onion and mushrooms for 5 minutes or until tender; remove from heat. Stir in flour and pepper. Add cream and milk gradually. Bring to a boil; reduce heat. Simmer for 4 to 5 minutes or until thickened, stirring constantly. Add cheese. Simmer until cheese is melted, stirring constantly; remove from heat. Stir in wine, 1 tablespoon lemon juice and parsley. Fold in scallops. Spoon into 8 scallop shells or into 1½-quart baking dish. Place shells on baking sheet. Toss bread crumbs with melted butter; sprinkle over scallops mixture. Broil 4 inches from heat source for 2 to 3 minutes or until golden brown. Yield: 8 servings.

Approx Per Serving: Cal 344; Prot 28 g; Carbo 15 g; Fiber 1 g;
T Fat 19 g; 50% Calories from Fat; Chol 92 mg; Sod 498 mg.

FETTUCINI ALFREDO WITH LEMON SCALLOPS

1   16-ounce package fettucini,
   cooked, drained
1/4 cup butter
1/4 cup olive oil
3 cloves of garlic, minced
1/2 cup half and half

1/2 cup grated Parmesan cheese
1 tablespoon minced fresh parsley
8 ounces scallops, rinsed, drained
1 tablespoon clarified butter
1/4 teaspoon salt
2 tablespoons lemon juice

Melt 1/4 cup butter with olive oil in saucepan. Sauté garlic for 3 minutes. Add half and half and parsley. Simmer until thickened, stirring constantly. Pour over fettucini, tossing to coat. Sauté scallops in clarified butter in skillet until tender. Add lemon juice and 1/4 teaspoon salt. Cook over high heat for 3 minutes, stirring constantly. Spoon over hot fettucini. Yield: 6 servings.

Approx Per Serving: Cal 538; Prot 20 g; Carbo 60 g; Fiber 3 g;
T Fat 24 g; 41% Calories from Fat; Chol 52 mg; Sod 365 mg.

SHRIMP ÉTOUFFÉE

1½ pounds shrimp, peeled,
  deveined
1 onion, chopped
1 green bell pepper, chopped
2 stalks celery, chopped
1 clove of garlic, minced

¼ cup butter
1 teaspoon tomato paste
Red pepper and white wine to
  taste
1 to 2 tablespoons cornstarch

Cook shrimp in boiling water to cover in medium saucepan until pink. Drain, reserving cooking liquid. Sauté onion, green pepper, celery and garlic in butter in large saucepan until tender. Add reserved cooking liquid, shrimp, tomato paste, red pepper and wine. Stir in enough cornstarch to obtain desired consistency. Simmer for 15 to 20 minutes or until thickened. Serve over rice. Yield: 8 servings.

Approx Per Serving: Cal 130; Prot 13 g; Carbo 4 g; Fiber 1 g;
  T Fat 7 g; 46% Calories from Fat; Chol 134 mg; Sod 194 mg.

SHRIMP AND CRAB ÉTOUFFÉE

1 pound whole shrimp
1 stalk celery
½ large onion
1½ cups water
4 cups chopped onion
½ cup butter
½ cup chopped celery

½ cup chopped green onions
1 tablespoon cornstarch
1 cup crab meat
Salt and pepper to taste
2 drops of Tabasco sauce
⅛ teaspoon cayenne pepper
½ cup chopped parsley

Peel and devein shrimp, reserving heads and shells. Place reserved heads and shells, celery stalk and ½ onion in saucepan with 1½ cups water. Bring to a boil. Cook until liquid is reduced to ¾ cup. Strain stock and set aside; set shrimp aside. Sauté 4 cups onion in butter in large heavy saucepan over low heat for 20 to 30 minutes or until lightly browned. Increase heat to medium. Reserve 2 tablespoons stock. Add remaining stock, ½ cup chopped celery and green onions. Stir cornstarch into reserved stock until paste forms. Stir into onion mixture. Add crab meat, shrimp, salt, pepper, Tabasco sauce and cayenne pepper. Reserve 2 tablespoons parsley. Add remaining parsley to étouffée. Cook for 2 to 3 minutes or until shrimp turn pink, stirring frequently. Serve over hot cooked rice, sprinkled with reserved parsley. May substitute crayfish for shrimp. Yield: 6 servings.

Approx Per Serving: Cal 264; Prot 18 g; Carbo 11 g; Fiber 3 g;
  T Fat 17 g; 56% Calories from Fat; Chol 169 mg; Sod 332 mg.

SHRIMP CASSEROLE

1¹/₂ pounds mushrooms
¹/₄ to ¹/₂ cup butter
1 pound shrimp, peeled, cooked
3 cups cooked rice
1 5-ounce can evaporated milk
¹/₃ cup catsup
1 teaspoon Worcestershire sauce

Salt, pepper, garlic and onion to
  taste
1 cup white wine
¹/₂ to ³/₄ cup shredded Swiss
  cheese
3 tablespoons grated Parmesan
  cheese

Sauté mushrooms in butter in large saucepan for 10 minutes or until tender. Combine with shrimp and rice. Mix evaporated milk, catsup, Worcestershire sauce, salt, pepper, garlic and onion in bowl. Stir in wine. Add to shrimp mixture, mixing well. Spoon into greased casserole. Sprinkle with Swiss cheese. Bake at 350 degrees for 35 minutes. Sprinkle with Parmesan cheese. Bake for 10 minutes longer. May substitute any cheese for Swiss cheese. Yield: 8 servings.

Approx Per Serving: Cal 352; Prot 17 g; Carbo 28 g; Fiber 2 g;
  T Fat 17 g; 46% Calories from Fat; Chol 126 mg; Sod 398 mg.

FETTUCINI PRIMAVERA

8 ounces chicken breast filets, cut
  into ¹/₂-inch cubes
¹/₂ cup sliced onion
2 tablespoons oil
1 cup red bell pepper, cut into
  julienne strips
1 cup zucchini, cut into julienne
  strips

2 cups small whole mushrooms
1 27-ounce can spaghetti sauce
8 ounces peeled deveined shrimp
2 cups shredded fresh spinach
8 ounces fettucini, cooked
¹/₂ to 1 cup shredded Provolone
  cheese

Sauté chicken and onion in hot oil until chicken is partially cooked. Add red bell pepper, zucchini and mushrooms. Sauté for 2 minutes. Add spaghetti sauce and shrimp. Cook for 10 minutes or until shrimp turn pink and chicken is cooked through. Stir in spinach. Cook for 3 to 5 minutes longer, stirring occasionally. Serve over cooked fettucini, topped with Provolone cheese. Yield: 6 servings.

Approx Per Serving: Cal 481; Prot 28 g; Carbo 53 g; Fiber 5 g;
  T Fat 18 g; 33% Calories from Fat; Chol 96 mg; Sod 904 mg.

TARRAGON-SHRIMP FETTUCINI

1/2 cup butter
2 pounds medium shrimp, peeled, deveined
4 cloves of garlic, minced
2 teaspoons dried crumbled tarragon
2 cups whipping cream

1 1/2 cups freshly grated Parmesan cheese
Cayenne pepper to taste
2 tablespoons dry white wine
16 ounces fettucini, cooked
3 tablespoons minced fresh parsley

Melt butter in large skillet over medium heat. Add shrimp, garlic and tarragon. Cook for 1 minute or until shrimp are just pink. Remove shrimp with slotted spoon to warm platter. Stir in cream, Parmesan cheese and cayenne pepper. Cook for 2 minutes or until bubbly, stirring often. Stir in wine; add shrimp. Cook for 1 minute or until heated through, tossing gently. Serve over cooked fettucini, tossing to coat. Sprinkle with parsley. Yield: 6 servings.

Approx Per Serving: Cal 894; Prot 42 g; Carbo 61 g; Fiber 3 g; T Fat 53 g; 54% Calories from Fat; Chol 376 mg; Sod 781 mg.

SHRIMP LINGUINE

1/2 cup Italian salad dressing
8 to 16 ounces shrimp, peeled, deveined
1 yellow squash, cut into julienne strips
1 zucchini, cut into julienne strips
1 carrot, cut into julienne strips

1 clove of garlic, minced
3 green onions, cut into strips
1/4 cup chopped parsley
2 teaspoons grated lemon rind
1 teaspoon salt
Cayenne pepper to taste
16 ounces linguine, cooked

Heat Italian dressing in wok. Add shrimp, squash, zucchini, carrot, garlic, green onions, parsley, lemon rind, salt and cayenne pepper. Stir-fry for 8 to 10 minutes or until vegetables are tender-crisp. Pour over cooked linguine, tossing to coat. Yield: 6 servings.

Approx Per Serving: Cal 448; Prot 22 g; Carbo 64 g; Fiber 5 g; T Fat 13 g; 26% Calories from Fat; Chol 105 mg; Sod 581 mg.

CURRIED SHRIMP POTPIE

2 tablespoons melted butter
6 sheets phyllo dough, cut into
  7x12-inch pieces
12 ounces frozen peeled shrimp,
  thawed
2 tablespoons butter
2 teaspoons curry powder
1 teaspoon cumin
1 onion, thinly sliced

1 clove of garlic, thinly sliced
1 tablespoon flour
1/2 cup chicken broth
1 cup small cauliflowerets
1 cup chick-peas, rinsed, drained
1/2 cup frozen green peas, thawed
1/4 teaspoon salt
1/4 teaspoon freshly ground pepper

Brush baking sheet with a small amount of melted butter. Brush each sheet of phyllo with remaining butter. Stack on prepared baking sheet. Cut a 4-inch "X" in center of dough layers; fold back 1 layer at a time onto uncut area to form opening in center. Bake at 425 degrees for 4 minutes or until golden brown. Remove to wire rack. Place shrimp in 7x12-inch microwave-safe baking dish; cover with waxed paper. Microwave on High for 3 minutes, stirring once. Drain in colander. Microwave 2 tablespoons butter with curry powder and cumin in same baking dish for 1 minute. Stir in onion, garlic and flour. Microwave for 1 minute longer. Stir in chicken broth and cauliflowerets. Microwave, covered, for 4 minutes, stirring once. Add drained shrimp and remaining ingredients. Microwave, covered, for 2 minutes or until heated through. Top casserole with phyllo crust; serve immediately. Yield: 4 servings.

Approx Per Serving: Cal 374; Prot 24 g; Carbo 40 g; Fiber 6 g;
  T Fat 14 g; 32% Calories from Fat; Chol 164 mg; Sod 621 mg.

SHRIMP SCAMPI

1 pound whole large shrimp
1/2 cup melted butter
1/2 teaspoon salt
6 cloves of garlic, crushed

2 tablespoons chopped parsley
1 teaspoon grated lemon rind
1 tablespoon lemon juice

Peel and devein shrimp, leaving tails. Combine melted butter, salt, garlic and 1 tablespoon parsley in 9x13-inch baking dish. Arrange shrimp over butter mixture in single layer. Bake at 400 degrees for 5 minutes; turn. Sprinkle with lemon rind, lemon juice and remaining parsley. Bake for 8 to 10 minutes longer or until shrimp are tender. Remove shrimp with slotted spoon to serving platter; drizzle with pan juices. Yield: 4 servings.

Approx Per Serving: Cal 292; Prot 18 g; Carbo 2 g; Fiber <1 g;
  T Fat 24 g; 73% Calories from Fat; Chol 220 mg; Sod 643 mg.

VEGETABLES & SIDE DISHES

SIMPLY ASPARAGUS

1 pound asparagus
1 teaspoon salt

1 to 2 teaspoons sugar

Combine asparagus and enough water to cover in skillet. Sprinkle with salt and sugar. Bring to a rolling boil. Cook for 2 minutes; remove from heat. Let stand until serving time; drain. Serve with lemon-butter sauce or Hollandaise sauce. Yield: 4 servings.

Approx Per Serving: Cal 33; Prot 4 g; Carbo 6 g; Fiber 2 g;
T Fat <1 g; 5% Calories from Fat; Chol 0 mg; Sod 535 mg.

DRUNKEN BEANS

12 ounces sliced bacon, chopped
3 large onions, chopped
6 15-ounce cans pinto beans, drained
3 12-ounce bottles of dark beer
3 cups beef stock

3 large tomatoes, chopped
1½ cups chopped fresh cilantro
3 jalapeño peppers, seeded, finely chopped
1 tablespoon sugar
Salt and pepper to taste

Cook bacon over medium-high heat in large heavy saucepan until crisp; remove bacon with slotted spoon to bowl. Sauté onions in pan drippings until tender, stirring frequently. Add beans, beer, beef stock, tomatoes, cilantro, jalapeño peppers, sugar and bacon bits; mix well. Season with salt and pepper. Bring to a boil; reduce heat. Simmer for 1½ hours or until slightly thickened, stirring occasionally. Yield: 12 servings.

Approx Per Serving: Cal 280; Prot 14 g; Carbo 40 g; Fiber 2 g;
T Fat 5 g; 18% Calories from Fat; Chol 7 mg; Sod 1226 mg.

To love what you do and feel that it matters—how could anything be more fun?

—Katherine Graham

BROCCOLI-MUSHROOM CASSEROLE

1 large onion, chopped
1 clove of garlic, minced
1/4 cup butter
4 cups bite-sized broccoli pieces
1 4-ounce can sliced mushrooms, drained

1/2 cup chopped almonds
1 10-ounce can cream of mushroom soup
7 ounces soft sharp Cheddar cheese
1/2 cup buttered bread crumbs

Sauté onion and garlic in butter in small skillet until tender. Steam broccoli in saucepan until tender-crisp. Add onion, garlic, mushrooms and half the almonds, mixing well. Mix mushroom soup and cheese in small bowl. Stir into broccoli mixture. Spoon into baking dish. Top with remaining almonds and bread crumbs. Bake at 350 degrees for 45 minutes. Yield: 10 servings.

Approx Per Serving: Cal 226; Prot 9 g; Carbo 11 g; Fiber 3 g;
T Fat 17 g; 66% Calories from Fat; Chol 34 mg; Sod 487 mg.

BROCCOLI LOVERS' CASSEROLE

2 cups crushed butter crackers
1/3 cup melted butter
2 10-ounce packages frozen chopped broccoli
1 1/2 cups shredded Cheddar cheese

1 10-ounce can cream of mushroom soup
3/4 cup mayonnaise
2 eggs, beaten
1/4 cup finely chopped onion

Toss cracker crumbs and melted butter in small bowl. Pat half the crumb mixture on bottom of 10-inch glass pie plate. Place broccoli in microwave-safe dish. Microwave on High for 5 to 6 minutes or until defrosted; drain. Combine with cheese, soup, mayonnaise, eggs and onion; mix well. Spoon into prepared plate. Top with remaining cracker crumbs. Microwave on Medium for 18 to 21 minutes or until set. Let stand for 5 to 8 minutes before serving. Yield: 8 servings.

Approx Per Serving: Cal 468; Prot 11 g; Carbo 21 g; Fiber 2 g;
T Fat 41 g; 74% Calories from Fat; Chol 109 mg; Sod 814 mg.

QUICK AND EASY BROCCOLI POTLUCK

2 10-ounce packages frozen
   chopped broccoli, thawed
2 10-ounce cans cream of
   mushroom soup
1 8-ounce can sliced water
   chestnuts, drained

1 8-ounce can bamboo shoots,
   drained
1 cup shredded Cheddar cheese
1 3-ounce can French-fried onions

Combine broccoli, soup, water chestnuts, bamboo shoots, half the cheese and half the onions in bowl; mix well. Add enough water for desired consistency. Spoon into 1½-quart baking dish. Bake, covered, at 350 degrees for 20 minutes. Sprinkle with remaining cheese and onions. Bake, uncovered, for 10 minutes longer. May substitute green beans for broccoli and cream of chicken or celery soup for mushroom soup. Yield: 8 servings.

Approx Per Serving: Cal 234; Prot 8 g; Carbo 18 g; Fiber 4 g;
  T Fat 15 g; 57% Calories from Fat; Chol 16 mg; Sod 752 mg.

BROCCOLI WITH LINGUINE AND GOAT CHEESE

Flowerets of 1 bunch broccoli
1 tablespoon minced garlic
3 tablespoons olive oil
1 cup whipping cream

4 ounces mild goat cheese,
   chopped
Salt and pepper to taste
16 ounces uncooked linguine

Cook broccoli in water to cover in saucepan for 3 minutes; rinse in cold water until cool and drain. Sauté garlic in olive oil in medium skillet until tender. Add cream. Bring to a boil; reduce heat. Stir in goat cheese until melted. Add broccoli; mix well. Remove from heat; season with salt and pepper. Cook pasta using package directions just until tender; drain. Toss with sauce in serving bowl; serve immediately. Yield: 6 servings.

Approx Per Serving: Cal 529; Prot 14 g; Carbo 63 g; Fiber 5 g;
  T Fat 25 g; 43% Calories from Fat; Chol 68 mg; Sod 134 mg.

CAULIFLOWER SURPRISE

1 head cauliflower
3/4 cup mayonnaise
1 to 1 1/2 teaspoons prepared
  horseradish
1 to 1 1/2 teaspoons Dijon mustard

1/2 to 1 teaspoon Worcestershire
  sauce
1 1/2 to 2 cups shredded Cheddar
  cheese

Steam cauliflower in saucepan until tender-crisp. Drain and break into bite-sized pieces. Arrange in baking dish. Combine mayonnaise, horseradish, mustard and Worcestershire sauce in small bowl. Spread over cauliflower. Cover with shredded cheese. Broil 5 inches from heat source until cheese is melted. Serve immediately. Yield: 6 servings.

Approx Per Serving: Cal 368; Prot 11 g; Carbo 5 g; Fiber 2 g;
  T Fat 35 g; 83% Calories from Fat; Chol 56 mg; Sod 442 mg.

CORN PUDDING

1/2 cup butter
1/4 cup sugar
3 tablespoons flour
1/2 cup evaporated milk

2 eggs, beaten
1 1/2 teaspoons baking powder
2   10-ounce packages frozen
  whole kernel corn, thawed

Melt butter in saucepan. Add mixture of sugar and flour, stirring until blended; remove from heat. Add evaporated milk, eggs and baking powder, stirring well. Stir in corn. Spoon into buttered 2-quart baking dish. Bake at 350 degrees for 45 minutes or until knife inserted near center comes out clean. May microwave on High for 10 to 15 minutes. Yield: 8 servings.

Approx Per Serving: Cal 236; Prot 5 g; Carbo 25 g; Fiber 3 g;
  T Fat 14 g; 52% Calories from Fat; Chol 89 mg; Sod 196 mg.

Live without making judgments. Acceptance brings joy.

 *Vegetables*

CUCUMBERS WITH SOUR CREAM-DILL SAUCE

2 tablespoons butter
1 tablespoon flour
1 teaspoon Bon Appetit seasoning
1/4 teaspoon white pepper
1 teaspoon chicken stock base
1/2 cup warm water

1 cup sour cream
1 teaspoon dillweed
3 to 4 cucumbers
2 tablespoons butter
1/2 teaspoon salt
1/4 teaspoon black pepper

Melt 2 tablespoons butter in 1-quart saucepan over low heat. Blend in flour, Bon Appetit seasoning and white pepper. Cook for several minutes, stirring constantly. Add stock base and warm water. Cook until thickened, stirring constantly; remove from heat. Stir in sour cream and dillweed. Cook over very low heat until heated through, stirring frequently. Peel cucumbers and cut into halves lengthwise. Scoop out seed; slice into 1/2-inch pieces. Melt 2 tablespoons butter in 2-quart saucepan over low heat. Add cucumbers, tossing to coat. Simmer, covered, for 10 minutes; remove from heat. Season with salt and black pepper. Serve with sour cream-dill sauce. Clarified butter is especially good for using in this recipe. Yield: 8 servings.

Approx Per Serving: Cal 137; Prot 2 g; Carbo 7 g; Fiber 2 g;
    T Fat 12 g; 76% Calories from Fat; Chol 28 mg; Sod 285 mg.
    Nutritional information does not include Bon Appetit seasoning.

STUFFED EGGPLANT

1/2 cup chopped celery
1/2 cup chopped green onions
2 tablespoons chopped fresh parsley
1/4 cup butter
3 medium eggplant
1 pound small shrimp, shelled

2 cups crab meat, flaked
Salt and pepper to taste
1/4 teaspoon thyme
1 teaspoon Worcestershire sauce
1 cup soft bread crumbs
1/2 cup water

Sauté celery, green onions and parsley in butter in large skillet. Cut eggplant into halves lengthwise. Scoop out centers, leaving 3/4-inch thick shells. Reserve shells. Cut removed centers into cubes. Add to skillet with shrimp, crab meat, salt, pepper, thyme and Worcestershire sauce. Cook for 5 minutes or until shrimp turn pink. Fold in bread crumbs. Spoon mixture into reserved eggplant shells. Place in baking pan filled with 1/2 cup water. Bake at 375 degrees for 30 to 35 minutes or until eggplant is tender and lightly browned. Yield: 6 servings.

Approx Per Serving: Cal 235; Prot 23 g; Carbo 15 g; Fiber 6 g;
    T Fat 10 g; 36% Calories from Fat; Chol 171 mg; Sod 374 mg.

Vegetables

JERRY'S GADO GADO

2 cups brown rice
1 onion, chopped
3 cups sliced green beans
3 cups cauliflowerets
3 cups chopped broccoli

2 cups chopped carrots
1 cup olive oil
2 cups crunchy peanut butter
2 tablespoons garlic powder
1/2 cup Spanish peanuts

Cook rice using package directions. Sauté onion in nonstick skillet until tender. Stir into rice. Spoon rice mixture around edge of circular platter. Steam green beans, cauliflowerets, broccoli and carrots until tender-crisp; drain. Spoon into center of platter. Heat oil, peanut butter and garlic powder in saucepan until mixture thins, stirring often. Pour over rice and vegetables. Top with peanuts. Yield: 8 servings.

Approx Per Serving: Cal 886; Prot 25 g; Carbo 63 g; Fiber 8 g; T Fat 65 g; 63% Calories from Fat; Chol 0 mg; Sod 341 mg.

MUSHROOM BAKE

16 ounces fresh mushrooms, sliced
1 8-ounce can pitted black
    olives, drained, sliced
1 cup shredded Cheddar cheese
1 1/2 tablespoons flour

1/2 teaspoon salt
1/8 teaspoon pepper
1/3 cup half and half
1 cup fresh bread crumbs
1 1/2 tablespoons melted butter

Layer mushrooms, olives and cheese in 2-quart baking dish. Combine flour, salt, pepper and half and half in small bowl; mix well. Pour over layers. Toss bread crumbs with melted butter. Sprinkle over top. Bake in preheated 350-degree oven for 30 minutes. May substitute evaporated milk for half and half. Yield: 8 servings.

Approx Per Serving: Cal 171; Prot 6 g; Carbo 8 g; Fiber 2 g; T Fat 15 g; 71% Calories from Fat; Chol 24 mg; Sod 488 mg.

Live in the moment. If you dwell on the past, you'll miss what is wonderful today.

 *Vegetables*

AUNT ADDIE'S ONION SHORTCAKE

1 7-ounce package corn muffin
  mix
1 egg, beaten
1/3 cup milk
1 8-ounce can creamed corn
1 large sweet onion, sliced

1/4 cup butter
1 cup sour cream
1/4 teaspoon salt
1 cup shredded sharp Cheddar
  cheese

Combine corn muffin mix, egg, milk and corn in bowl; mix well. Pour into greased 9x9-inch baking pan. Sauté onion in butter in saucepan; remove from heat. Stir in sour cream, salt and half the cheese. Spoon over batter. Sprinkle with remaining cheese. Bake at 425 degrees for 30 minutes. Yield: 6 servings.

Approx Per Serving: Cal 349; Prot 9 g; Carbo 23 g; Fiber 1 g;
  T Fat 25 g; 64% Calories from Fat; Chol 95 mg; Sod 564 mg.

BAKED POTATO ROSE

6 tablespoons unsalted butter
1 clove of garlic, peeled
2 pounds small red potatoes,
  peeled, sliced 1/4-inch thick
1 tablespoon oil

1 1/2 teaspoons salt
1/4 teaspoon white pepper
1 tablespoon finely chopped
  parsley

Melt butter in small skillet with garlic. Skim off white solids and discard with garlic, reserving clarified butter. Brush 9 or 10-inch pie plate with a small amount of clarified butter. Soak potatoes in cold water for 30 minutes, changing water when it becomes cloudy. Drain and dry thoroughly. Toss potatoes with reserved clarified butter, oil, salt and pepper in bowl. Arrange potato slices in overlapping concentric circles in prepared pie plate to resemble rose. Pour any excess butter over potatoes. Bake at 375 degrees for 45 to 55 minutes or until potatoes are browned and crisp. Sprinkle with parsley. Cut into wedges to serve. Yield: 8 servings.

Approx Per Serving: Cal 197; Prot 2 g; Carbo 25 g; Fiber 2 g;
  T Fat 10 g; 47% Calories from Fat; Chol 23 mg; Sod 407 mg.

Jeannine Stroth
Cousin's Cafe

CREAMY POTATO CASSEROLE

6 medium potatoes
1/4 cup butter
1 10-ounce can cream of chicken
   soup
2 cups sour cream

1/3 cup chopped green onions
1 1/2 cups shredded Cheddar cheese
1/2 to 1 cup crushed cornflakes
2 tablespoons melted butter

Cook potatoes until tender; cool. Peel and grate finely. Heat 1/4 cup butter with soup in saucepan until heated through. Add sour cream, green onions and cheese; mix well. Stir in grated potatoes. Spoon into buttered 2 1/2-quart baking dish. Toss cornflakes with melted butter; sprinkle over potato mixture. Bake at 350 degrees for 45 minutes. Yield: 8 servings.

Approx Per Serving: Cal 439; Prot 11 g; Carbo 33 g; Fiber 2 g;
  T Fat 30 g; 61% Calories from Fat; Chol 74 mg; Sod 624 mg.

HASHED BROWN POTATO CASSEROLE

1 2-pound package frozen
   hashed brown potatoes, thawed
1 10-ounce can cream of potato
   soup
1 10-ounce can cream of celery
   soup

1 cup sour cream
1 small onion, chopped
1/2 green bell pepper, chopped
Salt to taste
1 cup shredded Cheddar cheese

Combine potatoes, potato soup, celery soup, sour cream, onion and green pepper in bowl; mix well. Spoon into greased 9x13-inch baking dish. Season with salt; sprinkle with cheese. Bake at 300 degrees for 1 1/2 to 2 hours or until potatoes are tender and browned. May substitute 1/2 cup grated Parmesan cheese for Cheddar cheese. Yield: 10 servings.

Approx Per Serving: Cal 334; Prot 7 g; Carbo 32 g; Fiber 2 g;
  T Fat 21 g; 54% Calories from Fat; Chol 27 mg; Sod 554 mg.

Live in the moment. If you dwell on the future, you'll miss the freedom of today.

SCALLOPED POTATOES

1 2-pound package frozen
 hashed brown potatoes, thawed
1/2 cup margarine, softened
1 teaspoon salt
1/4 teaspoon pepper
1/2 cup chopped onions

1 10-ounce can cream of celery
 soup
1 cup milk
1 cup sour cream
11/2 cups cubed Velveeta cheese

Spread potatoes in buttered 9x13-inch baking dish. Combine margarine, salt, pepper, onions, celery soup, milk, sour cream and Velveeta cheese in large saucepan. Heat over medium heat until cheese is melted, stirring often. Pour over potatoes. Bake at 350 degrees for 1 hour. Let stand for several minutes before serving. Yield: 8 servings.

Approx Per Serving: Cal 517; Prot 10 g; Carbo 38 g; Fiber 3 g;
 T Fat 38 g; 64% Calories from Fat; Chol 67 mg; Sod 926 mg.

THINGS NOT MASHED

8 potatoes, boiled
2 cups sour cream
10 ounces sharp Cheddar cheese,
 shredded
1/4 cup chopped onion

3 tablespoons milk
1 teaspoon salt
1/8 teaspoon pepper
1/3 cup crushed croutons

Peel potatoes and grate into bowl. Add sour cream, cheese, onion, milk, salt and pepper; mix well. Spoon into 2-quart casserole. Top with crushed croutons. Bake at 300 degrees for 1 hour. Yield: 8 servings.

Approx Per Serving: Cal 402; Prot 14 g; Carbo 34 g; Fiber 2 g;
 T Fat 24 g; 54% Calories from Fat; Chol 64 mg; Sod 582 mg.

Accept others without conditions. It's the very essence of love.

TWICE-BAKED PARMESAN-CHIVE POTATOES

5 pounds russet potatoes	1/2 cup snipped fresh chives
1 cup milk	1/2 teaspoon salt
1/2 cup butter	1/2 teaspoon pepper
2 eggs, beaten	1/8 teaspoon ground nutmeg
3/4 cup grated Parmesan cheese	Paprika to taste

Pierce potatoes several times with fork. Place on baking sheet. Bake at 400 degrees for 50 to 60 minutes or until tender; cool for 15 minutes. Cut into halves lengthwise. Scoop out centers into mixer bowl, leaving 1/4-inch shells; set 18 shells aside. Heat milk and butter in saucepan until butter is melted. Pour over potatoes and beat with electric mixer until almost smooth. Add eggs, 1/2 cup Parmesan cheese, chives, salt, pepper and nutmeg. Whip until smooth. Spoon mixture into reserved shells. Sprinkle with remaining Parmesan cheese and paprika. Place on baking sheet. Bake at 350 degrees for 30 minutes or until puffed and lightly browned. Yield: 18 servings.

Approx Per Serving: Cal 215; Prot 6 g; Carbo 33 g; Fiber 3 g; T Fat 7 g; 30% Calories from Fat; Chol 42 mg; Sod 188 mg.

SPINACH CASSEROLE

2 10-ounce packages frozen chopped spinach, thawed, drained	Onion salt to taste
	1/4 teaspoon garlic salt
	1/4 teaspoon pepper
1 10-ounce can cream of mushroom soup	1/2 cup cracker crumbs
	2 tablespoons grated Parmesan cheese
2 eggs, beaten	

Combine spinach, soup, eggs, onion salt, garlic salt, pepper and half the cracker crumbs in bowl; mix well. Spoon into greased 8x8-inch baking dish. Sprinkle with remaining cracker crumbs and Parmesan cheese. Bake at 375 degrees for 20 minutes. Yield: 6 servings.

Approx Per Serving: Cal 138; Prot 7 g; Carbo 14 g; Fiber 3 g; T Fat 7 g; 42% Calories from Fat; Chol 75 mg; Sod 694 mg.

SPANOKOPETA (Spinach Pie)

4 pounds fresh spinach, finely
   chopped
1 onion, finely chopped
1/2 bunch parsley, finely chopped
1 bunch scallions, finely chopped
1/2 cup pine nuts

2 eggs, beaten
16 ounces feta cheese, crumbled
1/4 to 1/2 teaspoon ground nutmeg
Sea salt and pepper to taste
2 cups melted unsalted butter
16 ounces phyllo dough

Rinse spinach well; drain. Place in large saucepan, pressing down. Cook, covered, over medium heat until wilted. Drain in colander. Cool. Combine onion, parsley, scallions, pine nuts, eggs, feta cheese, nutmeg, salt and pepper in bowl. Mash until well mixed. Stir in spinach. Brush baking sheet with a small amount of melted butter. Layer with 6 sheets phyllo dough, brushing each sheet with melted butter. Spread with half the spinach mixture. Layer with 3 to 4 sheets of phyllo, brushing each with butter. Spread with remaining spinach mixture. Fold up loose ends of phyllo toward center of pan. Layer with remaining sheets of phyllo, brushing each sheet with butter. Bake at 350 degrees for 45 to 60 minutes or until golden brown. Cool for 10 minutes before slicing to serve. May substitute 16 ounces tofu mixed with 1/2 teaspoon white miso for feta cheese. Yield: 12 servings.

Approx Per Serving: Cal 566; Prot 17 g; Carbo 34 g; Fiber 8 g;
  T Fat 44 g; 66% Calories from Fat; Chol 152 mg; Sod 697 mg.

SPAGHETTI SQUASH ALFREDO

1 large spaghetti squash
2 tablespoons butter
2 tablespoons oil

1/2 cup half and half
1/2 cup grated Parmesan cheese
Salt and pepper to taste

Cook squash, covered, in water to cover in saucepan for 30 minutes or until squash can be pierced with tip of knife; drain. Let stand just until cool enough to handle. Cut squash into halves lengthwise; discard seed. Remove strands to bowl with fork. Add butter, oil, half and half, Parmesan cheese, salt and pepper; toss to mix well. Serve immediately. May microwave squash or reheat dish in microwave if desired. Yield: 6 servings.

Approx Per Serving: Cal 161; Prot 4 g; Carbo 8 g; Fiber 3 g;
  T Fat 13 g; 71% Calories from Fat; Chol 23 mg; Sod 185 mg.

SQUASH DRESSING

3 pounds yellow squash,
  sliced
1/2 cup margarine
2 cups yellow cornmeal
Salt and pepper to taste
1 large onion, chopped
2 stalks celery, chopped
1 10-ounce can cream of chicken
  soup

1 10-ounce can cream of
  mushroom soup
1 cup water
1 cup milk
3 eggs, beaten
1 pound chopped cooked chicken
  breasts

Cook squash in margarine in saucepan over low heat until tender; set aside. Combine cornmeal, salt, pepper, onion and celery in large bowl. Mix chicken soup, mushroom soup, water, milk and eggs in medium bowl. Add to cornmeal mixture, mixing well. Stir in squash and chicken. Spoon into 11x14-inch casserole. Bake at 375 degrees for 30 to 40 minutes or until browned. Yield: 10 servings.

Approx Per Serving: Cal 385; Prot 22 g; Carbo 35 g; Fiber 5 g;
  T Fat 18 g; 41% Calories from Fat; Chol 108 mg; Sod 635 mg.

VEGETABLES WITH HERBED TOPPING

1 teaspoon Mrs. Dash seasoning
4 ounces fresh green beans,
  trimmed, cut into halves
8 ounces broccoli flowerets
8 ounces cauliflowerets
1 small zucchini, sliced
1 2-ounce jar pimento, drained,
  cut into small squares
1/4 cup chopped onion

1/2 cup unsalted butter
2 cups soft bread crumbs
1/4 cup Mrs. Dash Crispy
  Coating Mix
2 teaspoons crushed dried tarragon
1/2 teaspoon dry mustard
2 tablespoons finely snipped
  fresh parsley
2 tablespoons lemon juice

Fill saucepan with 3/4 inch water; add Mrs. Dash seasoning. Place green beans, broccoli, cauliflowerets and zucchini in steamer basket. Steam, covered, for 5 to 7 minutes or until tender-crisp. Combine with pimento in serving bowl. Sauté onion in butter in skillet. Add bread crumbs, coating mix, tarragon and mustard. Simmer until heated through, tossing to coat with butter. Stir in parsley and lemon juice. Spoon mixture over vegetables. Yield: 6 servings.

Approx Per Serving: Cal 241; Prot 5 g; Carbo 20 g; Fiber 4 g;
  T Fat 17 g; 61% Calories from Fat; Chol 41 mg; Sod 97 mg.

VEGGIE ENCHILADAS

2 tablespoons olive oil
3 green onions, chopped
1 cup chopped mushrooms
1/2 cup frozen corn, thawed
1 8-ounce can black olives, chopped
1/2 teaspoon ground cumin

1/2 teaspoon ground oregano
1 tablespoon chili powder
16 ounces Cheddar cheese, shredded
2 cups canned enchilada sauce
12 corn or flour tortillas

Heat olive oil in skillet. Sauté green onions, mushrooms, corn and olives with cumin, oregano and chili powder for 2 minutes; remove from heat. Stir in 2/3 of the cheese. Heat enchilada sauce in saucepan. Dip tortillas into enchilada sauce. Spoon vegetable mixture evenly in center of each tortilla; roll up to enclose filling. Place seam side down in 9x13-inch baking dish. Pour remaining enchilada sauce over tortillas; sprinkle with remaining cheese. Bake at 350 degrees for 30 minutes. Yield: 12 servings.

Approx Per Serving: Cal 295; Prot 13 g; Carbo 19 g; Fiber 4 g; T Fat 21 g; 60% Calories from Fat; Chol 40 mg; Sod 552 mg.

SOUR CREAM ENCHILADAS

2 10-ounce cans cream of celery soup
2 6-ounce cans chopped green chilies, drained
2 bunches scallions, chopped
1 pound Longhorn cheese, shredded

1 pound Monterey Jack cheese, shredded
2 cups sour cream
24 tortillas
2 tablespoons oil

Combine soup, green chilies, scallions, cheeses and sour cream in bowl; mix well. Fry tortillas in oil in skillet for 30 seconds to soften. Spoon sour cream mixture evenly in center of each tortilla; roll up to enclose filling. Place seam side down in 9x13-inch baking dish. Bake at 300 degrees for 30 minutes. Yield: 24 servings.

Approx Per Serving: Cal 285; Prot 13 g; Carbo 17 g; Fiber 3 g; T Fat 19 g; 59% Calories from Fat; Chol 48 mg; Sod 509 mg.

MANICOTTI WITH RATATOUILLE SAUCE

8 ounces uncooked manicotti
32 ounces ricotta cheese
2 cups shredded mozzarella cheese
1/2 cup grated Parmesan cheese

2 eggs, slightly beaten
1/2 cup chopped parsley
Salt and pepper to taste
Ratatouille Sauce

Cook manicotti using package directions; drain. Place in single layer on waxed paper-lined surface to cool. Combine cheeses, eggs, parsley, salt and pepper in bowl; mix well. Spoon into manicotti. Spoon half the Ratatouille Sauce into 9x13-inch baking dish. Arrange filled manicotti in dish; spoon remaining sauce over manicotti. Bake at 350 degrees for 20 to 25 minutes or until bubbly. Yield: 8 servings.

Ratatouille Sauce

4 cups chopped peeled eggplant
2 cups sliced onions
2 cups green bell pepper strips
4 cloves of garlic, minced
6 tablespoons olive oil
4 cups sliced zucchini

1 teaspoon each oregano and basil
1/2 teaspoon marjoram
Salt and pepper to taste
2 15-ounce cans tomato sauce
2 15-ounce cans stewed tomatoes

Sauté eggplant, onions, green pepper and garlic in olive oil in skillet for 5 minutes. Add zucchini, oregano, basil, marjoram, salt, pepper, tomato sauce and tomatoes; mix well. Simmer for 5 minutes or until vegetables are tender-crisp. Yield: 8 servings.

Approx Per Serving: Cal 617; Prot 30 g; Carbo 50 g; Fiber 6 g;
   T Fat 34 g; 49% Calories from Fat; Chol 136 mg; Sod 1304 mg.

Offer someone love today. You will be pleased when it returns to you.

BASIL AND TOMATO FETTUCINI

¼ cup chopped onion
1 clove of garlic, minced
¼ cup olive oil
1 28-ounce can peeled tomatoes

6 fresh basil leaves, chopped
1 teaspoon salt
½ teaspoon pepper
1 12-ounce package fettucini

Sauté onion and garlic in oil in medium skillet until tender. Drain tomatoes, reserving juice. Chop finely. Add tomatoes, reserved tomato juice, basil, salt and pepper to onion mixture. Bring to a boil; reduce heat. Simmer for 15 to 20 minutes, stirring occasionally. Cook fettucini using package directions; drain. Toss with sauce to coat. Garnish with grated Parmesan cheese. Yield: 6 servings.

Approx Per Serving: Cal 318; Prot 8 g; Carbo 49 g; Fiber 4 g; T Fat 10 g; 28% Calories from Fat; Chol 0 mg; Sod 572 mg.

FRESH TOMATO PASTA

4 tomatoes, chopped
2 to 3 tablespoons olive oil
1 cup shredded mozzarella cheese
2 teaspoons salt

2 cloves of garlic, chopped
1 tablespoon fresh basil or
  1 teaspoon dried basil
12 ounces uncooked pasta

Combine tomatoes, olive oil, cheese, salt, garlic and basil in bowl; mix well. Let stand for 30 minutes. Cook pasta using package directions; drain. Toss with tomato mixture in bowl. Serve immediately. Yield: 4 servings.

Approx Per Serving: Cal 508; Prot 17 g; Carbo 70 g; Fiber 6 g; T Fat 17 g; 31% Calories from Fat; Chol 22 mg; Sod 1184 mg.

If I can stop one Heart from breaking
I shall not live in vain
If I can ease one Life the Aching
Or cool one Pain

Or help one fainting Robin
Unto his Nest again
I shall not live in Vain.

—Emily Dickinson

NOODLES FLORENTINE

2 pounds uncooked noodles
1/2 cup olive oil
2 cloves of garlic, finely chopped
Grated Parmesan cheese to taste
1/2 teaspoon freshly ground pepper
3 10-ounce packages frozen
   chopped spinach

1/2 to 2 teaspoons tarragon
2 tablespoons lemon juice
1/2 cup butter
Salt to taste
1/2 cup buttered toasted bread
   crumbs

Cook noodles using package directions; drain. Toss with olive oil, garlic, Parmesan cheese and pepper in large bowl; set aside. Microwave spinach in glass bowl; do not add water. Drain well. Mix with tarragon, lemon juice, butter and salt. Layer spinach and noodles in buttered baking dish. Sprinkle with bread crumbs and additional Parmesan cheese. Broil until lightly browned. Yield: 12 servings.

Approx Per Serving: Cal 443; Prot 14 g; Carbo 60 g; Fiber 2 g;
   T Fat 17 g; 34% Calories from Fat; Chol 143 mg; Sod 136 mg.

PIRATE RICE

2 ounces bacon, chopped
1 small onion, chopped
1 clove of garlic, chopped
2 ounces chopped celery
2 tablespoons olive oil
2 medium tomatoes, chopped

2 tablespoons tomato paste
Salt and pepper to taste
12 ounces uncooked rice
18 ounces chicken stock
6 ounces pigeon peas, cooked

Sauté bacon, onion, garlic and celery in olive oil in saucepan. Stir in tomatoes, tomato paste, salt and pepper. Add rice and chicken stock; mix well. Spoon into baking dish. Bake at 350 degrees until rice is tender. Stir in peas just before serving. Yield: 4 servings.

Approx Per Serving: Cal 479; Prot 14 g; Carbo 82 g; Fiber 5 g;
   T Fat 10 g; 20% Calories from Fat; Chol 4 mg; Sod 503 mg.

Chef Bruno Wehren
MGM Grand Hotel, Inc.

 Side Dishes

RISOTTO ALLA MILANESE

1 onion, finely chopped	¹/₄ teaspoon white pepper
¹/₄ cup butter	¹/₂ teaspoon saffron
1 cup dry white wine	4 to 5 cups chicken broth
2 cups uncooked white rice	1 cup freshly grated Parmesan
1 teaspoon salt	cheese

Sauté onion in butter in large saucepan until tender. Add wine. Bring to a boil. Cook until wine evaporates. Add rice, stirring to coat with butter. Add salt, pepper, saffron and half the broth. Simmer over medium heat until liquid is absorbed, stirring occasionally. Stir in remaining broth. Simmer until rice is cooked al dente. Spoon into serving bowl. Top with grated Parmesan cheese. Garnish with additional butter. May add 1 pound cooked ground round for main dish. Yield: 6 servings.

Approx Per Serving: Cal 420; Prot 15 g; Carbo 53 g; Fiber 1 g;
  T Fat 13 g; 28% Calories from Fat; Chol 32 mg; Sod 1323 mg.

Bob Barengo
Board of Trustees

SPANISH RICE

1¹/₂ cups uncooked long grain rice	1¹/₂ teaspoons salt
¹/₄ cup oil	Cayenne pepper to taste
1 clove of garlic, crushed	4 cups hot water
¹/₃ cup chopped celery	1¹/₂ to 2 pounds ground round
1 16-ounce can tomatoes	¹/₂ teaspoon chili powder
1 6-ounce can tomato paste	1 teaspoon sugar
1 small bay leaf	1 10-ounce can beef broth

Brown rice in hot oil in large skillet, stirring frequently. Add garlic and celery. Cook for 5 to 6 minutes longer, stirring often. Add tomatoes, tomato paste, bay leaf, salt, cayenne pepper and hot water. Simmer, covered, for 15 minutes. Brown ground round in skillet, stirring until crumbly; drain. Stir in chili powder, sugar and beef broth. Add to rice mixture, stirring well. Simmer for 40 minutes, stirring gently with fork. Discard bay leaf. May add additional water or tomato juice to moisten. Yield: 8 servings.

Approx Per Serving: Cal 451; Prot 25 g; Carbo 35 g; Fiber 2 g;
  T Fat 23 g; 47% Calories from Fat; Chol 74 mg; Sod 692 mg.

SPINACH AND RICE SOUFFLÉ

4 eggs, beaten
1 cup milk
8 ounces Cheddar cheese,
  shredded
1   10-ounce package frozen
  chopped spinach, cooked,
  drained
3 cups cooked rice

1/4 cup butter, softened
1 tablespoon chopped onion
1 tablespoon Worcestershire sauce
1/2 teaspoon marjoram
1/2 teaspoon thyme
1/2 teaspoon rosemary
1/2 teaspoon salt

Beat eggs and milk lightly in bowl. Stir in cheese, spinach and rice. Add butter, onion, Worcestershire sauce, marjoram, thyme, rosemary and salt; mix well. Pour into greased 2-quart baking dish. Place dish in pan of warm water. Bake at 350 degrees for 45 minutes. Yield: 8 servings.

Approx Per Serving: Cal 319; Prot 14 g; Carbo 23 g; Fiber 1 g;
  T Fat 19 g; 54% Calories from Fat; Chol 156 mg; Sod 454 mg.

Susan Molasky
Board of Trustees

ZUCCHINI RICE WITH LEMON

1/2 cup long grain rice
1 cup less 1 1/2 tablespoons
  chicken stock
1 1/2 tablespoons lemon juice

1/4 teaspoon grated lemon rind
8 ounces zucchini, thinly sliced
1 1/2 teaspoons fresh thyme
Freshly ground pepper to taste

Combine rice, chicken stock and lemon juice in heavy saucepan. Stir in lemon rind. Bring to a boil; reduce heat. Simmer, covered, for 10 minutes. Add zucchini, thyme and pepper. Cook for 17 minutes longer or until rice and zucchini are tender and liquid is absorbed. Yield: 2 servings.

Approx Per Serving: Cal 205; Prot 7 g; Carbo 42 g; Fiber 2 g;
  T Fat 1 g; 5% Calories from Fat; Chol <1 mg; Sod 356 mg.

Know that each day of your life is a gift.

ARTICHOKE-MUSHROOM QUICHE

1 9-ounce package frozen
   artichoke hearts
2 tablespoons reduced-calorie
   Italian salad dressing
8 ounces fresh mushrooms
1/2 cup fine dry bread
   crumbs
1/2 teaspoon paprika
1/8 teaspoon garlic powder
1/8 teaspoon salt

1/4 cup shredded low-fat Cheddar
   cheese
1/4 cup shredded part-skim
   mozzarella cheese
1 cup skim milk
2 eggs, beaten
1/8 teaspoon white pepper
2 tablespoons grated Parmesan
   cheese
Ground red pepper to taste

Cook artichoke hearts using package directions, omitting salt. Drain well; press between paper towels to remove moisture. Process in food processor until finely chopped. Combine with salad dressing in bowl; mix well. Chill, covered, for 3 hours. Process mushrooms in food processor until minced. Spray skillet with nonstick cooking spray. Heat over medium heat. Add mushrooms. Sauté for 15 minutes or until liquid evaporates, stirring frequently; remove from heat. Stir in bread crumbs, paprika, garlic powder and salt. Press mixture over bottom and up side of 9-inch pie plate sprayed with nonstick cooking spray. Bake at 350 degrees for 8 to 10 minutes or until dry. Spread artichoke mixture in mushroom shell. Sprinkle Cheddar and mozzarella cheeses evenly over top. Beat milk, eggs and white pepper in bowl. Pour over layers. Sprinkle with Parmesan cheese and red pepper. Bake at 350 degrees for 35 minutes or until knife inserted near center comes out clean. Let stand for 10 minutes before serving. Yield: 6 servings.

Approx Per Serving: Cal 138; Prot 10 g; Carbo 15 g; Fiber 4 g;
   T Fat 5 g; 32% Calories from Fat; Chol 79 mg; Sod 292 mg.

 It is one of the most beautiful compensations of this life that no man can sincerely try to help another without helping himself.

—Ralph Waldo Emerson

PUFFED CHEDDAR CHEESE OMELET

6 egg whites
6 egg yolks
1/2 cup mayonnaise
3 tablespoons water

2 tablespoons butter, softened
1 cup finely shredded Cheddar
cheese

Beat egg whites in mixer bowl until soft peaks form. Beat egg yolks with mayonnaise, water and butter in small bowl until lemon colored. Fold gently into egg whites. Pour into 10-inch nonstick skillet. Cook over low heat for 10 minutes. Bake in preheated 350-degree oven for 5 minutes. Sprinkle with cheese. Bake for 2 to 3 minutes longer or until cheese is melted. Yield: 4 servings.

Approx Per Serving: Cal 480; Prot 17 g; Carbo 2 g; Fiber 0 g;
T Fat 46 g; 86% Calories from Fat; Chol 381 mg; Sod 467 mg.

EGG CASSEROLE

4 slices white bread, cubed
4 eggs, beaten
2 cups milk

1/2 cup cubed Velveeta cheese
Salt and pepper to taste
6 slices bacon, crisp-fried, crumbled

Place bread cubes in 10x10-inch baking dish. Beat eggs, milk, Velveeta cheese, salt and pepper in bowl. Pour over bread cubes. Chill, covered, overnight. Sprinkle with bacon bits. Bake at 350 degrees for 40 to 50 minutes or until knife inserted near center comes out clean. Yield: 4 servings.

Approx Per Serving: Cal 323; Prot 18 g; Carbo 20 g; Fiber 1 g;
T Fat 19 g; 53% Calories from Fat; Chol 248 mg; Sod 567 mg.

BEST BARBECUE SAUCE

1 cup catsup
1/4 cup Dijon mustard
1 tablespoon lemon juice

1/4 cup packed brown sugar
Tabasco sauce to taste
1/4 cup Worcestershire sauce

Combine catsup, mustard, lemon juice, brown sugar, Tabasco sauce and Worcestershire sauce in saucepan. Cook over medium heat until of desired consistency, stirring frequently. Use for steak, chicken or shredded roast beef. May store in refrigerator for up to 1 week. Yield: 6 servings.

Approx Per Serving: Cal 116; Prot 2 g; Carbo 25 g; Fiber 1 g;
T Fat 2 g; 11% Calories from Fat; Chol 0 mg; Sod 844 mg.

QUICK BORDELAISE SAUCE

1½ tablespoons unsalted butter
2 tablespoons flour
2 cups beef stock

½ cup dry red wine
3 shallots, finely chopped
1 teaspoon finely chopped parsley

Melt butter in saucepan. Add flour; mix well. Cook over low heat until mixture is brown, stirring occasionally. Stir in beef stock gradually; mix well. Bring to a boil. Cook for 3 to 5 minutes or until thickened. Reduce heat. Simmer for 20 minutes. Skim off fat; strain. Combine wine and shallots in saucepan; mix well. Cook over medium heat until wine is reduced by ¾. Stir in 1 cup brown sauce. Simmer for 10 minutes. Stir in parsley. Yield: 1 cup.

Nutritional information for this recipe is not available.

NO-COOK CURRIED FRUIT RELISH

3 cups dried apricots
1 cup raisins
1 tablespoon dried minced onion
1 tablespoon curry powder
½ teaspoon salt

¼ cup sugar
2 cups boiling water
3 tea bags
¼ cup red wine vinegar

Snip each apricot into 4 or 5 pieces in medium bowl. Add raisins and minced onion, tossing to mix. Sprinkle with curry powder, salt and sugar. Pour boiling water over tea bags in small bowl. Let steep for 5 minutes; discard tea bags. Stir vinegar into tea; pour over fruit, tossing to coat. Chill, covered, for 18 hours, stirring occasionally. Spoon into small jars and store, covered, in refrigerator. Yield: 8 servings.

Approx Per Serving: Cal 207; Prot 3 g; Carbo 54 g; Fiber 5 g; T Fat <1 g; 2% Calories from Fat; Chol 0 mg; Sod 142 mg.

Susan Molasky
Board of Trustees

BREADS

APRICOT SWIRL SCONES

³/4 cup finely chopped dried
  apricots
2 tablespoons honey
2 2-inch strips lemon peel
1 tablespoon lemon juice
¹/4 cup water
3 cups flour

1 tablespoon baking powder
¹/4 teaspoon salt
1 cup unsalted butter, softened
¹/4 cup sugar
3 eggs
1 teaspoon vanilla extract
¹/3 cup buttermilk

Combine first 5 ingredients in saucepan. Simmer, covered, over low heat for 10 minutes or until apricots are very soft. Discard lemon peel. Mash apricots in saucepan until of purée consistency; set aside. Combine flour, baking powder and salt in bowl. Cream butter in mixer bowl at medium speed until pale and fluffy. Add eggs 1 at a time, beating well after each addition. Beat in vanilla. Add dry ingredients, beating at low speed until blended. Add buttermilk, beating gently. Fold apricot purée into mixture, swirling with spatula. Place by ¹/3 cupfuls 2 inches apart on ungreased baking sheet. Cover with plastic wrap; chill for 45 minutes. Remove plastic wrap. Bake at 350 degrees for 15 minutes; reduce heat to 325 degrees. Bake for 10 to 13 minutes longer or until pale golden brown. Cool on wire rack. May substitute plain yogurt for buttermilk. Yield: 12 servings.

Approx Per Serving: Cal 339; Prot 6 g; Carbo 42 g; Fiber 2 g;
  T Fat 17 g; 45% Calories from Fat; Chol 95 mg; Sod 155 mg.

Every day you should reach out and touch someone. People love that human touch . . . holding hands, a warm hug, or just a friendly pat on the back.

—from *Live and Learn and Pass It On*

DELUXE COFFEE CAKE

1 cup margarine, softened	1 cup sour cream
1 cup sugar	1 teaspoon vanilla extract
3 eggs, beaten	1/2 cup chopped pecans
2 1/2 cups flour	1/2 cup packed brown sugar
3 teaspoons baking powder	2 teaspoons cinnamon
1 teaspoon baking soda	2 tablespoons melted margarine

Cream margarine and sugar in mixer bowl until light and fluffy. Beat in eggs. Mix flour, baking powder and baking soda together. Add to creamed mixture alternately with sour cream, beating well after each addition. Beat in vanilla. Spoon half the batter into greased and floured tube pan. Sprinkle with half the pecans, half the brown sugar, half the cinnamon and half the melted margarine; repeat procedure with remaining ingredients. Bake at 350 degrees for 1 hour. Cool in pan. Invert onto serving plate. Yield: 12 servings.

Approx Per Serving: Cal 450; Prot 5 g; Carbo 50 g; Fiber 1 g; T Fat 26 g; 52% Calories from Fat; Chol 62 mg; Sod 385 mg.

OLD-FASHIONED SOUR CREAM COFFEE CAKE

1/2 cup sugar	1 teaspoon vanilla extract
2 to 3 tablespoons baking cocoa	2 cups sifted flour
1 tablespoon cinnamon	1 teaspoon baking powder
1/2 cup chopped pecans	1 teaspoon baking soda
1/2 cup butter, softened	1/4 teaspoon salt
1 cup sugar	1 cup sour cream
2 eggs	

Mix 1/2 cup sugar, baking cocoa, cinnamon and pecans in bowl; set aside. Cream butter and 1 cup sugar in mixer bowl until light and fluffy. Beat in eggs and vanilla. Sift flour, baking powder, baking soda and salt together. Add to butter mixture alternately with sour cream, mixing well after each addition. Layer batter and pecan mixture 1/2 at a time in lightly greased 10-inch tube pan. Bake at 350 degrees for 45 to 50 minutes. Yield: 16 servings.

Approx Per Serving: Cal 245; Prot 3 g; Carbo 32 g; Fiber 1 g; T Fat 12 g; 44% Calories from Fat; Chol 49 mg; Sod 171 mg.

BASIC SWEET DOUGH

1 quart milk, scalded, cooled to
   lukewarm
4 ounces dry or cake yeast
1 cup sugar
14 cups (or more) flour

1 cup sugar
1 teaspoon salt
1 pound unsalted butter
12 egg yolks

Combine milk, yeast, 1 cup sugar and 2 cups flour in bowl; mix well to form sponge. Let rise for 30 minutes. Sift remaining flour, 1 cup sugar and salt into large bowl. Work in butter with fingertips. Add egg yolks and yeast mixture; mix well. Knead on floured surface until smooth and elastic. Place in greased bowl, turning to coat surface. Let rise, covered, for 1 to 1½ hours or until doubled in bulk. Punch dough down and knead for several minutes. Let rise, covered, for 30 minutes. Use dough to make your favorite sweet rolls, cinnamon rolls or Pecan Rolls (recipe below). Yield: 24 servings.

Approx Per Serving: Cal 534; Prot 12 g; Carbo 74 g; Fiber 3 g;
   T Fat 20 g; 35% Calories from Fat; Chol 153 mg; Sod 116 mg.

PECAN ROLLS (Schnecken)

½ cup unsalted butter
8 ounces light brown sugar
¼ cup light corn syrup
120 pecan halves
1 recipe Basic Sweet Dough
   (recipe above)

½ cup melted unsalted butter
1 cup sugar
2 tablespoons cinnamon
1 cup pecan pieces

Combine ½ cup butter, brown sugar and corn syrup in saucepan. Cook over medium heat for 10 minutes. Spoon into 24 muffin cups; place 5 pecan halves in each prepared cup. Roll half the Sweet Dough at a time ½ inch thick on floured surface. Sprinkle with melted butter, sugar, cinnamon and pecan pieces. Roll up dough to enclose filling; cut into 1-inch slices. Place slices in prepared muffin cups. Let rise for 1 hour. Bake at 350 degrees for 45 minutes, switching muffin pans from top to bottom rack as rolls on top shelf begin to brown. Invert onto baking sheet; let stand for 1 minute before removing muffin pans. Yield: 24 servings.

Approx Per Serving: Cal 772; Prot 13 g; Carbo 97 g; Fiber 5 g;
   T Fat 37 g; 43% Calories from Fat; Chol 174 mg; Sod 123 mg.

STICKY BUN CAKE

Cinnamon to taste
1 4-ounce package vanilla
   instant pudding mix

²/₃ cup packed brown sugar
24 frozen rolls
¹/₂ cup melted butter

Combine cinnamon, pudding mix and brown sugar in small bowl. Layer half the frozen rolls in bundt pan. Sprinkle with half the cinnamon mixture; drizzle with half the butter. Repeat layers. Let rise in warm place for 4 hours. Bake at 350 degrees for 30 minutes. Yield: 12 servings.

Approx Per Serving: Cal 321; Prot 4 g; Carbo 49 g; Fiber 2 g; T Fat 12 g; 33% Calories from Fat; Chol 21 mg; Sod 429 mg.

AZTEC CORN BREAD

2¹/₂ cups stone-ground whole
   yellow cornmeal (not degermed)
3 cups hot water
1 envelope dry yeast

¹/₃ cup nonfat dry milk powder
¹/₂ cup sifted soy flour
2 teaspoons salt
4¹/₂ cups whole wheat flour

Mix cornmeal and hot water in large bowl. Let stand until lukewarm. Stir in yeast. Let stand for 5 minutes. Add milk powder, soy flour, salt and whole wheat flour, stirring with wooden spoon until stiff dough forms. Knead on floured surface for 3 to 5 minutes or until smooth. Place in bowl. Let rise, covered, until doubled in bulk. Knead on floured surface for 1 to 2 minutes. Divide into 2 equal portions; shape into loaves. Place in loaf pans. Let rise, covered, until doubled in bulk. Bake at 400 degrees for 10 minutes; reduce temperature to 350 degrees. Bake for 30 minutes longer. Cool on wire racks. Yield: 24 servings.

Approx Per Serving: Cal 137; Prot 5 g; Carbo 28 g; Fiber 4 g; T Fat 1 g; 67% Calories from Fat; Chol <1 mg; Sod 184 mg.

I've learned that for a happy day, look for something bright and beautiful in nature. Listen for a beautiful sound, speak a kind word to some person, and do something nice for someone without their knowledge.

—from *Live and Learn and Pass It On*

NEW ORLEANS HUSH PUPPIES

1 cup cornmeal
1 cup flour
1 egg
³/₄ cup 2% milk
1 tablespoon chopped chives
1 tablespoon minced onion

1 teaspoon salt
1 teaspoon sugar
1 teaspoon baking powder
Cayenne pepper to taste
Oil for frying

Combine cornmeal and flour in large bowl. Beat egg with milk in small bowl. Add to cornmeal mixture, stirring to moisten. Add chives, onion, salt, sugar, baking powder and cayenne pepper; mix well. Drop by spoonfuls into hot oil in skillet. Fry until golden brown; drain. Yield: 24 servings.

Approx Per Serving: Cal 48; Prot 2 g; Carbo 9 g; Fiber 1 g;
  T Fat 1 g; 10% Calories from Fat; Chol 10 mg; Sod 109 mg.
  Nutritional information does not include oil for frying.

LIGHT CRÊPES

¹/₂ cup plus 2 tablespoons flour
1¹/₃ cups skim milk

4 egg whites

Combine flour, milk and egg whites in blender container. Process for 30 seconds; scrape side of container. Process for 30 seconds longer. Chill batter for 1 hour. Spray 6-inch nonstick crêpe pan with nonstick cooking spray. Heat over medium heat. Pour 2 tablespoons batter into skillet, tilting to cover bottom with thin film of batter. Cook for 1 minute; shake skillet to loosen crêpe; turn. Cook for 30 seconds; repeat with remaining batter. Place crêpes on towel to cool. Stack between layers of waxed paper.
Yield: 16 servings.

Approx Per Serving: Cal 29; Prot 2 g; Carbo 5 g; Fiber <1 g;
  T Fat <1 g; 3% Calories from Fat; Chol <1 mg; Sod 23 mg.

NEW ORLEANS-STYLE FRENCH TOAST

5 eggs	2 tablespoons cream
1/3 to 1/2 cup sugar or honey	10 thick slices day-old French
2 tablespoons orange flower water	bread
1 to 3 tablespoons brandy	Oil for frying

Beat eggs and sugar in shallow bowl until light and frothy. Add orange flower water, brandy and cream, beating well. Soak bread slices in mixture. Heat 1/2 inch oil in skillet. Brown bread on both sides. Garnish with confectioners' sugar; serve with jam or syrup. Orange flower water is available in liquor stores or Middle Eastern markets. Yield: 10 servings.

Approx Per Serving: Cal 191; Prot 6 g; Carbo 27 g; Fiber 1 g;
 T Fat 5 g; 27% Calories from Fat; Chol 111 mg; Sod 239 mg.

ORANGE UPSIDE-DOWN FRENCH TOAST

2 tablespoons plus 2 teaspoons reduced-calorie margarine	1/2 teaspoon vanilla extract
Artificial sweetener equal to 2	1/2 teaspoon maple extract
tablespoons sugar	1/4 cup frozen unsweetened
1/2 teaspoon ground cinnamon	orange juice concentrate, thawed
4 eggs	1/4 cup water
1/2 teaspoon orange extract	4 slices white bread

Preheat oven to 400 degrees. Melt margarine in 8x8-inch baking dish in oven. Combine artificial sweetener and cinnamon; sprinkle in prepared dish. Beat eggs, orange extract, vanilla and maple flavorings, orange juice concentrate and water in shallow bowl. Soak bread slices in mixture. Arrange in baking dish; spoon any remaining egg mixture over bread. Bake for 25 minutes. Let stand for 1 minute before serving. Invert onto serving plates. May substitute whole wheat bread for white bread. Yield: 4 servings.

Approx Per Serving: Cal 218; Prot 9 g; Carbo 22 g; Fiber 1 g;
 T Fat 10 g; 43% Calories from Fat; Chol 213 mg; Sod 307 mg.

APPLE BREAD

½ cup butter
1 cup sugar
2 eggs
2 cups flour
½ teaspoon salt
½ teaspoon baking soda
1 teaspoon double acting baking
   powder

2 tablespoons buttermilk
1 cup coarsely chopped peeled
   apple
½ cup coarsely chopped pecans
1 teaspoon vanilla extract
2 teaspoons cinnamon

Cream butter until light and fluffy. Add sugar and eggs; beat well. Sift flour, salt, baking soda and baking powder together. Add to creamed mixture alternately with buttermilk, beating well after each addition. Fold in apple, pecans and vanilla. Spoon ⅓ of mixture into buttered 5x10-inch loaf pan. Sprinkle with half the cinnamon. Pour in ⅓ of the batter; sprinkle with remaining cinnamon. Top with remaining batter. Bake at 350 degrees for 50 to 60 minutes or until loaf tests done. Cool in pan for 5 minutes; remove to wire rack to cool completely. Yield: 12 servings.

Approx Per Serving: Cal 261; Prot 4 g; Carbo 35 g; Fiber 1 g;
   T Fat 12 g; 41% Calories from Fat; Chol 56 mg; Sod 230 mg.

BANANA BREAD

1 cup sugar
2 tablespoons liquid shortening
1 egg
1 teaspoon vanilla extract
2 cups flour
½ teaspoon salt

1 teaspoon baking powder
1 teaspoon baking soda
½ cup orange juice
2 large bananas, mashed
½ cup chopped pecans

Beat sugar, shortening, egg and vanilla in mixer bowl until smooth. Mix flour, salt, baking powder and baking soda together. Add to sugar mixture alternately with orange juice, beating well after each addition. Stir in bananas and pecans. Pour into greased 5x7-inch loaf pan. Bake at 325 degrees for 1 hour. Cool in pan for 5 minutes; remove to wire rack to cool completely. Yield: 12 servings.

Approx Per Serving: Cal 221; Prot 3 g; Carbo 39 g; Fiber 1 g;
   T Fat 6 g; 25% Calories from Fat; Chol 18 mg; Sod 192 mg.

WHOLE WHEAT-BANANA BREAD

1/2 cup melted butter	1 teaspoon baking soda
1 cup sugar	1/2 teaspoon salt
2 eggs, slightly beaten	1 cup whole wheat flour
1 cup mashed bananas	1/3 cup hot water
1 cup sifted all-purpose flour	1/2 cup chopped walnuts

Blend melted butter and sugar in mixer bowl. Beat in eggs and bananas. Sift all-purpose flour together with baking soda and salt. Stir in whole wheat flour. Add to batter alternately with hot water, mixing well after each addition. Stir in chopped walnuts. Spoon into greased 5x9-inch loaf pan. Bake at 325 degrees for 1 hour and 10 minutes or until bread tests done. Remove to wire rack to cool. This bread is moist with a light cake-like texture. Yield: 12 servings.

Approx Per Serving: Cal 263; Prot 4 g; Carbo 36 g; Fiber 2 g;
T Fat 12 g; 40% Calories from Fat; Chol 56 mg; Sod 235 mg.

POPPY SEED BREAD

1/2 cup orange juice	1 1/2 teaspoons almond extract
3/4 cup confectioners' sugar	1 1/2 teaspoons butter flavoring
1/2 teaspoon butter flavoring	3 cups flour
1/2 teaspoon almond extract	1 1/2 teaspoons salt
1/2 teaspoon vanilla extract	1 1/2 teaspoons baking powder
3 eggs, beaten	1 1/2 cups milk
2 1/4 cups sugar	1 1/2 teaspoons poppy seed
1 1/2 teaspoons vanilla extract	

Mix orange juice, confectioners' sugar, 1/2 teaspoon butter flavoring, 1/2 teaspoon almond extract and 1/2 teaspoon vanilla in small bowl, stirring until smooth; set aside. Combine eggs, sugar, 1 1/2 teaspoons vanilla, 1 1/2 teaspoons almond extract, 1 1/2 teaspoons butter flavoring, flour, salt, baking powder, milk and poppy seed in mixer bowl. Beat for 2 minutes on medium speed. Pour into 2 greased and floured large loaf pans. Bake at 350 degrees for 40 to 60 minutes. Cool in pans for 5 minutes. Remove to breadboard. Pierce several holes in loaves. Pour orange glaze over hot bread. Yield: 24 servings.

Approx Per Serving: Cal 169; Prot 3 g; Carbo 36 g; Fiber <1 g;
T Fat 1 g; 8% Calories from Fat; Chol 29 mg; Sod 170 mg.

 *Breads*

CHOCOLATE CHIP-PUMPKIN LOAF

$^{1}/_{2}$ cup butter, softened
1 cup sugar
2 eggs
1 teaspoon vanilla extract
$1^{1}/_{2}$ cups flour
1 teaspoon baking soda
1 teaspoon cinnamon
$^{1}/_{2}$ teaspoon nutmeg
$^{1}/_{4}$ teaspoon each ginger and cloves

$^{1}/_{2}$ teaspoon salt
$^{3}/_{4}$ cup pumpkin
$^{3}/_{4}$ cup chocolate chips
$^{1}/_{2}$ cup chopped walnuts
$^{1}/_{2}$ cup confectioners' sugar
$^{1}/_{8}$ teaspoon each cinnamon and nutmeg
1 tablespoon (or more) cream

Cream butter in mixer bowl until light. Add sugar; beat until fluffy. Beat in eggs 1 at a time. Add vanilla. Sift flour, baking soda, 1 teaspoon cinnamon, $^{1}/_{2}$ teaspoon nutmeg, ginger, cloves and salt together. Add to butter mixture alternately with pumpkin, mixing well after each addition. Fold in chocolate chips and half the walnuts. Spoon into greased and floured 5x9-inch loaf pan; sprinkle with remaining walnuts. Bake at 350 degrees for 1 hour or until loaf tests done. Cool in pan for 15 minutes; remove to wire rack to cool completely. Mix confectioners' sugar, $^{1}/_{8}$ teaspoon cinnamon and $^{1}/_{8}$ teaspoon nutmeg in bowl. Add enough cream to make of glaze consistency. Drizzle over completely cooled loaf. Yield: 12 servings.

Approx Per Serving: Cal 318; Prot 4 g; Carbo 42 g; Fiber 1 g;
 T Fat 16 g; 44% Calories from Fat; Chol 58 mg; Sod 237 mg.

PUMPKIN BREAD

$3^{1}/_{3}$ cups flour
2 teaspoons baking soda
$1^{1}/_{2}$ teaspoons salt
2 teaspoons cinnamon
2 teaspoons nutmeg

3 cups sugar
$^{2}/_{3}$ cup water
1 cup oil
4 eggs, beaten
1   16-ounce can pumpkin

Combine flour, baking soda, salt, cinnamon, nutmeg and sugar in large bowl. Beat water, oil, eggs and pumpkin in medium bowl. Add to dry ingredients, beating well. Pour into 2 greased and floured loaf pans. Bake at 350 degrees for 1 hour or until loaves test done. May add raisins, nuts or dried fruit. Yield: 24 servings.

Approx Per Serving: Cal 259; Prot 3 g; Carbo 40 g; Fiber 1 g;
 T Fat 10 g; 35% Calories from Fat; Chol 36 mg; Sod 215 mg.

MONKEY BREAD

3¹/₂ to 4¹/₂ cups flour
1 tablespoon sugar
1 teaspoon salt
2 envelopes dry yeast
¹/₂ cup butter

1 cup milk
¹/₂ cup water
3 eggs, at room temperature
¹/₂ cup melted butter

Combine 1¹/₂ cups flour, sugar, salt and yeast in mixer bowl, stirring to mix. Heat ¹/₂ cup butter, milk and water in saucepan to 90 to 100 degrees. Stir into dry ingredients. Beat at medium speed for 2 minutes. Add eggs and 1 cup flour. Beat at high speed for 2 minutes, scraping bowl. Add enough remaining flour to make soft dough. Let rise, covered, in warm place until doubled in bulk. Divide into halves. Roll out each portion to ¹/₃-inch thickness. Cut into 3-inch diamond shapes. Dip in ¹/₂ cup melted butter. Layer in 9-inch tube pan. Let rise, covered, until almost doubled in bulk. Bake at 400 degrees for 35 to 45 minutes or until golden brown. Cool in pan for 5 minutes; invert onto serving plate. Yield: 16 servings.

Approx Per Serving: Cal 259; Prot 6 g; Carbo 29 g; Fiber 1 g;
T Fat 13 g; 47% Calories from Fat; Chol 73 mg; Sod 251 mg.

NANNE (Indian Bread)

1 envelope dry yeast
2 tablespoons warm water
4 cups whole wheat flour
¹/₂ teaspoon salt

1 teaspoon sugar
¹/₂ cup yogurt
¹/₂ cup lukewarm milk
2 to 4 tablespoons peanut oil

Dissolve yeast in warm water. Combine flour, salt and sugar in bowl. Mix yogurt and lukewarm milk in small bowl; add yeast mixture, stirring well. Add to dry ingredients, mixing thoroughly. Add oil a little at a time, kneading to form smooth elastic dough. Let stand, covered, for 1 hour. Knead several times. Divide into 4 portions. Shape into balls; pat into 9 to 10-inch circles. Line oven rack with foil. Preheat oven to 375 degrees. Place circles on rack in middle of oven. Bake for 15 to 18 minutes or until puffed and lightly browned. Serve hot or cold; keeps well wrapped in plastic. Yield: 16 servings.

Approx Per Serving: Cal 141; Prot 5 g; Carbo 22 g; Fiber 4 g;
T Fat 4 g; 27% Calories from Fat; Chol 2 mg; Sod 74 mg.

Susan Molasky
Board of Trustees

 *Breads*

WAIOLI BREAD

3 envelopes dry yeast
1/3 cup water
1/2 cup all-purpose flour
1/2 cup sugar
2 cups milk

3/4 cup shortening
3 eggs, beaten
3 teaspoons salt
51/2 cups all-purpose flour
2 cups whole wheat flour

Mix first 3 ingredients in bowl. Let stand overnight. Add sugar, milk, shortening, eggs and salt; mix well. Add 51/2 cups all-purpose flour and wheat flour gradually, stirring after each addition. Knead on floured surface. Let rise, covered, in warm place for 1 hour. Divide into 4 portions. Knead each portion and shape into loaf. Place in 4 greased loaf pans. Let rise, covered, until doubled in bulk. Bake at 350 degrees for 45 minutes. Yield: 48 servings.

Approx Per Serving: Cal 122; Prot 3 g; Carbo 18 g; Fiber 1 g;
  T Fat 4 g; 30% Calories from Fat; Chol 15 mg; Sod 143 mg.

Muriel Stevens
Board of Trustees

ROSEMARY BREAD

2 envelopes active dry yeast
2 cups warm water
1 teaspoon honey
3 eggs, slightly beaten
11/4 cups oil

1/2 cup honey
11/2 cups whole wheat flour
4 teaspoons salt
2 to 3 tablespoons minced rosemary
7 to 8 cups unbleached flour

Combine first 3 ingredients in large bowl. Let stand for 5 to 10 minutes. Reserve 2 tablespoons eggs. Stir remaining eggs into oil and 1/2 cup honey in bowl. Add to yeast mixture, stirring well. Add whole wheat flour 1/2 cup at a time, stirring well after each addition. Add salt and rosemary, stirring with wooden spoon. Add unbleached flour, stirring until dough is sticky. Knead on floured surface for several minutes until dough is elastic. Place in greased bowl, turning to grease surface. Let rise, covered, in warm place for 1 to 11/2 hours or until doubled in bulk. Divide dough into halves. Divide each half into 3 equal portions. Roll each portion into an 18-inch rope. Braid 3 ropes together to form loaves, sealing ends. Place on greased baking sheets. Let stand, covered with damp towel, for 40 minutes. Brush with reserved egg. Bake at 350 degrees for 1 hour or until golden brown. Yield: 30 servings.

Approx Per Serving: Cal 234; Prot 5 g; Carbo 31 g; Fiber 1 g;
  T Fat 10 g; 39% Calories from Fat; Chol 21 mg; Sod 293 mg.

GARLIC-CHEESE BREAD

1 cup margarine, softened
8 ounces extra-sharp Cheddar
   cheese, shredded
1/3 cup freshly grated Romano
   cheese

1 tablespoon finely chopped garlic
2 1-pound round loaves
   sourdough bread, sliced

Cream margarine in mixer bowl until light and fluffy. Add Cheddar cheese, Romano cheese and garlic; stir well. Chill, covered, overnight. Remove from refrigerator and let stand for 15 to 20 minutes. Spread over bread slices; place on broiler pan. Broil for 5 to 6 minutes or until bubbly and lightly browned. Yield: 24 servings.

Approx Per Serving: Cal 213; Prot 7 g; Carbo 19 g; Fiber <1 g;
   T Fat 12 g; 52% Calories from Fat; Chol 11 mg; Sod 393 mg.

APPLE-PECAN MUFFINS

1¼ cups flour
1 teaspoon baking soda
1/2 teaspoon ground cinnamon
1/8 teaspoon salt
1 cup sugar
1/2 cup oil
1 egg, beaten

2 tablespoons lemon juice
1½ teaspoons vanilla extract
3/4 teaspoon grated lemon rind
2 cups coarsely grated peeled
   green apples
1/2 cup chopped toasted pecans

Sift flour, baking soda, cinnamon and salt into medium bowl. Combine sugar, oil, egg, lemon juice, vanilla and lemon rind in large bowl, whisking well. Add sifted dry ingredients, stirring well. Fold in apples and pecans. Spoon 1/3 cup batter into each greased muffin cup. Bake at 350 degrees for 35 minutes or until muffins test done. Remove to wire racks to cool. Yield: 12 servings.

Approx Per Serving: Cal 258; Prot 2 g; Carbo 34 g; Fiber 2 g;
   T Fat 13 g; 45% Calories from Fat; Chol 18 mg; Sod 97 mg.

GINGER-YOGURT MUFFINS

2 cups biscuit mix
1/4 cup sugar
1/2 teaspoon baking soda
1/4 teaspoon ginger

1 egg, beaten
1 cup orange yogurt
1/4 cup melted butter
1/4 cup chopped pecans

Combine biscuit mix, sugar, baking soda and ginger in bowl, stirring to mix. Add egg, yogurt and butter, stirring until moistened. Stir in pecans carefully. Fill greased muffin cups 2/3 full. Bake at 400 degrees for 15 minutes. Remove to wire rack to cool. Yield: 12 servings.

Approx Per Serving: Cal 185; Prot 3 g; Carbo 22 g; Fiber <1 g;
  T Fat 9 g; 46% Calories from Fat; Chol 28 mg; Sod 403 mg.

OATMEAL MUFFINS

1 cup rolled oats
1 cup buttermilk
1/3 cup butter flavored shortening,
  softened
1/2 cup packed brown sugar
1 egg, beaten

1 cup sifted flour
1 teaspoon baking powder
1/2 teaspoon baking soda
1 teaspoon salt
1 cup chopped pecans

Combine oats with buttermilk in bowl; soak for 1 hour. Cream shortening, brown sugar and egg in mixer bowl until light and fluffy. Sift flour, baking powder, baking soda and salt together. Add to creamed mixture alternately with buttermilk mixture, stirring well after each addition. Fold in pecans. Fill greased muffin cups 2/3 full. Bake at 350 degrees for 20 to 25 minutes or until muffins test done. Remove to wire rack to cool. Yield: 12 servings.

Approx Per Serving: Cal 235; Prot 4 g; Carbo 26 g; Fiber 2 g;
  T Fat 14 g; 51% Calories from Fat; Chol 19 mg; Sod 272 mg.

DESSERTS

APPLE CRISP

This is a traditional favorite made with pure and wholesome ingredients.

8 large apples, peeled, sliced
Juice and zest of 1/2 lemon
1/4 cup brown rice syrup
1/4 cup barley malt syrup
1/4 cup arrowroot
1/2 cup raisins
1/4 cup roasted chopped walnuts
1/4 teaspoon vanilla extract
1/2 teaspoon cinnamon
1/4 teaspoon sea salt
1/4 cup unrefined corn oil
1 cup each whole wheat pastry
  flour and unbleached flour
1/2 teaspoon vanilla extract
1/4 cup rice syrup
1/4 teaspoon cinnamon

Combine apples with next 10 ingredients in large bowl; mix lightly. Spread evenly in oiled 9x13-inch baking dish; press lightly. Combine corn oil with whole wheat flour and unbleached flour in bowl; mix until crumbly. Blend 1/2 teaspoon vanilla into rice syrup. Add to crumb mixture with 1/4 teaspoon cinnamon; mix well. Spread evenly over apple mixture; press firmly. Bake at 350 degrees for 45 minutes or until topping is crisp and golden brown and apples are tender. Serve hot or cold. Yield: 8 servings.

Approx Per Serving: Cal 379; Prot 5 g; Carbo 72 g; Fiber 5 g; T Fat 10 g; 23% Calories from Fat; Chol 0 mg; Sod 74 mg.

RANCH HAND APPLE DUMPLINGS

3 cups baking mix
1 cup milk
5 to 6 apples, grated
1/2 cup sugar
1 teaspoon cinnamon
1 cup sugar
1 1/2 cups water
3 cups milk
1/2 cup sugar
1 tablespoon vanilla extract
1/2 teaspoon nutmeg

Combine baking mix and 1 cup milk in bowl; mix to form soft dough. Roll to 12x16-inch rectangle on floured surface. Spread apples over dough; sprinkle with 1/2 cup sugar and cinnamon. Roll from long side to enclose filling. Cut into 1-inch slices; arrange in baking pans. Bring 1 cup sugar and water to a boil in saucepan. Pour over slices. Bake at 400 degrees for 20 to 25 minutes or until golden brown. Mix milk with remaining ingredients in bowl. Serve dumplings hot or cold with milk sauce. Yield: 14 servings.

Approx Per Serving: Cal 303; Prot 4 g; Carbo 58 g; Fiber 1 g; T Fat 6 g; 19% Calories from Fat; Chol 9 mg; Sod 370 mg.

APRICOT-CREAM CHEESE MOLD

2 3-ounce packages apricot
  gelatin
2 cups boiling water
1 pint vanilla ice cream

1 16-ounce can juice-pack apricot
  halves
3 ounces cream cheese, softened

Dissolve gelatin in boiling water in bowl. Chill until slightly thickened. Combine ice cream, apricots and cream cheese in blender container; process until smooth. Add to gelatin; mix well. Spoon into mold. Chill until firm. Unmold onto serving plate; garnish with cherries and whipped cream. May substitute ice milk or frozen yogurt for ice cream or light sour cream or cream cheese for regular cream cheese. Yield: 8 servings.

Approx Per Serving: Cal 210; Prot 4 g; Carbo 34 g; Fiber 1 g;
  T Fat 7 g; 30% Calories from Fat; Chol 26 mg; Sod 130 mg.

BANANAS GUADALUPE

4 large bananas
6 tablespoons unsalted butter
1/2 cup sugar
1 cup whipping cream

2 to 3 tablespoons white rum
3/4 teaspoon vanilla extract
Cloves or freshly ground nutmeg
  to taste

Peel bananas and slice into halves lengthwise. Sauté gently in butter in skillet until golden brown. Drain on paper towel. Place on shallow serving platter. Cool. Sprinkle bananas with 1/4 cup sugar. Beat whipping cream in mixer bowl until soft peaks form. Fold in remaining 1/4 cup sugar, rum and vanilla. Spoon over bananas to cover completely. Chill in refrigerator. Sprinkle lightly with cloves or nutmeg just before serving. Yield: 4 servings.

Approx Per Serving: Cal 583; Prot 3 g; Carbo 53 g; Fiber 2 g;
  T Fat 40 g; 62% Calories from Fat; Chol 128 mg; Sod 26 mg.

The heart that has truly loved never forgets.
—Thomas More

BUTTERFINGER DESSERT

1/2 cup margarine, softened
2 cups confectioners' sugar
4 egg yolks
1 teaspoon vanilla extract

1 pint whipping cream, whipped
1 angel food cake
6 3-ounce Butterfinger bars,
 crushed

Combine margarine, confectioners' sugar, egg yolks and vanilla in bowl; mix well. Fold in whipped cream. Tear cake into small pieces. Layer cake pieces, whipped cream mixture and candy 1/2 at a time in 12x16-inch dish. Freeze until firm. Let stand at room temperature for 5 to 10 minutes before serving. May use egg substitute in place of uncooked egg yolks if preferred. Yield: 12 servings.

Approx Per Serving: Cal 622; Prot 8 g; Carbo 78 g; Fiber <1 g;
 T Fat 33 g; 47% Calories from Fat; Chol 125 mg; Sod 450 mg.

WHITE CHOCOLATE CHEESECAKE

Don't count the calories in this recipe.

32 ounces cream cheese, softened
1 cup sugar
1 tablespoon vanilla extract
4 eggs
8 ounces white chocolate, melted,
 cooled

2 cups thawed frozen raspberries
1 cup sugar
1/2 cup Framboise or Chambord

Beat cream cheese in mixer bowl until smooth. Add 1 cup sugar and vanilla; mix well. Beat in eggs. Fold in chocolate. Spoon into 10-inch springform pan; place in larger pan with 1 inch hot water. Bake at 300 degrees for 1 hour or until wooden pick inserted in center comes out clean. Cool on wire rack. Chill in refrigerator. Combine raspberries, 1 cup sugar and Framboise in blender container; process until smooth. Strain into bowl. Serve over cheesecake. Garnish with whipped cream. Yield: 12 servings.

Approx Per Serving: Cal 602; Prot 9 g; Carbo 62 g; Fiber 2 g;
 T Fat 34 g; 52% Calories from Fat; Chol 158 mg; Sod 264 mg.

Desserts

LIGHT HEAVEN CHEESECAKE

2 envelopes unflavored gelatin	1 cup ricotta cheese
1 cup fructose	1 recipe graham cracker crust
2 cups plain yogurt	2 cups sliced strawberries

Combine gelatin, fructose, yogurt and ricotta cheese in blender container; process until smooth. Chill until partially set. Spoon into dish lined with graham cracker crust. Chill until firm. Top with strawberries. May substitute other fruit for strawberries. Yield: 10 servings.

Approx Per Serving: Cal 353; Prot 7 g; Carbo 52 g; Fiber 2 g; T Fat 14 g; 34% Calories from Fat; Chol 18 mg; Sod 234 mg.

SOUR CREAM CHEESECAKE

2 cups graham cracker crumbs	1 teaspoon vanilla extract
1/4 cup sugar	3 eggs
1/2 cup melted butter	2 cups sour cream
16 ounces cream cheese, softened	1/2 cup sugar
1/2 cup sugar	1 teaspoon vanilla extract

Combine graham cracker crumbs, 1/4 cup sugar and butter in bowl; mix well. Press mixture into springform pan. Beat cream cheese, 1/2 cup sugar and 1 teaspoon vanilla in mixer bowl until smooth. Beat in eggs 1 at a time by hand. Spoon into prepared pan. Bake at 375 degrees for 30 minutes or until set. Cool on wire rack. Spread mixture of sour cream, 1/2 cup sugar and 1 teaspoon vanilla over top. Bake for 10 minutes longer. Cool on wire rack. Chill until serving time. Yield: 12 servings.

Approx Per Serving: Cal 468; Prot 8 g; Carbo 39 g; Fiber 1 g; T Fat 32 g; 62% Calories from Fat; Chol 132 mg; Sod 337 mg.

The highest reward for a person's toil is not what they get for it, but what they become by it.

—John Ruskin

 *Desserts*

BRANDIED CHOCOLATE FONDUE

4 ounces German's sweet chocolate
2 ounces semisweet chocolate chips
2 tablespoons water
2 tablespoons half and half

2 tablespoons brandy
1½ teaspoons instant coffee granules
Cinnamon to taste

Combine chocolate, chocolate chips and water in double boiler. Cook over hot but not boiling water until chocolate melts, stirring to blend well. Add half and half, brandy, coffee granules and cinnamon; mix well. Cook until heated through. Spoon into fondue pot. Serve with pineapple cubes, mandarin orange sections, banana chunks, apple slices, strawberries, pretzels, cookies, pound cake cubes or marshmallows and forks for dipping. May substitute orange juice or Cointreau for brandy and omit cinnamon if preferred. May melt chocolate in microwave on Medium. Yield: 4 servings.

Approx Per Serving: Cal 242; Prot 2 g; Carbo 28 g; Fiber <1 g;
T Fat 16 g; 54% Calories from Fat; Chol 3 mg; Sod 7 mg.

CHOCOLATE DREAM DESSERT

1 cup flour
½ cup chopped walnuts
½ cup margarine
8 ounces cream cheese, softened
1 teaspoon vanilla extract
2 12-ounce containers whipped topping

2 4-ounce packages chocolate instant pudding mix
2½ cups milk
½ cup chopped walnuts

Combine flour, ½ cup walnuts and margarine in bowl; mix well. Press mixture into 9x13-inch baking dish. Bake at 450 degrees until golden brown. Cool on wire rack. Beat cream cheese and vanilla in mixer bowl until smooth. Fold in half the whipped topping. Spread over crust. Combine pudding mix with milk in bowl; mix well. Spread over cream cheese layer. Top with remaining whipped topping; sprinkle with ½ cup walnuts. Freeze for 8 to 10 hours. May top with chocolate slivers if preferred. Yield: 15 servings.

Approx Per Serving: Cal 414; Prot 5 g; Carbo 35 g; Fiber 1 g;
T Fat 29 g; 62% Calories from Fat; Chol 22 mg; Sod 247 mg.

Desserts

CUPCAKE BLINTZES

16 ounces small curd cottage
   cheese
3 tablespoons sour cream
3 eggs

½ cup baking mix
2 tablespoons sugar
¼ cup melted butter

Combine cottage cheese, sour cream, eggs, baking mix, sugar and butter in mixer bowl; beat until smooth. Spoon into greased muffin cups. Bake at 350 degrees for 35 to 40 minutes or until golden brown. Serve with sour cream and cherry or blueberry sauce. Yield: 12 servings.

Approx Per Serving: Cal 131; Prot 7 g; Carbo 7 g; Fiber 0 g;
   T Fat 8 g; 58% Calories from Fat; Chol 71 mg; Sod 271 mg.

MINTED FRUIT DESSERT

1 cup ³/₄-inch pineapple pieces
1 cup sliced kiwifruit
2 tablespoons chopped mint leaves

2 tablespoons each white and
   green Crème de Menthe
1 pint pineapple sherbet

Combine pineapple, kiwifruit and mint in bowl; mix well. Add Crème de Menthe; mix gently. Add sherbet; mix gently. Spoon into stemmed glasses. Garnish with fresh raspberries and additional mint leaves. Yield: 8 servings.

Approx Per Serving: Cal 119; Prot 1 g; Carbo 23 g; Fiber 1 g;
   T Fat 1 g; 9% Calories from Fat; Chol 4 mg; Sod 24 mg.

AVOCADO ICE CREAM

1 14-ounce can evaporated milk,
   chilled
½ cup orange juice

½ cup lemon juice
1½ cups sugar
1 cup mashed avocado

Beat evaporated milk in chilled bowl until almost doubled in volume. Add mixture of juices, sugar and avocado; mix well. Spoon into freezer container. Freeze until firm. May double recipe to freeze in ice cream freezer. Yield: 4 servings.

Approx Per Serving: Cal 536; Prot 8 g; Carbo 95 g; Fiber 6 g;
   T Fat 17 g; 27% Calories from Fat; Chol 29 mg; Sod 114 mg.

LEMON ICE CREAM

3 cups sugar
4 cups milk
¾ cup lemon juice

Juice of 1 orange
2 cups whipping cream, whipped

Combine sugar and milk in large bowl; mix well. Stir in mixture of lemon juice and orange juice. Fold in whipped cream. Spoon into airtight container. Freeze until firm. Yield: 8 servings.

Approx Per Serving: Cal 579; Prot 5 g; Carbo 85 g; Fiber <1 g; T Fat 26 g; 39% Calories from Fat; Chol 98 mg; Sod 75 mg.

LEMON MOUSSE

8 egg yolks
3 cups sugar
2 envelopes unflavored gelatin
½ cup cold water
2 teaspoons cornstarch

Juice and grated rind of 6 lemons
½ cup Grand Marnier
3 cups whipping cream
6 tablespoons confectioners' sugar
8 egg whites

Beat egg yolks with sugar in mixer bowl until thick and lemon colored. Soften gelatin in cold water in double boiler. Heat over hot water, stirring until gelatin dissolves. Blend cornstarch with ⅓ of the lemon juice in large bowl. Add remaining lemon juice, lemon rind and gelatin mixture; mix well. Add to egg mixture. Pour into double boiler. Cook over hot water until thickened, stirring constantly. Stir in half the liqueur. Cook for 1 minute longer; do not boil. Chill until mixture begins to set. Beat remaining liqueur with whipping cream and confectioners' sugar in mixer bowl until soft peaks form. Beat egg whites in mixer bowl until stiff but not dry. Fold whipped cream mixture and egg whites into lemon mixture. Spoon into soufflé dish or individual serving dishes. Chill until serving time. Garnish with toasted slivered almonds. Yield: 16 servings.

Approx Per Serving: Cal 375; Prot 5 g; Carbo 46 g; Fiber <1 g; T Fat 19 g; 46% Calories from Fat; Chol 168 mg; Sod 48 mg.

COLD GRAND MARNIER SOUFFLÉ

2 envelopes unflavored gelatin	1/4 cup Grand Marnier
3/4 cup orange juice	1/4 cup lemon juice
6 egg yolks	Salt to taste
Grated rind of 2 oranges and 1 lemon	6 egg whites
	3/4 cup sugar
1 1/4 cups sugar	2 1/2 cups whipping cream

Cut a piece of waxed paper long enough to serve as collar of soufflé dish.
Fold paper into halves, oil inside and tie around dish. Soften gelatin in 1/2
cup orange juice in small bowl. Place in hot water; stir until gelatin dissolves.
Combine remaining orange juice with egg yolks, orange rind, lemon rind,
1 1/4 cups sugar, liqueur, lemon juice and salt in heavy saucepan; mix well.
Cook until sugar dissolves and mixture coats spoon; remove from heat. Beat
in gelatin mixture. Cool over ice or in refrigerator just until mixture is syrupy.
Beat egg whites in mixer bowl until soft peaks form. Add 3/4 cup sugar
gradually, beating until stiff peaks form. Whip cream in mixer bowl until
soft peaks form. Reserve a small amount of whipped cream for topping.
Fold remaining whipped cream and beaten egg whites into gelatin mixture.
Spoon into prepared dish. Chill overnight or until firm. Remove collar carefully. Pipe reserved whipped cream into rosettes on top; garnish with candied
violets. Yield: 12 servings.

Approx Per Serving: Cal 365; Prot 5 g; Carbo 39 g; Fiber <1 g;
T Fat 21 g; 52% Calories from Fat; Chol 174 mg; Sod 50 mg.

*The future belongs to those who believe in the beauty of
their dreams.*

—Eleanor Roosevelt

CRANBERRY STEAMED PUDDING

*This is a traditional holiday dessert from my
great-grandmother, Hazel Rogers.*

1 egg	2¹/₂ teaspoons baking powder
²/₃ cup sugar	2¹/₂ cups (about) flour
1 tablespoon shortening	1¹/₂ cups whole cranberries
1 cup milk	Cinnamon Sauce

Combine egg, sugar, shortening, milk, baking powder and enough flour to make a thick batter in bowl; mix well. Fold in cranberries. Spoon into greased 3-pound coffee can. Place coffee can in large stockpot. Fill stockpot with hot water nearly to top of coffee can. Cover coffee can tightly with foil. Steam for 1¹/₂ hours. Serve warm with Cinnamon Sauce. Yield: 12 servings.

Cinnamon Sauce

¹/₄ cup cornstarch	¹/₂ cup butter
2 cups sugar	¹/₄ teaspoon salt
4 cups boiling water	Cinnamon to taste

Mix cornstarch and sugar in bowl. Stir into boiling water in saucepan. Add butter, salt and cinnamon. Cook until thickened, stirring constantly. Yield: 12 servings.

Approx Per Serving: Cal 409; Prot 3 g; Carbo 67 g; Fiber 2 g; T Fat 11 g; 24% Calories from Fat; Chol 43 mg; Sod 232 mg.

When one door of happiness closes, another opens; but often we look so long at the closed door that we do not see the one which has been opened for us.

—Helen Keller

GRAHAM CRACKER PUDDING

18 to 20 cinnamon crisp graham
  crackers, finely crushed
5 tablespoons brown sugar
3 tablespoons margarine, softened
1 cup sugar
3 tablespoons flour

1/8 teaspoon salt
2²/3 cups milk
3 egg yolks, beaten
1 teaspoon vanilla extract
3 egg whites

Pat half the graham cracker crumbs in bottom of 8x8-inch pan. Mix brown sugar and margarine in small bowl. Drop by teaspoonfuls over graham cracker crumbs; set aside. Combine sugar, flour and salt in saucepan. Add 1/2 cup milk. Cook over medium heat, stirring until smooth. Add a small amount of mixture to beaten egg yolks. Stir egg yolks into milk mixture, beating constantly. Add remaining milk. Cook until mixture begins to boil and thicken, stirring constantly. Stir in vanilla; remove from heat. Pour over graham cracker crumbs. Beat egg whites in mixer bowl until stiff peaks form. Spread over custard mixture. Sprinkle with remaining graham cracker crumbs. Chill for 4 hours to overnight. Yield: 16 servings.

Approx Per Serving: Cal 150; Prot 3 g; Carbo 23 g; Fiber <1 g;
  T Fat 5 g; 31% Calories from Fat; Chol 45 mg; Sod 98 mg.

OZARK PUDDING

1 egg
3/4 cup sugar
2 tablespoons flour
1¹/4 teaspoons baking powder

1/8 teaspoon salt
1/2 cup chopped pecans
1/2 cup chopped apples
1 teaspoon vanilla extract

Beat egg and sugar in bowl until smooth. Mix flour, baking powder and salt together. Stir into egg mixture. Add pecans, apples and vanilla, stirring well. Pour into greased 8x8-inch pan. Bake at 350 degrees for 35 minutes. Serve topped with ice cream or whipped cream. Yield: 6 servings.

Approx Per Serving: Cal 192; Prot 2 g; Carbo 31 g; Fiber 1 g;
  T Fat 8 g; 35% Calories from Fat; Chol 36 mg; Sod 125 mg.

BAKED HALVA (Wheat Pudding)

3³/4 cups farina
2 teaspoons flour
3¹/2 teaspoons baking powder
2 cups melted butter
1¹/4 cups sugar
1¹/4 cups milk

12 egg yolks, beaten
1 tablespoon almond extract
12 egg whites
4 cups sugar
4 cups water
1 teaspoon vanilla extract

Mix farina, flour and baking powder together. Combine butter and 1¹/4 cups sugar in mixer bowl; mix until smooth. Add milk, egg yolks and almond extract; mix well. Stir in farina mixture. Beat egg whites in mixer bowl until stiff peaks form. Fold into pudding. Spoon into greased 9x13-inch baking dish. Bake at 375 degrees for 25 minutes. Cool for 5 minutes. Cut into squares in pan. Combine 4 cups sugar and water in saucepan. Cook over medium heat for 15 minutes. Cool for 5 minutes. Stir in vanilla. Pour over halva. Let stand, covered with foil, until cool. Store in refrigerator. Yield: 15 servings.

Approx Per Serving: Cal 729; Prot 11 g; Carbo 106 g; Fiber <1 g;
T Fat 30 g; 37% Calories from Fat; Chol 239 mg; Sod 341 mg.

BLACKBERRY COBBLER DELIGHT

2 cups sifted flour
2 tablespoons sugar
¹/4 teaspoon baking powder
¹/4 teaspoon salt
¹/2 cup butter

4 cups blackberries
1 cup sugar
³/4 teaspoon cinnamon
1 cup sour cream
2 egg yolks

Sift flour, 2 tablespoons sugar, baking powder and salt into bowl. Cut in butter with pastry blender or work in with fingers until crumbly. Press firmly over bottom and halfway up sides of 8x8-inch baking pan. Chill in refrigerator. Spread blackberries in prepared pan. Sprinkle with mixture of 1 cup sugar and cinnamon. Bake at 400 degrees for 15 minutes. Combine sour cream and egg yolks in bowl; mix well. Pour over blackberries. Bake for 25 to 30 minutes longer or until set. Serve at room temperature.
Yield: 9 servings.

Approx Per Serving: Cal 381; Prot 5 g; Carbo 54 g; Fiber 5 g;
T Fat 17 g; 40% Calories from Fat; Chol 86 mg; Sod 171 mg.

Desserts

OLD-FASHIONED PEACH COBBLER

¼ cup cornstarch	½ cup flour
1¼ cups unsweetened apple juice	⅛ teaspoon salt
10 cups sliced fresh peaches	⅛ teaspoon nutmeg
½ cup sugar	2 tablespoons margarine
½ teaspoon ground nutmeg	1 to 1½ tablespoons cold water
½ teaspoon almond extract	1 tablespoon flour

Combine cornstarch and ¼ cup apple juice; mix well and set aside. Combine peaches, remaining 1 cup apple juice, sugar and ½ teaspoon nutmeg in large saucepan. Bring to a boil; reduce heat. Simmer, covered, for 8 to 10 minutes or until peaches are tender. Stir in cornstarch mixture. Cook until thickened and bubbly, stirring constantly; remove from heat. Stir in almond extract. Let mixture stand to cool. Combine ½ cup flour, salt and ⅛ teaspoon nutmeg in medium bowl. Cut in margarine until mixture is crumbly. Sprinkle cold water over mixture 1 tablespoon at a time, stirring with fork until moistened. Shape dough into a ball. Sprinkle 1 tablespoon flour over flat surface. Roll out dough to 8-inch square; cut into ½-inch strips. Spoon cooled peach mixture into 8x8-inch baking dish sprayed with nonstick cooking spray. Arrange pastry strips lattice-style over peaches, sealing to edges of dish. Bake at 425 degrees for 20 minutes or until golden brown and bubbly. Garnish with fresh sprig of mint. Serve warm. Yield: 6 servings.

Approx Per Serving: Cal 306; Prot 3 g; Carbo 68 g; Fiber 5 g;
  T Fat 4 g; 12% Calories from Fat; Chol 0 mg; Sod 93 mg.

RASPBERRY DELIGHT

32 marshmallows	1 cup raspberries
½ cup raspberry juice	18 graham crackers, crushed
1 cup whipped cream	2 tablespoons melted butter

Combine marshmallows and raspberry juice in top of double boiler. Cook over boiling water until marshmallows are melted, stirring frequently. Set aside to cool. Fold in whipped cream and raspberries. Toss graham cracker crumbs with melted butter. Reserve 2 to 3 tablespoons mixture. Pat remaining graham cracker crumb mixture into 6x12-inch glass dish. Pour raspberry mixture over graham cracker crust; sprinkle with reserved crumbs. Chill for several hours before serving. Yield: 8 servings.

Approx Per Serving: Cal 248; Prot 2 g; Carbo 39 g; Fiber 1 g;
  T Fat 10 g; 36% Calories from Fat; Chol 28 mg; Sod 151 mg.

RHUBARB CRUNCH

1 cup flour
3/4 cup rolled oats
1 cup packed brown sugar
1 teaspoon cinnamon
2 cups melted butter

2 cups chopped rhubarb
1/2 cup sugar
1 teaspoon cornstarch
1/2 cup water
1/2 teaspoon vanilla extract

Combine flour, oats, brown sugar, cinnamon and melted butter in bowl, stirring until crumbly. Pat half the mixture into 9x9-inch pan. Arrange rhubarb over crust. Combine sugar, cornstarch, water and vanilla in saucepan. Cook until thickened and clear, stirring frequently. Pour over rhubarb. Top with remaining crumb mixture. Bake at 350 degrees for 1 hour. May substitute any fruit desired for rhubarb. Yield: 8 servings.

Approx Per Serving: Cal 676; Prot 4 g; Carbo 64 g; Fiber 2 g; T Fat 47 g; 61% Calories from Fat; Chol 124 mg; Sod 404 mg.

SUMMER TRIFLE

This is a gorgeous dessert and very elegant if ladyfingers are used.

1 6-ounce package vanilla
  instant pudding mix
1 cup sour cream
1 cup milk
1 teaspoon grated orange rind

2 cups whipping cream, whipped
1/2 prepared angel food cake, cut
  into cubes
4 cups sliced strawberries

Combine pudding mix, sour cream, milk and orange rind in bowl. Beat until thickened. Fold in whipped cream. Layer 1/2 of the cake, 1/3 of the strawberries and 1/2 of the pudding mixture in clear glass trifle bowl; repeat layers, topping with remaining strawberries. Garnish with whipped cream. Chill for 1 hour before serving. May substitute raspberries or other berries for strawberries and line bowl with ladyfingers instead of cake. Yield: 10 servings.

Approx Per Serving: Cal 403; Prot 5 g; Carbo 45 g; Fiber 3 g; T Fat 24 g; 52% Calories from Fat; Chol 79 mg; Sod 317 mg.

 *I shall hear in Heaven.*

—Ludwig Van Beethoven, last words

RASPBERRY ZABAGLIONE

6 egg yolks
1 egg
3 tablespoons sugar
1/2 cup anisette

1 cup fresh raspberries
1/4 cup maraschino liqueur
1 tablespoon sugar

Combine egg yolks, egg and 3 tablespoons sugar in top of double boiler. Cook over boiling water until pale yellow and fluffy, beating constantly with wire whisk. Add anisette gradually. Cook until mixture is thickened, whisking constantly; remove from heat. Combine raspberries, maraschino liqueur and 1 tablespoon sugar in small bowl; mix well. Layer custard mixture and a small amount of raspberry mixture in tall stemmed glass. Repeat layers. Yield: 6 servings.

Approx Per Serving: Cal 242; Prot 4 g; Carbo 25 g; Fiber 1 g; T Fat 7 g; 25% Calories from Fat; Chol 248 mg; Sod 22 mg.

FLAT APPLE PIE

1 cup shortening
3 cups flour
1 teaspoon salt
1 egg yolk
1/2 cup milk
10 apples, sliced
11/2 cups sugar
3/4 cup raisins
1/2 cup walnuts

2 tablespoons lemon juice
3 tablespoons flour
1 teaspoon cinnamon
1/2 teaspoon each cloves and mace
2 tablespoons margarine
1 egg white
1 tablespoon sugar
1 teaspoon vanilla extract
1/2 cup confectioners' sugar

Cut shortening into mixture of 3 cups flour and salt in bowl. Add egg yolk and milk; mix to form soft dough. Divide into 1/3 and 2/3 portions. Roll larger portion on floured surface to fit 10x15-inch baking pan. Fit into pan. Combine apples, 11/2 cups sugar, raisins, walnuts, lemon juice, 3 tablespoons flour, cinnamon, cloves and mace in bowl; mix lightly. Spread in prepared pan; dot with margarine. Roll remaining pastry on floured surface. Place over apple mixture. Pastry need not fit perfectly; do not seal edges. Beat egg white with 1 tablespoon sugar and vanilla in bowl. Spread over pastry. Bake at 375 degrees for 50 to 60 minutes or until golden brown. Mix confectioners' sugar with enough water to make of drizzling consistency in bowl. Drizzle over hot pie. Yield: 16 servings.

Approx Per Serving: Cal 409; Prot 4 g; Carbo 62 g; Fiber 3 g; T Fat 18 g; 40% Calories from Fat; Chol 14 mg; Sod 159 mg.

SOUR CREAM-APPLE PIE

1½ cups sugar
1 cup water
1 teaspoon cinnamon
¼ teaspoon each allspice and
  nutmeg
1 tablespoon cornstarch

1 tablespoon fresh lemon juice
8 cups thinly sliced Golden
  Delicious apples
1 unbaked 10-inch pie shell
2 tablespoons butter
1 cup sour cream

Combine first 5 ingredients in saucepan. Cook over low heat until sugar dissolves. Bring to a rolling boil; boil for 5 minutes. Dissolve cornstarch in lemon juice in cup. Stir into hot syrup. Cook until thickened and clear, stirring constantly. Add apple slices. Simmer until apples are tender, stirring frequently. Spoon into pie shell; dot with butter. Bake at 425 degrees for 30 minutes. Beat sour cream in mixer bowl until smooth. Spread over apples. Bake for 5 minutes or until sour cream is set. Yield: 8 servings.

Approx Per Serving: Cal 432; Prot 3 g; Carbo 70 g; Fiber 3 g;
  T Fat 18 g; 35% Calories from Fat; Chol 21 mg; Sod 193 mg.

GERMAN CHOCOLATE ANGEL PIE

2 egg whites
⅛ teaspoon salt
⅛ teaspoon cream of tartar
½ cup sugar
1 teaspoon vanilla extract
½ cup finely chopped pecans

4 ounces German's sweet
  chocolate
3 tablespoons water
1 teaspoon vanilla extract
1 cup whipping cream, whipped

Beat egg whites with salt and cream of tartar in mixer bowl until foamy. Add sugar gradually, beating until stiff. Fold in 1 teaspoon vanilla and pecans. Spread over bottom and side of greased 8-inch pie plate. Bake at 300 degrees for 50 to 55 minutes. Cool completely. Melt chocolate with water in saucepan over low heat, stirring constantly. Add remaining 1 teaspoon vanilla; mix well. Fold in whipped cream. Pour into prepared pie shell. Chill in refrigerator for 2 hours. Yield: 8 servings.

Approx Per Serving: Cal 276; Prot 3 g; Carbo 23 g; Fiber <1 g;
  T Fat 21 g; 64% Calories from Fat; Chol 41 mg; Sod 58 mg.

THE WILLOWS SKY-HIGH COCONUT CREAM PIE

1/2 cup sugar	1 teaspoon vanilla extract
1/4 cup cornstarch	1/2 cup shredded coconut
1/8 teaspoon salt	1 baked 9-inch pie shell, cooled
2 cups milk	6 egg whites, at room temperature
4 egg yolks	6 tablespoons sugar
1 tablespoon butter	1/4 cup shredded coconut

Mix 1/2 cup sugar, cornstarch and salt in 11/2-quart saucepan. Add milk gradually, stirring until smooth. Cook over low heat until thickened, stirring constantly; do not boil. Remove from heat. Whisk egg yolks in small bowl until thick. Stir a small amount of hot mixture into egg yolks; stir egg yolks into hot mixture. Cook over low heat until very thick, whisking constantly; do not boil. Remove from heat. Stir in butter, vanilla and 1/2 cup coconut; cool to room temperature. Spoon into pie shell. Beat egg whites in large mixer bowl until frothy. Add 6 tablespoons sugar, beating constantly until stiff peaks form. Spread evenly over filling; sprinkle with 1/4 cup coconut. Bake at 350 degrees for 4 to 5 minutes or until light brown. Cool for 2 to 3 hours before serving. May prepare in advance and store in refrigerator for up to 4 days, adding meringue on day to be served. Yield: 8 servings.

Approx Per Serving: Cal 350; Prot 8 g; Carbo 43 g; Fiber 1 g;
  T Fat 17 g; 43% Calories from Fat; Chol 119 mg; Sod 273 mg.

RECIPE FOR RAPTURE (Fresh Huckleberry Pie)

4 cups huckleberries	2 tablespoons lemon juice
1/2 cup water	1 baked 9-inch pie shell
2 tablespoons cornstarch	3 ounces cream cheese, softened
3/4 cup sugar	2 cups whipped cream

Combine 1 cup huckleberries and water in saucepan. Bring to a boil; reduce heat. Simmer for 2 minutes to make syrup. Combine cornstarch and sugar in bowl. Add to syrup gradually. Cook until thickened and clear, stirring constantly. Cool slightly; add lemon juice. Spread pie shell with cream cheese. Cover cream cheese with remaining 3 cups fresh huckleberries. Pour cooled sauce over huckleberries. Top with whipped cream. Yield: 8 servings.

Approx Per Serving: Cal 366; Prot 3 g; Carbo 39 g; Fiber 3 g;
  T Fat 23 g; 54% Calories from Fat; Chol 52 mg; Sod 181 mg.

BUTTERMILK-LEMON PIE

1/2 cup margarine	1 cup buttermilk
Juice of 1 lemon	2 teaspoons grated lemon rind
3 egg yolks	1 baked 8 or 9-inch pie shell
2 tablespoons flour	3 egg whites
1 cup sugar	1/4 cup sugar
1/4 teaspoon salt	

Melt margarine in saucepan; remove from heat. Add lemon juice and egg yolks, mixing well. Add mixture of flour, 1 cup sugar and salt alternately with buttermilk, mixing well after each addition. Stir in lemon rind. Cook until thickened, stirring constantly. Spoon into pie shell. Beat egg whites with 1/4 cup sugar in mixer bowl until stiff peaks form. Spread over pie, sealing to edge. Bake at 350 degrees for 15 minutes or until golden brown. Yield: 6 servings.

Approx Per Serving: Cal 514; Prot 7 g; Carbo 60 g; Fiber 1 g;
  T Fat 28 g; 49% Calories from Fat; Chol 108 mg; Sod 523 mg.

TWO-CRUST LEMON PIE

1 lemon	3 eggs
1/2 cup water	1 recipe 2-crust pie pastry
11/4 cups sugar	1 tablespoon egg white
1/4 cup butter	1 tablespoon sugar
2 tablespoons flour	Cinnamon to taste
1/8 teaspoon salt	

Peel and seed lemon, reserving 1/3 of the rind. Cut lemon into quarters. Combine with reserved rind and water in blender container; process until well chopped. Add 11/4 cups sugar, butter, flour and salt; process until smooth. Add eggs; process until smooth. Spoon into pastry-lined pie plate; top with remaining pastry. Brush with egg white; sprinkle with mixture of 1 tablespoon sugar and cinnamon. Bake at 400 degrees for 30 minutes. Cool on wire rack. Yield: 6 servings.

Approx Per Serving: Cal 560; Prot 7 g; Carbo 70 g; Fiber 1 g;
  T Fat 28 g; 45% Calories from Fat; Chol 127 mg; Sod 517 mg.

MACADAMIA NUT CREAM PIE

1 cup milk
¼ cup sugar
¼ cup chopped macadamia nuts
Salt to taste
1 teaspoon vanilla extract
⅓ cup milk
1 egg

5 teaspoons cornstarch
2 egg whites
½ cup sugar
1 baked 9-inch pie shell
1 cup whipping cream, whipped
¼ cup sugar
¼ cup chopped macadamia nuts

Combine 1 cup milk, ¼ cup sugar, ¼ cup macadamia nuts, salt and vanilla in saucepan. Cook just to the simmering point; remove from heat. Blend ⅓ cup milk with egg and cornstarch in bowl. Stir a small amount of hot mixture into egg mixture; stir egg mixture into hot mixture. Cook for 5 minutes or until thickened, stirring constantly. Cool for 1 hour. Beat egg whites in mixer bowl until soft peaks form. Add ½ cup sugar, beating constantly until stiff peaks form. Fold into cooled filling. Spoon into pie shell. Chill until serving time. Top with mixture of whipped cream and ¼ cup sugar; sprinkle with ¼ cup macadamia nuts. Yield: 8 servings.

Approx Per Serving: Cal 410; Prot 6 g; Carbo 40 g; Fiber 1 g;
T Fat 26 g; 56% Calories from Fat; Chol 73 mg; Sod 188 mg.

PEANUT PIE

¾ cup packed brown sugar
2 tablespoons flour
2 tablespoons cornstarch
½ teaspoon salt
2 cups milk
3 egg yolks, beaten
1 teaspoon vanilla extract

1 tablespoon butter
1 cup roasted peanuts, chopped
1 baked 8 or 9-inch pie shell
3 egg whites
1 tablespoon sugar
Salt to taste

Mix brown sugar, flour, cornstarch and ½ teaspoon salt in saucepan. Add milk; mix well. Cook over low heat until thickened, stirring constantly. Stir a small amount of hot mixture into egg yolks; stir egg yolks into hot mixture. Cook for 2 to 3 minutes or until thickened, stirring constantly. Add vanilla, butter and peanuts. Cool slightly. Spoon into pie shell. Beat egg whites with sugar and salt to taste in mixer bowl until stiff peaks form. Spread over pie, sealing to edge. Bake at 425 degrees just until golden brown. Yield: 8 servings.

Approx Per Serving: Cal 414; Prot 11 g; Carbo 46 g; Fiber 2 g;
T Fat 22 g; 47% Calories from Fat; Chol 92 mg; Sod 344 mg.

 *Pies*

SOUR CREAM PEACH PIE

½ cup butter	1 egg
1½ cups flour	¼ teaspoon salt
½ teaspoon salt	½ teaspoon vanilla extract
4 cups sliced peaches	1 cup sour cream
1 cup sugar	Cinnamon Topping
2 tablespoons flour	

Cut butter into mixture of 1½ cups flour and ½ teaspoon salt until crumbly. Pat into bottom of 9-inch pie plate. Combine peaches and ¼ cup sugar in bowl; mix well. Combine ¾ cup sugar, 2 tablespoons flour, egg, ¼ teaspoon salt and vanilla in bowl; mix well. Add peaches; mix well. Fold in sour cream. Pour into prepared pie plate. Bake at 400 degrees for 15 minutes. Reduce temperature to 350 degrees. Bake for 20 minutes longer. Sprinkle with Cinnamon Topping. Increase temperature to 400 degrees. Bake for 10 minutes. Cool before cutting. May substitute apples for peaches.
Yield: 8 servings.

Cinnamon Topping

⅓ cup sugar	1 teaspoon cinnamon
⅓ cup flour	¼ cup butter

Combine sugar, flour and cinnamon in bowl; mix well. Cut in butter until crumbly. Yield: 8 servings.

Approx Per Serving: Cal 500; Prot 6 g; Carbo 67 g; Fiber 2 g;
    T Fat 24 g; 43% Calories from Fat; Chol 86 mg; Sod 371 mg.

How beautifully the leaves grow old. How full of light and colour are their last days.

—John Burroughs

MERRYFIELD APPLE CAKES

3 cups flour
2 cups sugar
1 cup oil
3 eggs
1 teaspoon baking soda
1 teaspoon salt

2 teaspoons vanilla extract
3 cups chopped peeled apples
1 cup chopped California walnuts
1/2 cup chopped dark seedless
  raisins
1/2 cup confectioners' sugar

Combine flour, sugar, oil, eggs, baking soda, salt and vanilla in mixer bowl. Beat at low speed until well mixed, scraping bowl constantly. Beat for 3 minutes longer, scraping bowl occasionally. Stir in apples, walnuts and raisins. Spread evenly in 2 greased and floured 8-inch round cake pans. Bake at 325 degrees for 1 hour or until golden brown. Cool in pans on wire rack for 10 minutes. Remove to wire racks to cool completely. Chill, wrapped, for up to 1 week. Place paper doily over cake surface. Sprinkle with confectioners' sugar. Remove doily. Yield: 18 servings.

Approx Per Serving: Cal 378; Prot 4 g; Carbo 53 g; Fiber 2 g;
  T Fat 18 g; 41% Calories from Fat; Chol 36 mg; Sod 178 mg.

BANANA CAKE

2 1/4 cups flour
1 2/3 cups sugar
1 1/4 teaspoons baking powder
1/4 teaspoon baking soda
1 teaspoon salt

2/3 cup shortening
2/3 cup milk
3 eggs
1 1/4 cups mashed bananas

Sift flour, sugar, baking powder, baking soda and salt in bowl. Add shortening, milk and eggs; mix well. Stir in bananas. Pour into nonstick bundt pan. Bake at 350 degrees for 1 hour. Cool in pan for 35 minutes. Invert onto serving plate. Yield: 16 servings.

Approx Per Serving: Cal 257; Prot 4 g; Carbo 39 g; Fiber 1 g;
  T Fat 10 g; 35% Calories from Fat; Chol 41 mg; Sod 177 mg.

 *Cakes*

BUTTER CAKE

1 2-layer package yellow cake
   mix
2 eggs
1/2 cup melted butter

8 ounces cream cheese, softened
1 1-pound package confectioners'
   sugar
2 eggs

Combine cake mix, 2 eggs and melted butter in bowl; mix well. Spread in greased 9x13-inch cake pan. Mix cream cheese, confectioners' sugar and 2 eggs in bowl. Spoon over cake mix mixture. Bake at 350 degrees for 30 minutes or until lightly browned. Yield: 15 servings.

Approx Per Serving: Cal 414; Prot 4 g; Carbo 65 g; Fiber 0 g;
   T Fat 16 g; 34% Calories from Fat; Chol 90 mg; Sod 325 mg.

CARROT CAKES

2 cups flour
1/4 teaspoon salt
2 teaspoons baking soda
2 teaspoons cinnamon
4 eggs
2 cups sugar
1 1/2 cups oil

3 cups grated carrots
1 cup chopped walnuts
1 1-pound package confectioners'
   sugar
8 ounces cream cheese, softened
1 teaspoon vanilla extract
1/2 cup margarine, softened

Sift flour, salt, baking soda and cinnamon together. Cream eggs, sugar and oil in mixer bowl until light and fluffy. Stir in carrots. Add flour mixture gradually, beating well after each addition. Stir in walnuts. Pour into 2 greased and floured loaf pans. Bake at 350 degrees for 35 to 40 minutes or until wooden pick inserted in center comes out clean. Combine confectioners' sugar, cream cheese and vanilla in bowl; mix well. Beat in margarine. Spread over cooled loaves. Yield: 24 servings.

Approx Per Serving: Cal 429; Prot 4 g; Carbo 50 g; Fiber 1 g;
   T Fat 25 g; 51% Calories from Fat; Chol 46 mg; Sod 181 mg.

Don't wait for your ship to come in. Swim out to it.

Cakes

FAMOUS PINEAPPLE-CARROT CAKE

3 cups flour
2 cups sugar
2 teaspoons baking powder
2 teaspoons baking soda
2 teaspoons salt
4 eggs
1¹/₃ cups oil
2 cups finely shredded carrots

1 cup crushed pineapple
2 teaspoons vanilla extract
3 tablespoons butter, softened
12 ounces cream cheese, softened
1 tablespoon vanilla extract
6 cups confectioners' sugar
¹/₂ cup pecan pieces

Sift flour, sugar, baking powder, baking soda and salt together. Combine eggs, oil, carrots, pineapple with juice and 2 teaspoons vanilla in mixer bowl. Add flour mixture gradually, beating well after each addition. Beat at medium speed for 2 minutes. Pour into greased and floured 11x15-inch cake pan. Bake at 350 degrees for 45 minutes. Cream butter and cream cheese in mixer bowl until light and fluffy. Beat in 1 tablespoon vanilla and confectioners' sugar. Stir in pecans. Spread over cooled cake.
Yield: 16 servings.

Approx Per Serving: Cal 677; Prot 6 g; Carbo 94 g; Fiber 2 g;
  T Fat 32 g; 43% Calories from Fat; Chol 83 mg; Sod 515 mg.

CHOCOLATE TRUFFLE CAKE

1 pound semisweet chocolate,
  coarsely chopped
10 tablespoons unsalted butter
5 egg yolks, at room temperature
5 egg whites, at room
  temperature, stiffly beaten

3 cups whipping cream
2 tablespoons sugar
¹/₂ teaspoon vanilla extract

Melt chocolate and butter in bowl in microwave; mix well. Blend in egg yolks. Fold in egg whites ¹/₄ at a time. Pour into buttered 12-inch springform pan. Bake at 375 degrees for 12 minutes. Do not overbake; cake will be loose. Cool in pan. Remove side of pan. Beat whipping cream, sugar and vanilla in bowl until stiff peaks form. Spread over top and side of cake. May serve with raspberry sauce. Yield: 16 servings.

Approx Per Serving: Cal 384; Prot 4 g; Carbo 20 g; Fiber 0 g;
  T Fat 35 g; 77% Calories from Fat; Chol 147 mg; Sod 37 mg.

MISSISSIPPI MUD CAKE

4 eggs
2 cups sugar
1 cup melted butter
1½ cups flour
⅓ cup baking cocoa
1 teaspoon vanilla extract
1 cup coconut
2 cups chopped pecans

1 7-ounce jar marshmallow creme
½ cup melted butter
⅓ cup baking cocoa
1 teaspoon vanilla extract
1 1-pound package confectioners' sugar
6 tablespoons milk

Beat eggs and sugar in large bowl until thick. Combine 1 cup butter, flour, ⅓ cup baking cocoa, 1 teaspoon vanilla, coconut and pecans in bowl; mix well. Add to egg mixture; mix well. Pour into greased and floured 9x13-inch cake pan. Bake at 350 degrees for 30 to 40 minutes or until cake tests done. Spread hot cake with marshmallow creme. Combine ½ cup melted butter, ⅓ cup baking cocoa and 1 teaspoon vanilla in bowl; mix well. Beat in confectioners' sugar. Add enough milk to make of spreading consistency. Spread over cake. May add 1 cup chopped pecans to frosting. Yield: 16 servings.

Approx Per Serving: Cal 616; Prot 5 g; Carbo 84 g; Fiber 3 g; T Fat 31 g; 45% Calories from Fat; Chol 101 mg; Sod 175 mg.

CHOCOLATE SHEET CAKE

½ cup baking cocoa
1 cup margarine
1 cup water
2 cups sugar
2 cups flour
½ cup buttermilk
2 eggs
1 teaspoon vanilla extract

1 teaspoon baking soda
¼ cup baking cocoa
6 tablespoons milk
½ cup margarine
1 1-pound package confectioners' sugar
1 teaspoon vanilla extract
1 cup chopped walnuts

Bring ½ cup baking cocoa, 1 cup margarine and water to a boil in saucepan. Simmer until margarine is melted. Stir in mixture of sugar, flour, buttermilk, eggs, 1 teaspoon vanilla and baking soda. Pour into greased and floured sheet cake pan. Bake at 350 degrees for 20 minutes. Bring ¼ cup baking cocoa, milk and ½ cup margarine to a boil in saucepan. Simmer until margarine is melted. Remove from heat. Beat in confectioners' sugar and 1 teaspoon vanilla. Stir in walnuts. Spread over cooled cake. Yield: 16 servings.

Approx Per Serving: Cal 512; Prot 5 g; Carbo 75 g; Fiber 2 g; T Fat 23 g; 40% Calories from Fat; Chol 28 mg; Sod 274 mg.

GINGERBREAD CAKE

1/2 cup butter
5 tablespoons unsulphured
  molasses (treacle)
1/4 cup golden syrup
3 tablespoons (heaping) brown
  sugar
5 tablespoons milk
1 tablespoon marmalade

1 cup self-rising flour
1/4 teaspoon baking soda
2 teaspoons (heaping) ginger
1 teaspoon (heaping) pumpkin
  pie spice
1/4 cup (heaping) whole wheat
  flour
2 eggs

Combine butter, molasses, golden syrup, brown sugar, milk and marmalade in medium saucepan. Cook over low heat until butter melts, stirring constantly. Cool to lukewarm. Sift flour, baking soda, ginger and pumpkin pie spice into bowl. Stir in oats. Add eggs and cooled syrup mixture; mix well. Spoon into 7x7-inch or 8-inch round cake pan lined with paper. Place on center shelf of oven preheated to 335 degrees. Bake for 1½ to 1¾ hours or until cake tests done. Cool in pan for 2 to 3 minutes; remove to wire rack to cool completely, removing paper. May substitute whole wheat flour for oats. Yield: 9 servings.

Approx Per Serving: Cal 250; Prot 4 g; Carbo 35 g; Fiber 1 g;
  T Fat 12 g; 43% Calories from Fat; Chol 76 mg; Sod 295 mg.

MANDARIN ORANGE CAKE

1 2-layer package yellow cake
   mix
1 cup oil
3 eggs
1 11-ounce can mandarin oranges

8 ounces whipped topping
1 16-ounce can crushed pineapple
1 4-ounce package vanilla
   instant pudding mix

Combine cake mix, oil, eggs and mandarin oranges with juice in mixer bowl; mix well. Pour into 2 greased and floured cake pans. Bake at 375 degrees for 25 minutes or until wooden pick inserted in center comes out clean. Cool in pans for several minutes. Remove to wire rack to cool completely. Mix whipped topping, pineapple with juice and pudding mix in bowl. Spread between layers and over top and side of cake. Garnish with coconut. Yield: 12 servings.

Approx Per Serving: Cal 504; Prot 4 g; Carbo 61 g; Fiber 9 g;
  T Fat 28 g; 49% Calories from Fat; Chol 53 mg; Sod 349 mg.

 *Cakes*

HOMEMADE CAKE MIX

3 pounds sugar
3¹/₄ pounds cake flour

6 tablespoons baking powder
2 teaspoons salt

Sift sugar, cake flour, baking powder and salt together 3 times. Store in airtight container. Yield: enough for eight 9-inch cake layers.

Nutritional information for this recipe is not available.

CAKE MIX YELLOW CAKE

1 cup milk
3 eggs
¹/₂ cup butter, softened

1 teaspoon vanilla extract
4¹/₂ cups (1¹/₂ pounds) Homemade
    Cake Mix

Combine milk, eggs, butter and vanilla in mixer bowl; mix well. Add Cake Mix gradually, beating constantly until smooth. Spoon into 2 greased and floured paper-lined 9-inch cake pans. Bake at 350 degrees for 25 to 30 minutes. Remove to wire rack to cool. Frost as desired. Yield: 16 servings.

For **Cake Mix Chocolate Cake**: Increase milk by 2 tablespoons and add 6 tablespoons baking cocoa and 1 teaspoon baking soda.

Nutritional information for this recipe is not available.

CAKE MIX MARBLE CAKES

1¹/₂ cups milk
5 eggs
1 teaspoon vanilla extract
³/₄ cup butter, softened

7¹/₂ cups (2¹/₂ pounds) Homemade
    Cake Mix
1 ounce baking chocolate, melted
2 tablespoons milk

Grease and flour 2 waxed paper-lined 5x9-inch loaf pans. Combine 1¹/₂ cups milk, eggs, vanilla and butter in mixer bowl; mix well. Add Cake Mix gradually, beating at medium speed for 2 minutes. Combine ¹/₃ of the batter with chocolate and 2 tablespoons milk in bowl. Spoon a small amount of the white batter into each prepared loaf pan. Top with chocolate batter and remaining white batter; swirl gently with knife. Bake at 350 degrees for 50 minutes or until loaves test done. Yield: 24 servings.

Nutritional information for this recipe is not available.

VODKA POUND CAKE

5 to 8 ounces candied ginger
1/2 cup finely chopped pecans
3 cups cake flour
3 teaspoons baking powder

1 cup butter, softened
1³/₄ cups sugar
8 egg whites
³/₄ cup 80 proof vodka

Grease 4x11-inch pan. Line with greased waxed paper. Rinse ginger with hot water to remove sugar and soften; pat dry. Cut into tiny pieces to measure 1 cup. Combine ginger, pecans and 1/2 cup flour in small bowl. Sift remaining flour and baking powder together. Cream butter and sugar in mixer bowl until light and fluffy. Add egg whites 2 at a time, beating well after each addition. Add flour mixture to creamed mixture alternately with vodka 1/3 at a time, stirring well with spatula after each addition. Fold in ginger mixture. Spoon batter into prepared pan. Bake at 325 degrees for 1¼ hours or until cake tests done. Cool in pan on wire rack for 30 minutes. Turn out onto serving plate. The batter will look curdled or strange, but don't worry. Taste mellows if allowed to stand, wrapped, overnight. Yield: 16 servings.

Approx Per Serving: Cal 366; Prot 4 g; Carbo 52 g; Fiber 1 g;
T Fat 14 g; 37% Calories from Fat; Chol 31 mg; Sod 184 mg.

Muriel Stevens
Board of Trustees

PUMPKIN CAKE

1 2-layer package yellow cake
   mix
2/3 cup oil
4 eggs

2/3 cup sugar
1/2 teaspoon nutmeg
1 teaspoon cinnamon
1 16-ounce can pumpkin

Combine cake mix, oil, eggs, sugar, nutmeg and cinnamon in bowl; mix well. Stir in pumpkin. Pour into greased 10-inch tube pan. Bake at 350 degrees for 1 hour or until cake tests done. Yield: 16 servings.

Approx Per Serving: Cal 279; Prot 3 g; Carbo 38 g; Fiber 1 g;
T Fat 13 g; 42% Calories from Fat; Chol 53 mg; Sod 215 mg.

 *Cakes*

STRAWBERRY MERINGUE CAKE

1 2-layer package yellow cake
  mix
1 cup orange juice
1/3 cup water
4 egg yolks
1 teaspoon grated orange rind

4 egg whites
1/4 teaspoon cream of tartar
1 cup sugar
2 cups whipping cream
1/4 cup sugar
1 quart fresh strawberries, sliced

Combine cake mix, orange juice, water, egg yolks and orange rind in mixer bowl. Beat for 4 minutes. Pour into 2 greased and waxed paper-lined round cake pans. Beat egg whites with cream of tartar in mixer bowl until soft peaks form. Add 1 cup sugar gradually, beating constantly until stiff peaks form. Spread gently over batter. Bake at 350 degrees for 35 to 40 minutes or until layers test done. Cool completely in pans. Remove from pans, keeping meringue side up. Beat whipping cream and 1/4 cup sugar in mixer bowl until stiff peaks form. Spread 2/3 of the whipped cream over bottom layer. Arrange sliced berries over whipped cream. Add top layer. Spread with remaining whipped cream. Garnish with whole strawberries.
Yield: 12 servings.

Approx Per Serving: Cal 450; Prot 5 g; Carbo 63 g; Fiber 1 g;
  T Fat 20 g; 40% Calories from Fat; Chol 125 mg; Sod 297 mg.

STRAWBERRY SURPRISE CAKE

1 2-layer package golden vanilla
  yellow cake mix
1 6-ounce package vanilla
  instant pudding mix

1 quart fresh strawberries
1 16-ounce jar strawberry glaze
16 ounces whipped topping

Prepare and bake yellow cake using package directions in 9x13-inch cake pan. Cool in pan. Prepare vanilla pudding mix using package directions. Chill. Reserve 6 to 8 whole strawberries. Slice remaining strawberries. Spread pudding over cooled cake. Layer with sliced strawberries, strawberry glaze and whipped topping. Top with reserved whole strawberries.
Yield: 16 servings.

Approx Per Serving: Cal 348; Prot 2 g; Carbo 61 g; Fiber 1 g;
  T Fat 11 g; 28% Calories from Fat; Chol 0 mg; Sod 276 mg.

TOMATO SOUP CAKE

1   10-ounce can tomato soup
1/2 cup oil
1 cup sugar
2 cups flour
1 teaspoon nutmeg
1 teaspoon cinnamon
1/2 teaspoon cloves
1 teaspoon baking soda

2 teaspoons baking powder
1 teaspoon vanilla extract
1 cup chopped walnuts
1 cup raisins
1 1/2 cups confectioners' sugar
3 ounces cream cheese, softened
1/2 teaspoon vanilla extract

Combine soup, oil and sugar in small bowl; mix well. Combine flour, nutmeg, cinnamon, cloves, baking soda and baking powder in large bowl. Add soup mixture, stirring to moisten. Stir in 1 teaspoon vanilla. Fold in walnuts and raisins. Pour into greased and floured 9x13-inch cake pan. Bake at 325 degrees for 45 minutes or until cake tests done. Cool in pan. Cream confectioners' sugar, cream cheese and vanilla in mixer bowl until light and fluffy. Spread over cooled cake. Yield: 16 servings.

Approx Per Serving: Cal 319; Prot 4 g; Carbo 48 g; Fiber 2 g;
    T Fat 14 g; 39% Calories from Fat; Chol 6 mg; Sod 234 mg.

WEST HEAVEN CAKE

8 ounces dates, chopped
1 teaspoon baking soda
1 cup boiling water
1/2 cup shortening
1 cup sugar
2 eggs, beaten

1 teaspoon vanilla extract
1 1/3 cups flour
2 tablespoons baking cocoa
1/4 teaspoon salt
1 cup chocolate chips
1/2 cup chopped walnuts

Place dates in small bowl. Sprinkle with baking soda; pour in boiling water. Let stand to cool. Cream shortening and sugar in mixer bowl until light and fluffy. Add eggs and vanilla; beat well. Sift flour, baking cocoa and salt together. Add to creamed mixture alternately with dates, stirring well after each addition. Pour into greased and floured 9x13-inch cake pan. Sprinkle with chocolate chips and walnuts. Bake at 350 degrees for 40 minutes. Cool in pan for several minutes. Garnish with confectioners' sugar.
Yield: 16 servings.

Approx Per Serving: Cal 271; Prot 3 g; Carbo 38 g; Fiber 2 g;
    T Fat 13 g; 43% Calories from Fat; Chol 26 mg; Sod 97 mg.

WALDORF RED CAKE

1/2 cup butter, softened
1 1/2 cups sugar
2 eggs, beaten
2 ounces red food coloring
2 tablespoons baking cocoa
1/4 teaspoon salt

1 cup buttermilk
2 1/4 cups sifted cake flour
1 teaspoon vanilla extract
1 teaspoon baking soda
1 tablespoon vinegar
Waldorf Frosting

Cream butter and sugar in mixer bowl. Add eggs. Beat until light and fluffy. Stir food coloring and baking cocoa together until paste forms. Stir into creamed mixture with salt. Add buttermilk alternately with flour, beating after each addition. Add vanilla. Dissolve baking soda in vinegar. Add to mixture, stirring gently. Pour into 2 greased and floured 8-inch cake pans. Bake at 350 degrees for 40 minutes or until layers test done. Cool in pans for several minutes; invert onto wire rack to cool completely. Split cooled layers into halves. Spread Waldorf Frosting between layers and over side and top of cake. Yield: 16 servings.

Waldorf Frosting

1 cup butter, softened
1 cup sugar
5 tablespoons flour

1 cup milk
1 teaspoon vanilla extract

Cream butter and sugar in mixer bowl until smooth. Combine flour and milk in saucepan. Cook over medium heat until mixture thickens, stirring constantly. Add creamed mixture, beating until smooth. Stir in vanilla. Yield: 16 servings.

Approx Per Serving: Cal 331; Prot 3 g; Carbo 52 g; Fiber 1 g;
   T Fat 13 g; 35% Calories from Fat; Chol 60 mg; Sod 214 mg.

Hope sees the invisible, feels the intangible and achieves the impossible.

MOCK BUTTERFINGER CANDY BARS

1 cup sugar
1 cup honey
2 cups peanut butter

6 cups cornflakes
1/2 to 1 cup semisweet chocolate chips

Combine sugar and honey in saucepan. Cook over low heat until sugar is melted, stirring frequently. Add peanut butter, stirring until smooth. Stir in cornflakes. Spread in ungreased 9x13-inch pan. Sprinkle chocolate chips over warm mixture, spreading when melted. Cool; cut into bars. Yield: 30 servings.

Approx Per Serving: Cal 206; Prot 6 g; Carbo 25 g; Fiber 3 g; T Fat 11 g; 48% Calories from Fat; Chol 0 mg; Sod 92 mg.

CREAM CHEESE FUDGE

6 ounces cream cheese, softened
2 tablespoons whipping cream
4 cups confectioners' sugar
4 1-ounce squares baking chocolate, melted

1 teaspoon rum
1 teaspoon vanilla extract
Salt to taste
1½ cups chopped pecans

Beat cream cheese and cream in mixer bowl until smooth. Beat in confectioners' sugar gradually. Blend in chocolate. Add remaining ingredients; mix well. Press into lightly buttered 8x11-inch dish. Chill. Yield: 80 servings.

Approx Per Serving: Cal 54; Prot 1 g; Carbo 7 g; Fiber <1 g; T Fat 3 g; 49% Calories from Fat; Chol 3 mg; Sod 7 mg.

UNCOOKED CHOCOLATE FUDGE

1/4 cup butter
4 ounces baking chocolate, broken into pieces
1 1-pound package confectioners' sugar, sifted

3 tablespoons light cream
1 teaspoon vanilla extract
4 ounces semisweet chocolate, melted

Melt butter and baking chocolate in saucepan over low heat. Combine with confectioners' sugar, cream and vanilla in bowl; mix well. Press into greased 8x8-inch dish. Let stand until firm. Cut into squares. Decorate with melted semisweet chocolate. Yield: 36 servings.

Approx Per Serving: Cal 103; Prot 1 g; Carbo 18 g; Fiber <1 g; T Fat 4 g; 33% Calories from Fat; Chol 4 mg; Sod 12 mg.

 *Candy*

PEANUT BUTTER CANDY BALLS

1/2 cup butter, softened
1 1/2 cups creamy peanut butter
3 cups confectioners' sugar

2 cups semisweet chocolate chips
4 ounces paraffin wax

Cream butter, peanut butter and confectioners' sugar in mixer bowl until smooth. Shape into 1-inch balls; place on cookie sheet. Chill for 20 minutes. Melt chocolate chips and paraffin in top of double boiler, stirring constantly. Dip peanut butter balls into chocolate mixture to coat completely. Cool on wax-paper lined cookie sheets. Store in refrigerator. Yield: 60 servings.

Approx Per Serving: Cal 103; Prot 2 g; Carbo 10 g; Fiber 1 g;
T Fat 7 g; 56% Calories from Fat; Chol 4 mg; Sod 40 mg.

PECAN CANDY

1 5-ounce can evaporated milk
2 cups sugar
1/2 cup butter

1/4 teaspoon vanilla extract
1 cup chopped pecans

Cook first 3 ingredients in heavy saucepan over medium heat until mixture coats spoon, stirring frequently. Stir in vanilla and pecans. Cook until mixture thickens. Drop by spoonfuls onto buttered waxed paper. Yield: 12 servings.

Approx Per Serving: Cal 278; Prot 2 g; Carbo 36 g; Fiber 1 g;
T Fat 15 g; 48% Calories from Fat; Chol 24 mg; Sod 78 mg.

Jeanne R. Jones
Board of Trustees

BROWNIES

1 cup butter
3 squares unsweetened chocolate
6 eggs, beaten
2 cups sugar

1 cup flour
1 teaspoon vanilla extract
2 cups chopped pecans
Favorite frosting (optional)

Melt butter and chocolate in heavy saucepan over low heat. Beat eggs, sugar, flour and vanilla in bowl. Stir in pecans. Fold in chocolate mixture. Pour into 7x11-inch baking pan. Bake at 350 degrees for 30 minutes or until edges pull away from sides of pan. Frost. Cool in pan. Yield: 15 servings.

Approx Per Serving: Cal 408; Prot 5 g; Carbo 38 g; Fiber 2 g;
T Fat 28 g; 60% Calories from Fat; Chol 118 mg; Sod 132 mg.

BUTTERMILK BROWNIES

2 cups sugar
2 cups flour
1/2 cup margarine
1/4 cup baking cocoa
1/2 cup oil
1 cup water
2 eggs, beaten
1/2 cup buttermilk

1 teaspoon baking soda
1 teaspoon vanilla extract
2 tablespoons baking cocoa
2 tablespoons margarine
3 tablespoons milk
1 teaspoon vanilla extract
1 1/2 cups confectioners' sugar
1/2 cup chopped pecans

Combine sugar and flour in bowl; set aside. Melt 1/2 cup margarine in saucepan with 1/4 cup baking cocoa, oil and water, stirring frequently. Pour into sugar mixture, stirring well. Add eggs, buttermilk, baking soda and 1 teaspoon vanilla, stirring until smooth. Pour into greased 11x14-inch baking pan. Bake at 400 degrees for 12 to 15 minutes or until edges pull away from sides of pan. Cool in pan. Combine 2 tablespoons baking cocoa, 2 tablespoons margarine and milk in small saucepan. Cook until smooth, stirring constantly; remove from heat. Stir in 1 teaspoon vanilla and confectioners' sugar. Spread over brownies; sprinkle with pecans. Yield: 25 servings.

Approx Per Serving: Cal 234; Prot 3 g; Carbo 32 g; Fiber 1 g; T Fat 11 g; 42% Calories from Fat; Chol 18 mg; Sod 99 mg.

GRANDMÈRE'S CHOCOLATE CHIP COOKIES

2 1/4 cups whole wheat pastry flour
1 teaspoon baking soda
1/2 teaspoon salt
1 cup unsalted butter, softened
1/2 cup sugar
1/2 cup packed light brown sugar
1/2 cup plain yogurt
1 egg, beaten

2 teaspoons vanilla extract
1/2 teaspoon cream of tartar
1 1/2 cups granola
2 cups semisweet chocolate chips
2/3 cup chopped pecans
2/3 cup chopped walnuts
2/3 cup chopped almonds

Combine flour, baking soda and salt in small bowl; set aside. Cream butter, sugar and brown sugar in mixer bowl until light and fluffy. Add yogurt, egg, vanilla and cream of tartar. Beat until smooth. Stir in flour mixture and remaining ingredients. Drop by rounded tablespoonfuls 1 1/2 inches apart onto greased cookie sheet. Bake at 375 degrees for 15 minutes or until golden brown. Remove to wire rack to cool. Yield: 60 servings.

Approx Per Serving: Cal 127; Prot 2 g; Carbo 13 g; Fiber 1 g; T Fat 8 g; 55% Calories from Fat; Chol 12 mg; Sod 42 mg.

 *Cookies*

LOW-CALORIE CHOCOLATE DREAMS

3 egg whites
¹/₂ teaspoon cream of tartar

1 cup fine granulated sugar
2 tablespoons baking cocoa

Beat egg whites in mixer bowl until foamy. Add cream of tartar; beat until soft peaks form. Add sugar gradually, beating until stiff peaks form. Fold in baking cocoa 1 tablespoon at a time. Drop by level teaspoonfuls onto greased cookie sheet. Bake at 275 degrees for 20 minutes. Cool slightly on cookie sheet. Remove with spatula to wire rack to cool completely. Store in airtight container in dry place for up to 10 days. Yield: 108 servings.

Approx Per Serving: Cal 8; Prot <1 g; Carbo 2 g; Fiber <1 g;
    T Fat <1 g; 2% Calories from Fat; Chol 0 mg; Sod 1 mg.

CRUNCHY CARROT COOKIES

2 cups sifted flour
1 teaspoon baking powder
¹/₄ teaspoon baking soda
¹/₂ teaspoon nutmeg
1 teaspoon cinnamon
¹/₄ teaspoon salt
2 cups slightly crushed cornflakes
¹/₂ cup butter, softened

¹/₂ cup sugar
¹/₂ cup packed light brown sugar
2 eggs
1 cup finely shredded carrots
1 cup raisins
1 cup coarsely chopped pecans
¹/₃ cup milk

Sift flour, baking powder, baking soda, nutmeg, cinnamon and salt into bowl. Stir in cornflakes. Cream butter, sugar and brown sugar in large mixer bowl until light and fluffy. Beat in eggs. Stir in carrots, raisins, pecans and milk. Add flour mixture, mix well. Drop by teaspoonfuls 2 inches apart onto lightly greased cookie sheet. Bake at 375 degrees for 12 minutes or until light brown. Remove to wire rack to cool. Yield: 144 servings.

Approx Per Serving: Cal 33; Prot <1 g; Carbo 5 g; Fiber <1 g;
    T Fat 1 g; 35% Calories from Fat; Chol 5 mg; Sod 27 mg.

DREAM BARS

1/2 cup butter, softened
11/2 cups packed brown sugar
1 cup flour
2 eggs, beaten
1 teaspoon vanilla extract

2 tablespoons flour
1/2 teaspoon baking powder
1/4 teaspoon salt
11/2 cups flaked coconut
1 cup chopped walnuts

Combine butter, 1/2 cup brown sugar and flour in small bowl, stirring until crumbly. Pat into 9x13-inch baking pan. Bake at 375 degrees for 10 minutes. Beat eggs and 1 cup brown sugar in medium bowl until frothy. Add vanilla, flour, baking powder, salt, coconut and walnuts; mix well. Pour over warm crust. Bake for 20 minutes. Cool slightly before cutting into bars. Sweet dreams! Yield: 16 servings.

Approx Per Serving: Cal 269; Prot 3 g; Carbo 36 g; Fiber 2 g; T Fat 13 g; 43% Calories from Fat; Chol 42 mg; Sod 114 mg.

FRUIT SLICES

1 cup margarine
11/4 cups sugar
2 eggs, beaten
1/2 cup molasses
1/2 cup water
1 teaspoon baking soda
11/2 cups raisins

11/2 cups currants
1 cup chopped pecans
1 teaspoon cinnamon
1 teaspoon ground cloves
1 teaspoon allspice
5 cups flour

Cream margarine and sugar in mixer bowl until light and fluffy. Add eggs, beating well. Mix molasses, water and baking soda in small bowl. Add to creamed mixture, stirring well. Fold in raisins, currants and pecans. Add cinnamon, cloves, allspice and flour, stirring well. Press into greased 10x15-inch baking pan. Bake at 375 degrees for 20 minutes. May frost with confectioners' sugar icing when cool. Yield: 36 servings.

Approx Per Serving: Cal 209; Prot 3 g; Carbo 33 g; Fiber 1 g; T Fat 8 g; 33% Calories from Fat; Chol 12 mg; Sod 89 mg.

JAN HAGELS

1 cup butter, softened
1 cup sugar
1 egg yolk
2 cups sifted flour

½ teaspoon cinnamon
1 egg white
1 teaspoon water
8 ounces sliced almonds

Cream butter, sugar and egg yolk in mixer bowl until light and fluffy. Add flour and cinnamon, mixing well. Separate dough into 3 portions. Spread thinly over 3 small cookie sheets. Beat egg white and water in bowl until frothy. Spread over dough. Arrange almonds in mosaic pattern over top. Bake at 325 degrees for 15 to 20 minutes or until golden brown. Slice while hot. Yield: 50 servings.

Approx Per Serving: Cal 93; Prot 2 g; Carbo 8 g; Fiber 1 g;
T Fat 6 g; 58% Calories from Fat; Chol 14 mg; Sod 33 mg.

SOFT MOLASSES COOKIES

3 cups sifted flour
2 teaspoons baking soda
1 teaspoon cinnamon
1 teaspoon ginger
1 teaspoon nutmeg
¼ teaspoon ground cloves
¾ teaspoon salt

½ cup shortening
½ cup sugar
1 egg, beaten
1 cup molasses
1 tablespoon vinegar
½ cup boiling water

Sift flour, baking soda, cinnamon, ginger, nutmeg, cloves and salt together. Cream shortening and sugar in mixer bowl until light and fluffy. Add egg and molasses, beating well. Mix vinegar with boiling water. Add alternately with sifted dry ingredients to creamed mixture, beating well after each addition. Drop by spoonfuls 2 inches apart onto ungreased cookie sheet. Bake at 375 degrees for 12 to 15 minutes or until browned. Cool on wire rack. Yield: 24 servings.

Approx Per Serving: Cal 138; Prot 2 g; Carbo 23 g; Fiber <1 g;
T Fat 5 g; 30% Calories from Fat; Chol 9 mg; Sod 140 mg.

LEMON BAR COOKIES

24 graham crackers
1 cup melted butter
1 cup sugar
1/2 cup milk
1 egg, slightly beaten
1 cup chopped pecans

1 cup shredded coconut
1 cup graham cracker crumbs
2 cups confectioners' sugar
1/2 cup melted butter
Juice of 1 lemon

Line bottom of 9x13-inch baking dish with 12 whole graham crackers. Combine 1 cup butter, sugar, milk and egg in saucepan; mix well. Bring to a boil, stirring constantly. Stir in pecans, coconut and graham cracker crumbs. Spread in prepared dish. Top with remaining whole graham crackers. Frost with mixture of confectioners' sugar, 1/2 cup butter and lemon juice. Cut into bars. Yield: 25 servings.

Approx Per Serving: Cal 272; Prot 1 g; Carbo 29 g; Fiber 1 g;
T Fat 17 g; 56% Calories from Fat; Chol 39 mg; Sod 179 mg.

MACADAMIA NUT-CHOCOLATE CHIP COOKIES

10 pounds butter, softened
7 1/2 pounds confectioners' sugar
10 pounds brown sugar
30 eggs
16 pounds and 14 ounces White Rose
5 pounds and 10 ounces cake flour

5 1/4 ounces baking soda
6 1/2 ounces salt
3 pounds and 12 ounces pecans
10 pounds macadamia nuts
13 pounds and 2 ounces chocolate chips

Cream butter, confectioners' sugar and brown sugar in very large bowl until light and fluffy. Beat in eggs. Sift in flour, baking soda and salt; mix well. Stir in pecans, macadamia nuts and chocolate chips. Drop batter into 5 to 5 1/2-ounce cookies on cookie sheet. Bake in moderate oven until light golden brown. Cool on cookie sheet for several minutes; remove to wire rack to cool completely. Yield: 256 servings.

Approx Per Serving: Cal 695; Prot 8 g; Carbo 81 g; Fiber 3 g;
T Fat 41 g; 51% Calories from Fat; Chol 64 mg; Sod 580 mg.

Chef Bruno Wehren
MGM Grand Hotel, Inc.

 *Cookies*

OATMEAL-DATE BARS

1¹/₂ cups chopped dates
³/₄ cup water
2¹/₂ tablespoons lemon juice
¹/₃ cup margarine, softened
²/₃ cup packed brown sugar
1 teaspoon vanilla extract

1 cup rolled oats
³/₄ cup all-purpose flour
¹/₄ cup whole wheat flour
¹/₂ teaspoon baking soda
¹/₈ teaspoon salt

Combine dates, water and lemon juice in saucepan. Bring to a boil; reduce heat. Simmer for 5 minutes or until mixture thickens, stirring frequently. Cream margarine in mixer bowl. Add brown sugar, beating at medium speed until light and fluffy. Stir in vanilla. Combine oats, all-purpose flour, whole wheat flour, baking soda and salt. Add to creamed mixture, stirring until crumbly. Press 2 cups mixture into 9x9-inch baking pan sprayed with non-stick cooking spray. Bake at 375 degrees for 5 minutes. Spread date mixture over prepared crust; top with remaining crumb mixture. Bake for 20 minutes longer or until golden brown. Cool in pan on wire rack. Cut into bars. Yield: 16 servings.

Approx Per Serving: Cal 170; Prot 2 g; Carbo 33 g; Fiber 2 g; T Fat 4 g; 22% Calories from Fat; Chol 0 mg; Sod 93 mg.

PEANUT BUTTER COOKIES

2 cups shortening
2 cups sugar
2 cups brown sugar
4 eggs, beaten
2 teaspoons vanilla extract

2 cups peanut butter
6 cups flour
4 teaspoons baking soda
1 teaspoon salt

Cream shortening, sugar, brown sugar, eggs and vanilla in mixer bowl until light and fluffy. Stir in peanut butter. Add flour, baking soda and salt, mixing well. Drop by tablespoonfuls onto cookie sheet. Bake at 350 degrees for 10 minutes or until golden brown. Cool on wire rack. Yield: 48 servings.

Approx Per Serving: Cal 277; Prot 5 g; Carbo 33 g; Fiber 1 g; T Fat 15 g; 46% Calories from Fat; Chol 18 mg; Sod 167 mg.

PERSIMMON COOKIES

1 cup margarine
1 cup sugar
1 egg, beaten
1 cup persimmon pulp
1 cup raisins
1 cup chopped pecans
1/2 cup glazed fruit

2 cups flour
1 teaspoon baking soda
1 teaspoon cinnamon
1 teaspoon nutmeg
1/2 teaspoon ground cloves
1/4 teaspoon salt

Cream margarine and sugar in mixer bowl until light and fluffy. Add egg, beating well. Fold in persimmon, raisins, pecans and glazed fruit. Mix flour, baking soda, cinnamon, nutmeg, cloves and salt together. Add to creamed mixture, stirring well. Drop by teaspoonfuls onto greased cookie sheet. Bake at 375 degrees for 12 to 15 minutes. Cool on wire rack. Yield: 36 servings.

Approx Per Serving: Cal 145; Prot 1 g; Carbo 19 g; Fiber 1 g; T Fat 8 g; 46% Calories from Fat; Chol 6 mg; Sod 136 mg.

PUMPKIN COOKIES

1 cup oil
3 cups sugar
2 eggs, beaten
5 cups flour
2 teaspoons baking powder
2 teaspoons baking soda
2 teaspoons nutmeg
2 teaspoons cinnamon

1 teaspoon allspice
1/4 teaspoon ginger
1 3/4 teaspoons salt
1   29-ounce can solid-pack pumpkin
2 cups semisweet chocolate chips
1 cup chopped walnuts
3 teaspoons vanilla extract

Beat oil and sugar in mixer bowl. Add eggs, beating well. Sift flour, baking powder, baking soda, nutmeg, cinnamon, allspice, ginger and salt together. Add to sugar mixture alternately with pumpkin, beating well after each addition. Fold in chocolate chips, walnuts and vanilla. Drop by teaspoonfuls onto greased cookie sheets. Bake at 350 degrees for 10 to 12 minutes or until golden brown. Cool on wire rack. Yield: 60 servings.

Approx Per Serving: Cal 158; Prot 2 g; Carbo 23 g; Fiber 1 g; T Fat 7 g; 40% Calories from Fat; Chol 7 mg; Sod 105 mg.

 *Cookies*

COOKIE MIX

Use Cookie Mix for the following cookie recipes.

6 cups sifted flour
1 tablespoon salt

2¹/₃ cups shortening

Mix flour and salt in large bowl. Cut in shortening until mixture resembles coarse meal. Store in refrigerator or cool place. Yield: 8 cups.

Approx Per Cup: Cal 843; Prot 9 g; Carbo 66 g; Fiber 2 g; T Fat 61 g; 65% Calories from Fat; Chol 0 mg; Sod 801 mg.

COOKIE MIX BROWNIES

1¹/₂ cups Cookie Mix
1¹/₂ cups sugar
¹/₂ teaspoon baking powder
3 eggs

3 1-ounce squares baking chocolate, melted
1 teaspoon vanilla extract
¹/₂ cup chopped pecans

Combine Cookie Mix, sugar, baking powder, eggs, chocolate and vanilla in bowl; mix well. Stir in pecans. Spread in greased 9x9-inch baking pan. Bake at 375 degrees for 25 to 30 minutes or until brownies test done. Cool on wire rack. Garnish with confectioners' sugar. Cut into 1¹/₂-inch squares. Yield: 36 servings.

Approx Per Serving: Cal 97; Prot 1 g; Carbo 12 g; Fiber 1 g; T Fat 5 g; 47% Calories from Fat; Chol 18 mg; Sod 44 mg.

COOKIE MIX DATE BARS

¹/₂ cup Cookie Mix
¹/₂ cup packed brown sugar
¹/₄ teaspoon baking powder
1 egg

1 tablespoon milk
1 teaspoon vanilla extract
¹/₂ cup chopped dates
¹/₂ cup chopped walnuts

Combine Cookie Mix, brown sugar and baking powder in bowl. Add egg, milk and vanilla; mix well. Stir in dates and walnuts. Spoon into greased 8x8-inch baking pan. Bake at 375 degrees for 20 to 25 minutes or until tester comes out clean. Cool on wire rack. Cut into bars. Yield: 32 servings.

Approx Per Serving: Cal 52; Prot 1 g; Carbo 8 g; Fiber <1 g; T Fat 2 g; 30% Calories from Fat; Chol 7 mg; Sod 20 mg.

COOKIE MIX SPICY FRUIT DROPS

2 cups Cookie Mix
1 cup packed light brown sugar
1/2 teaspoon baking powder
1 teaspoon cinnamon
1/2 teaspoon ground cloves

1/2 teaspoon allspice
2 eggs
2 tablespoons orange juice
1   8-ounce jar glazed fruit
1 cup chopped walnuts

Combine Cookie Mix, brown sugar, baking powder, cinnamon, cloves and allspice in bowl. Add eggs and orange juice; mix well. Stir in fruit and walnuts. Drop by teaspoonfuls 2 inches apart onto ungreased cookie sheet. Bake at 375 degrees for 10 to 12 minutes or until light brown. Cool on wire rack. Yield: 48 servings.

Approx Per Serving: Cal 88; Prot 1 g; Carbo 11 g; Fiber <1 g; T Fat 4 g; 45% Calories from Fat; Chol 9 mg; Sod 43 mg.

COOKIE MIX FUDGE DROPS

2 cups Cookie Mix
1/2 cup sugar
1/4 teaspoon baking soda
2   1-ounce squares baking
    chocolate, melted

1 egg
1/2 cup milk
1 teaspoon vanilla extract
1/2 cup chopped pecans

Combine Cookie Mix, sugar and baking soda in bowl. Add chocolate, egg, milk and vanilla; mix well. Stir in pecans. Drop by teaspoonfuls 2 1/2 inches apart onto greased cookie sheet. Bake at 375 degrees for 10 to 12 minutes or until set. Cool on wire rack. May frost as desired. Yield: 40 servings.

Approx Per Serving: Cal 73; Prot 1 g; Carbo 7 g; Fiber <1 g; T Fat 5 g; 60% Calories from Fat; Chol 6 mg; Sod 48 mg.

We cannot direct the wind...But we can adjust the sails.

 *Cookies*

COOKIE MIX MOLASSES CRISPS

2 cups Cookie Mix
1/4 cup flour
3/4 cup sugar
1 1/2 teaspoons baking soda
1 teaspoon cinnamon

1/2 teaspoon ground cloves
1/2 teaspoon ginger
1 egg
3 tablespoons molasses

Combine first 7 ingredients in bowl. Add egg and molasses; mix well to form dough. Chill for 1 hour to overnight. Roll 1/4 inch thick on floured surface. Cut out as desired; place on cookie sheet. Bake at 375 degrees for 8 to 10 minutes or until golden brown. Cool on wire rack. Yield: 48 servings.

Approx Per Serving: Cal 54; Prot 1 g; Carbo 7 g; Fiber <1 g;
 T Fat 3 g; 44% Calories from Fat; Chol 4 mg; Sod 61 mg.

COOKIE MIX NUT BALLS

2 cups Cookie Mix
1/2 cup sifted confectioners' sugar
1 tablespoon orange juice

1 teaspoon vanilla extract
1/4 cup chopped walnuts

Combine all ingredients in bowl; mix well to form crumbly dough, adding additional orange juice if needed to bind. Shape into 1-inch balls; place 1 inch apart on ungreased cookie sheet. Bake at 375 degrees for 12 to 15 minutes or until golden bown. Cool on wire rack. Yield: 36 servings.

Approx Per Serving: Cal 58; Prot 1 g; Carbo 5 g; Fiber <1 g;
 T Fat 4 g; 60% Calories from Fat; Chol 0 mg; Sod 45 mg.

COOKIE MIX SUGAR COOKIES

2 cups Cookie Mix
3/4 cup sugar
1/4 cup flour

1 teaspoon baking powder
1 egg
1 teaspoon vanilla extract

Combine Cookie Mix, sugar, flour and baking powder in bowl; mix well. Add egg and vanilla; mix to form soft dough. Chill if necessary for easy handling. Roll 1/8 to 1/4 inch thick on floured cloth or surface. Cut out as desired; place on lightly greased cookie sheet. Bake at 375 degrees for 8 to 10 minutes or until light brown. Cool on wire rack. Yield: 48 servings.

Approx Per Serving: Cal 51; Prot 1 g; Carbo 6 g; Fiber <1 g;
 T Fat 3 g; 46% Calories from Fat; Chol 4 mg; Sod 42 mg.

The butterfly is the symbol of the Nathan Adelson Hospice. It is an ancient symbol of immortality. The butterfly represents change, progression, evolution, and a passing from one stage to another.

The editors have attempted to present these family recipes in a form that allows approximate nutritional values to be computed. Persons with dietary or health problems or whose diets require close monitoring should not rely solely on the nutritional information provided. They should consult their physicians or a registered dietitian for specific information.

Abbreviations for Nutritional Profile

Cal — Calories	Dietary Fiber — Fiber	Sod — Sodium
Prot — Protein	T Fat — Total Fat	g — gram
Carbo — Carbohydrates	Chol — Cholesterol	mg — milligrams

Nutritional information for these recipes is computed from information derived from many sources, including materials supplied by the United States Department of Agriculture, computer databanks and journals in which the information is assumed to be in the public domain. However, many specialty items, new products and processed foods may not be available from these sources or may vary from the average values used in these profiles. More information on new and/or specific products may be obtained by reading the nutrient labels. Unless otherwise specified, the nutritional profile of these recipes is based on all measurements being level.

- **Artificial sweeteners** vary in use and strength so should be used "to taste," using the recipe ingredients as a guideline. Sweeteners using aspartame (NutraSweet and Equal) should not be used as a sweetener in recipes involving prolonged heating which reduces the sweet taste. For further information on the use of these sweeteners, refer to package information.
- **Alcoholic ingredients** have been analyzed for basic ingredients, although cooking causes the evaporation of alcohol thus decreasing caloric content.
- **Buttermilk, sour cream** and **yogurt** are the types available commercially.
- **Cake mixes** which are prepared using package directions include 3 eggs and ½ cup oil.
- **Chicken,** cooked for boning and chopping, has been roasted; this method yields the lowest caloric values.
- **Cottage cheese** is cream-style with 4.2% creaming mixture. Dry-curd cottage cheese has no creaming mixture.
- **Eggs** are all large. To avoid raw eggs that may carry salmonella as in eggnog or 6-week muffin batter, use an equivalent amount of commercial egg substitute.
- **Flour** is unsifted all-purpose flour.
- **Garnishes,** serving suggestions and other optional additions and variations are not included in the profile.
- **Margarine** and **butter** are regular, not whipped or presoftened.
- **Milk** is whole milk, 3.5% butterfat. Lowfat milk is 1% butterfat. Evaporated milk is whole milk with 60% of the water removed.
- **Oil** is any type of vegetable cooking oil. Shortening is hydrogenated vegetable shortening.
- **Salt** and other ingredients to taste as noted in the ingredients have not been included in the nutritional profile.
- If a choice of ingredients has been given, the nutritional profile information reflects the first option. If a choice of amounts has been given, the nutritional profile reflects the greater amount.

Substitution Chart

	Instead of	Use
Baking	1 teaspoon baking powder	¼ teaspoon soda plus ½ teaspoon cream of tartar
	1 tablespoon cornstarch (for thickening)	2 tablespoons flour or 1 tablespoon tapioca
	1 cup sifted all-purpose flour	1 cup plus 2 tablespoons sifted cake flour
	1 cup sifted cake flour	1 cup minus 2 tablespoons sifted all-purpose flour
	1 cup dry bread crumbs	¾ cup cracker crumbs
Dairy	1 cup buttermilk	1 cup sour milk or 1 cup yogurt
	1 cup heavy cream	¾ cup skim milk plus ⅓ cup butter
	1 cup light cream	⅞ cup skim milk plus 3 tablespoons butter
	1 cup sour cream	⅞ cup sour milk plus 3 tablespoons butter
	1 cup sour milk	1 cup milk plus 1 tablespoon vinegar or lemon juice or 1 cup buttermilk
Seasoning	1 teaspoon allspice	½ teaspoon cinnamon plus ⅛ teaspoon cloves
	1 cup catsup	1 cup tomato sauce plus ½ cup sugar plus 2 tablespoons vinegar
	1 clove of garlic	⅛ teaspoon garlic powder or ⅛ teaspoon instant minced garlic or ¾ teaspoon garlic salt or 5 drops of liquid garlic
	1 teaspoon Italian spice	¼ teaspoon each oregano, basil, thyme, rosemary plus dash of cayenne
	1 teaspoon lemon juice	½ teaspoon vinegar
	1 tablespoon mustard	1 teaspoon dry mustard
	1 medium onion	1 tablespoon dried minced onion or 1 teaspoon onion powder
Sweet	1 1-ounce square chocolate	¼ cup cocoa plus 1 teaspoon shortening
	1⅔ ounces semisweet chocolate	1 ounce unsweetened chocolate plus 4 teaspoons granulated sugar
	1 cup honey	1 to 1¼ cups sugar plus ¼ cup liquid or 1 cup corn syrup or molasses
	1 cup granulated sugar	1 cup packed brown sugar or 1 cup corn syrup, molasses or honey minus ¼ cup liquid

Herb and Spice Chart

Allspice	Pungent aromatic spice, whole or in powdered form. It is excellent in marinades, particularly in game marinade, or in curries.
Basil	Can be chopped and added to cold poultry salads. If the recipe calls for tomatoes or tomato sauce, add a touch of basil to bring out a rich flavor.
Bay leaf	The basis of many French seasonings. It is added to soups, stews, marinades and stuffings.
Bouquet garni	A must in many Creole cuisine recipes. It is a bundle of herbs, spices and bay leaf tied together and added to soups, stews or sauces.
Celery seed	From wild celery rather than domestic celery. It adds pleasant flavor to bouillon or a stock base.
Chervil	One of the traditional *fines herbes* used in French-derived cooking. (The others are tarragon, parsley and chives.) It is good in omelets or soups.
Chives	Available fresh, dried or frozen, it can be substituted for raw onion or shallot in any poultry recipe.
Cinnamon	Ground from the bark of the cinnamon tree, it is important in desserts as well as savory dishes.
Coriander	Adds an unusual flavor to soups, stews, chili dishes, curries and some desserts.
Cumin	A staple spice in Mexican cooking. To use, rub seeds together and let them fall into the dish just before serving. Cumin also comes in powdered form.
Garlic	One of the oldest herbs in the world, it must be carefully handled. For best results, press or crush garlic clove.
Marjoram	An aromatic herb of the mint family, it is good in soups, sauces, stuffings and stews.
Mustard (dry)	Brings a sharp bite to sauces. Sprinkle just a touch over roast chicken for a delightful flavor treat.
Oregano	A staple herb in Italian, Spanish and Mexican cuisines. It is very good in dishes with a tomato foundation; it adds an excellent savory taste.

216

Herb and Spice Chart

Paprika	A mild pepper that adds color to many dishes. The very best paprika is imported from Hungary.
Rosemary	A tasty herb important in seasoning stuffing for duck, partridge, capon and other poultry.
Sage	A perennial favorite with all kinds of poultry and stuffings. It is particularly good with goose.
Tarragon	One of the *fines herbes*. Goes well with all poultry dishes whether hot or cold.
Thyme	Usually used in combination with bay leaf in soups, stews and sauces.

ALLSPICE	BASIL	BAY LEAF	CELERY SEED	CHERVIL	CHIVES
CINNAMON	CORIANDER	CUMIN	GARLIC	MARJORAM	MUSTARD
OREGANO	PAPRIKA	ROSEMARY	SAGE	TARRAGON	THYME

Index

Chicken Diablo, 110
Chicken Enchiladas with Tomato
  Sauce, 112
Chicken in Black Bean Sauce, 111
Chicken Kashmir, 113
Chicken "Margarita," 114
Chicken Marsala, 14
Chicken Quick, 115
Chicken Salad Aïoli, 74
Chicken Scarpariello alla Dolce
  Vita, 115
Chicken Tamale Casserole, 116
Chicken with Macadamia Nuts, 113
Creamy Chicken 'n Cheese
  Enchiladas, 112
Crusted Dijon Chicken, 111
Fruited Chicken Salad with Curried
  Ginger Dressing, 73
Herb Broiled Chicken, 108
Honey Chicken Wings, 49
Honey Roasted Chicken, 117
Maw Maw's Chicken Stew, 118
Orange Chicken, 118
"Penicillin" Soup with Noodles, 68
Roasted Chicken, 116
Rosemary Chicken, 32
Samoan Seafood Salad, 44
Sour Cream Chicken and Broccoli, 109
Southern Fried Chicken with Gravy, 117
Springtime Chicken Salad, 31
Teriyaki Chicken, 119
Teriyaki-Chicken Salad, 74
White Chili, 65

CHILI
Firestarter Chili, 63
Ranch House Chili, 64
Two-Bean Chili con Carne, 64
White Chili, 65

COFFEE CAKES
Deluxe Coffee Cake, 159
Old-Fashioned Sour Cream Coffee
  Cake, 159

COOKIE MIX COOKIES
Brownies, 210
Date Bars, 210
Fudge Drops, 211
Mix, 210
Molasses Crisps, 212
Nut Balls, 212
Spicy Fruit Drops, 211
Sugar Cookies, 212

COOKIES. *See also* Cookie Mix Cookies
Brownies, 202
Buttermilk Brownies, 203
Crunchy Carrot Cookies, 204
Dream Bars, 205
Fruit Slices, 205
Grandmère's Chocolate Chip Cookies, 203
Jan Hagels, 206
Lemon Bar Cookies, 207
Low-Calorie Chocolate Dreams, 204
Macadamia Nut-Chocolate Chip
  Cookies, 207
Oatmeal-Date Bars, 208
Peanut Butter Cookies, 208
Persimmon Cookies, 209
Pumpkin Cookies, 209
Soft Molasses Cookies, 206

CRAB MEAT
Crab Dip with Sauterne, 50
Crab Meat Crêpes, 128
Creole Crab and Rice, 129
Deep-South Crab Cakes, 127
Shrimp and Crab Étouffée, 131
Zesty Crab Cakes with Seafood
  Sauce, 127

DESSERTS. *See also* Cakes; Candy;
  Cheesecakes; Cookies; Pies;
  Puddings
Amaretto Custard, 22
Apple Crisp, 172
Apricot-Cream Cheese Mold, 173
Avocado Ice Cream, 177
Bananas Guadalupe, 173
Blackberry Cobbler Delight, 182
Brandied Chocolate Fondue, 176
Bread Pudding, 46
Butterfinger Dessert, 174
Chocolate Dream Dessert, 176
Cinnamon Sauce, 180
Cold Grand Marnier Soufflé, 179
Cupcake Blintzes, 177
Fruit-Filled Cocoa Tacos, 15
Ginger Crème Brûlée, 24
Lemon Ice Cream, 178
Minted Fruit Dessert, 177
Old-Fashioned Peach Cobbler, 183
Phyllo with Fresh Berries, 30
Ranch Hand Apple Dumplings, 172
Raspberry Delight, 183
Rhubarb Crunch, 184
Summer Trifle, 184
Tuaca Tiramisu, 34

Index

Order Form

I would like to order additional copies of *BEST BETS*.

☐ FOR MYSELF, QUANTITY _____   ☐ AS A GIFT, QUANTITY _____

MAIL TO NAME _____

ADDRESS_____

CITY/STATE/ZIP _____

IF GIFT, GIFT CARD SHOULD READ _____

ENCLOSED IS MY CHECK FOR **$14.95** PLUS **$2.40** FOR
SHIPPING AND HANDLING.

The tax deductible portion of the cookbook price is $7.75

Mail to: Nathan Adelson Hospice
BEST BETS • 4141 S. Swenson • Las Vegas, NV 89119
or call: 1-702-796-3132

Order Form

I would like to order additional copies of *BEST BETS*.

☐ FOR MYSELF, QUANTITY _____   ☐ AS A GIFT, QUANTITY _____

MAIL TO NAME _____

ADDRESS_____

CITY/STATE/ZIP _____

IF GIFT, GIFT CARD SHOULD READ _____

ENCLOSED IS MY CHECK FOR **$14.95** PLUS **$2.40** FOR
SHIPPING AND HANDLING.

The tax deductible portion of the cookbook price is $7.75

Mail to: Nathan Adelson Hospice
BEST BETS • 4141 S. Swenson • Las Vegas, NV 89119
or call: 1-702-796-3132

Notes